With Bold Strokes

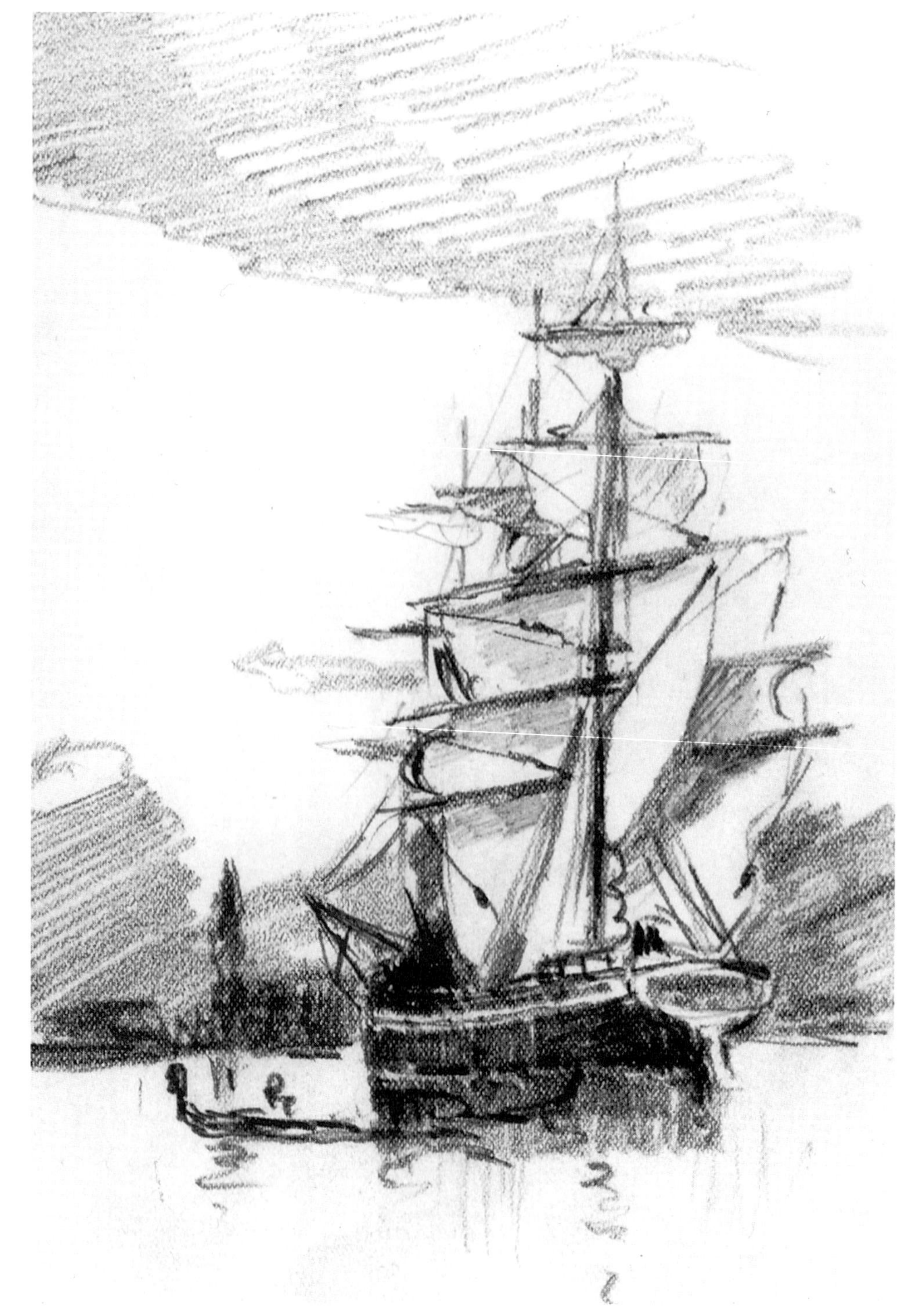

With Bold Strokes

BOYER GONZALES, 1864–1934

Edward Simmen

TEXAS A&M UNIVERSITY PRESS
COLLEGE STATION

All photographs courtesy Rosenberg Library, Galveston, Texas.

Publication of this volume is made possible by a generous grant
from the Rosenberg Library, Galveston, Texas.

The paper used in this book meets the minimum requirements
of the American National Standard for Permanence
of Paper for Printed Library Materials, Z39.48-1984.
Binding materials have been chosen for durability.

Frontis photo: Untitled., ca. 1907

Library of Congress Cataloging-in-Publication Data

Simmen, Edward.
    With bold strokes : Boyer Gonzales, 1864–1934 / Edward Simmen.
      p.   cm.
    Includes bibliographical references and index.
    ISBN 0-89096-739-3
    1. Gonzales, Boyer—Criticism and interpretation.
    2. Impressionism (Art)—United States.   I. Title.
ND237.G6115S56   1997   96-46066
759.13—dc20   CIP

For Lise

CONTENTS

ILLUSTRATIONS

THE PLATES

PREFACE

When I first began my research into the life and times of the Texas artist Boyer Gonzales, I never expected to uncover such a rich amount of information in the form of a variety of documents. Fortunately for me, the majority of the members of the Gonzales family were avid collectors and savers. Beginning with Boyer's father, Thomas (1829–96), one Gonzales after another kept these documents, added to them, and then, upon death, passed them on to the next Gonzales. In 1989, they found their way to the Galveston and Texas History Center at the Rosenberg Library in Galveston where they have been carefully organized, catalogued, and filed. That, of course, made conducting research so much easier.

Then, too, I had available the Rosenberg's excellent collection of Galveston city directories, newspapers, maps, and reference books as well as the complete records of Trinity Episcopal Church, where so many of the members of the family were christened, confirmed, married, and buried.

Most exciting to me was to discover that the History Center also holds a unique collection of ten letters, never before made public, that Winslow Homer wrote to Boyer Gonzales over a period of fourteen years, beginning with one written in December of 1893 after Boyer Gonzales had been to the World's Columbian Exposition in Chicago and ending with one written in October of 1907 following Gonzales's marriage. Indeed, those letters became a central point in the biography of Gonzales because of the tremendous influence that Homer had on Gonzales as a person, as well as an artist, when Gonzales was first beginning to paint.

In an attempt to find the Gonzales letters to Homer, which from his comments to Gonzales Homer so obviously enjoyed, I spent a week in the fall of 1992 at the Winslow Homer Museum in Prout's Neck, Maine, and at the Homer Archives at the Bowdoin College Museum of Art in Brunswick, but I found nothing. The letters were evidently discarded either by Homer himself or by his heirs. They would have proved, like Gonzales's other letters and diary entries, to be very interesting and revealing. However, while I was unable to find them, my stay in Maine offered me the opportunity to have very helpful conversations with several Homer scholars, including his biographer, Philip Beam. Those conversations did much to help me understand the relationship that an aspiring young artist had with one of the world's most renowned painters.

Also related to Homer is another document in the Rosenberg's collection of Gonzales memorabilia: the rough, type-written draft of an essay about the times he and Homer spent together at the artist's studio in Maine beginning with Gonzales's first visit to Prout's Neck. Parts of that essay are included in this biography.

On other occasions, my research on Gonzales took me far beyond the confines of Galveston, Texas. Twice, I went to work in the archives of the Louisiana Collection at the New Orleans Public Library and the Historic New Orleans Collection. I also made several very productive visits to Washington, D.C., to the Archives of American Art at the National Portrait Gallery, which during the summer of 1993 had mounted a comprehensive exhibit of paintings by American artists—pictures that were originally displayed at the Columbian Exposition held in Chicago in 1893 to celebrate the 400th anniversary of Columbus's discovery of America. Boyer Gonzales was in Chicago for the exposition and was inspired by the paintings by Whistler, Sargent, and Homer. That visit to Chicago helped Gonzales to take his painting more seriously; the same exhibit, a century later in Washington, did much to bring me closer to Gonzales.

In 1992, on my way to Maine to search for the lost letters of Gonzales's correspondence with Homer, I took time to research in the archives of the city of New York and at the "Little Church around the Corner" where Boyer and Nell Hertford were married in 1907. I even had the opportunity during the spring of 1994 to visit the antiquarian library at the Royal Academy of Art in London and browse through the illustrated catalogue of an exhibit that Gonzales had seen during his trip to Europe in 1892. On another occasion, I had a most memorable time retracing Gonzales's footsteps through Germany and Switzerland, sailing down the Rhine, visiting places he had visited, and looking for buildings and monuments he had sketched.

I soon found it necessary to go to Corpus Christi to search for information regarding ancestors of the Gonzales family. And it was my good fortune on another occasion to locate, quite by accident, distant relatives of the Gonzales family, the Blossmans of Corpus Christi and Houston. These relatives were so distant that they were quite unaware that Boyer Gonzales ever existed, much less that he was one of America's most highly praised artists during the last thirty years of his life; they were kind enough to supply me with documents that revealed a great deal about Boyer Gonzales's Spanish ancestry, information that even Boyer Gonzales's son, Boyer, Jr., never knew.

Indeed, it was Boyer Gonzales, Jr., who, beginning in 1980, bequeathed to the Rosenberg Library a large number of his father's oil paintings and watercolors, many of which are reproduced in this book. Gonzales, Jr., likewise saw to it that, upon the death of his wife, Elizabeth, the Gonzales family papers would also be given to the library's Galveston and Texas History Center. Mrs. Gonzales died in Seattle in 1989.

Granted, the Gonzales collection at the Rosenberg is not an especially large one, but it is so diverse in the type of documents it contains that it is, indeed, a rare one. Nearly every type of useful document is there: diaries, invitations, scrapbooks, sketch pads, letters, postal cards, train tickets, envelopes, newspapers, travel brochures, pencil drawings, pen and ink sketches, clippings, stock certificates, tintypes, and photographs of family and friends. Several were taken in the late 1880s of the interior of their Galveston home. There are even several snapshots taken by Boyer's younger brother, Alcie, showing the damage caused to their home during the 1900 storm which devastated the island city.

People who keep such things do not, generally, do so with the idea in mind that someone a hundred years later might be reading them with the intent of using them to see what kind of light each one might be able to shed on that individual. Much of the material—the clippings in the scrapbooks, for example—is not dated. I found that I had to date items using both internal evidence and divine guidance.

What had been saved proved to be extremely valuable, especially the diaries and letters. Together, all the documents bring to life a sensitive, intelligent, industrious, witty, gentle, and talented group of people, family as well as friends.

The material in the Gonzales family papers brings to life more than a hundred fifty years of the history of that family, and in so doing gives a firsthand glimpse into what life was like in those Victorian times when Galveston was in its prime. The world of the Gonzales family is not limited just to Galveston; that world stretches from the northwest, when the states of Oregon and Washington were still the Washington Territory, to the northeast and the rocky coast of Maine. Then it takes in the states that come in between: Georgia, New Mexico, Michigan, Illinois, California, Florida, and Colorado, as well as the interior of Mexico.

The world of Boyer Gonzales also crossed the Atlantic and took in Germany, England, Italy, the Netherlands, and France. There were visits to the Royal Academy of Art and the National Gallery in London, the Louvre in Paris, the Uffizi in Florence, and the Rijksmuseum in Amsterdam. The vibrant descriptions in the letters and diaries of Boyer and his wife, especially during the time they spent in Venice, recreate those places as they were in the last decades of the nineteenth century and the years prior to the First World War.

What an imaginative family they were! They were sometimes so imaginative that their records get in the way of the historian's obligation to distinguish truth from myth. One of the great obstacles I encountered was how to deal with Gonzales's relationship with the Dutch marine painter Hendrik Willem Mesdag, who was born in 1831 and died at the Hague in 1915. At the beginning of my study, I found numerous references to their personal relationship and later realized that Mesdag had a profound influence on Gonzales as a painter.

On February 8, 1981, Boyer Gonzales, Jr., addressed a special meeting of the Friends of the Rosenberg Library as part of the inauguration of an exhibition of the works of both father and son. At that time, he spoke of his father's relationship with the Dutch artist: "One of my father's principal teachers was a very distinguished gentleman named Mesdag. My father used to go to Europe frequently in the summer to sell cotton, and I think that he sold very little cotton and spent a lot of time in museums and studied.[1] He studied with Mr. Mesdag at the Hague and maybe on several occasions, I don't know. But one of the best family stories [is about Mesdag]. My mother and father were married in 1907 and went to Europe in 1908, and Dad took my mother to call on the Mesdags and they were very cordial. Mrs. Mesdag served tea, and Mr. Mesdag brought a series of his paintings out for them to see. My father was a gentleman of the old school, a very difficult kind of man . . . and he had tremendous respect for his elders and particularly for someone as famous as Mr. Mesdag. One of the paintings came before them, and Daddy said, 'Mr. Mesdag, I think that's awfully good.' Mr. Mesdag's rejoinder was, 'They are *all* good.'"[2]

It is a good story. Unfortunately, it is not true. Or it is at least a gross exaggeration of fact. During the summer of 1892, Boyer Gonzales, at the age was twenty-seven, did go to Europe, spending nearly a month at a spa in Germany. Letters to his father indicate that on his way there he passed two days in the Netherlands, but he spent most of that time in Amsterdam with clients of his father. As a tourist, he was bewitched—as his diary reveals—by the beauty of the city and the picturesque countryside, and while he notes that he visited museums in London and Venice, never did he record visiting a museum or art gallery in Amsterdam or even mention, for that matter, being in the Hague. Nor does he make note of meeting any painters, let alone Mesdag. Had he met him and painted with him, he would have surely been impressed enough to mention it in his diary. It is safe to assume that in 1892 he did not know of the Dutch painter's existence, let alone his work.

With regard to the trip that Boyer and Nell Gonzales took to Europe in 1908, there are documents—a comment in a letter which she wrote to her sister and an entry in her diary which she kept during the trip—that show they did visit Mesdag's museum and studio. The entry notes: "Mesdag's Gallery, although small, is the most artistic of any we've seen. It is attached to his studio and residence which are most picturesque." She adds, ". . . we had the extreme pleasure of visiting Mr. Mesdag in his studio. . . ."[3] No mention is made of Boyer Gonzales's studying with the Dutch marine painter nor of taking tea and "visiting" with the Mesdags. Indeed, the latter would have been most difficult, if not impossible, as they would have had no means of communication, entrapped as they were in their English and touring French.

Still, it is, as I said, a good story. And it is precisely that vivid imagination which was part of Boyer Gonzales's charm and personality. Like most writers and artists, he loved to invent and embellish. On the occasion of the father-son exhibition of paintings at the Rosenberg Library in 1981, Boyer, Jr., told the gathering that his father was "not only interested in the sea, he knew the sea and he shipped once, as I suppose a teen-ager or a very young man, as a supercargo on a barkentine to Philadelphia with a load of his father's cotton. They got into a hurricane and were blown out of the Yucatan channel, and they were 42 days [getting from Galveston] to Philadelphia. He had some marvelous sea experiences to tell about. He also had a great imagination and I think his stories got better with the years."[4] They must have been good stories. I find the lives of all the family to be exciting and fascinating on their own, even eliminating the myth.

One other problem I uncovered had to do with the birth dates of both Boyer Gonzales and his wife, Eleanor Eliza Hertford. Official records for vital statistics for that period either do not exist or they are very hard to come by. To add to the dilemma, the dates of birth, especially for Boyer, vary depending upon the document. Sometimes, he reports be-

ing born September 22, 1867. On other occasions, it appears, as it does in his obituary, as being 1877. *The National Cyclopaedia of American Biography,* which was published in 1935, the year following his death, records his being born on September 22, 1874. Another biographical sketch published in 1976 indicates he was born in 1878. Not having the correct information seems to have frustrated more than one biographer. On July 18, 1972, a research assistant at the Texas State Historical Survey Committee wrote to Boyer Gonzales, Jr., in Seattle to inform him of a project that was being undertaken regarding prominent Texas artists. He found, "Our biographical and professional data on his [father's] life and career is scanty; we do not even have the exact dates of his life."[5] Being helpful, Boyer, Jr., informed his corespondent what he had always known to be correct: his father had been born in 1867.

It was not until after I had read the record of their marriage that I found the correct date of birth. The wedding took place on the morning of September 21, 1907, in the Church of the Transfiguration in New York City, better known as "The Little Church around the Corner."[6] The marriage record states he is forty-three years old. In his own handwriting, Gonzales gives his birth date as September 22, 1864. Several hours later, the bride and groom went to the Department of Health of the city of New York to sign their certificate of marriage.[7] This document also indicates that Gonzales was forty-three years old.

It is important to realize that he did not begin his career as a serious artist until after their marriage. Of course, most successful artists begin painting seriously long before they are middle-aged. But not Boyer Gonzales. That is when he started. The day after they were married, the couple left to spend their honeymoon in Woodstock, New York, where Gonzales studied watercolor with the noted painter, Birge Harrison, at an art colony sponsored by the Art Students League of New York. His son later admitted, and photographs attest to the fact, that Boyer Gonzales was decades older than his fellow "students."

The birth date of his wife, Eleanor, presented a very different problem. Whereas with Boyer, I had many different dates to deal with, with his wife, I had none. In none of the Gonzales family papers or other documents in the Rosenberg Library, including the *Galveston Daily News,* was a date mentioned. At first, I had to rely on information supplied by friends of the Gonzaleses who were under the impression that Nell, as she was called, was much younger that her husband. Several indicated that she could have been fifteen years younger. It was not until I found the marriage record at the Episcopal Church in New York City that I came to the conclusion she was more his contemporary than she would have liked others to know. The document issued by the City of New York, signed just hours after the ceremony, states she was thirty years old.[8] But the marriage certificate of the church contradicts that. That paper, which she signed, gives her birth date as March 8, 1869.[9] That made Nell thirty-eight years old, just five years younger than her husband. Additional evidence appears in vital statistics records in the Rosenberg's collection; these indicate that Nell's father, John Hertford, a teller at the First National Bank, died of dysentery in April of 1869, just one month following the birth of his daughter.

There is one other reason to accept their birth dates as recorded on the marriage certificate, signed in the presence of the Episcopal priest who conducted the ceremony. At the bottom of the page is printed: "We, the undersigned, in the PRESENCE OF GOD, hereby solemnly declare, without reservation or evasion, that the above facts, and all other statements, whether in writing or given orally are TRUE in every particular to the best of our knowledge and belief."[10] Following are the signatures of the bride and groom. It should be noted that the words that are written in capital letters appear so in the document.

Indeed, each one had reasons for concealing correct birth dates. Perhaps each felt the pressure of age. As for Boyer Gonzales, at forty-three, it was certainly late for him to begin a career as an artist. And Eleanor Hertford, at thirty-eight, certainly could not have been looked upon as a blushing, young bride. The certificate does much to explain why they had only one child; they were both late in beginning their life together.

One special point should be made about the sketches and water colors that Boyer Gonzales painted during his trip to Mexico in the spring of 1895. In the light of today, the scenes of village life he captured may seem commonplace: adobe buildings, dusty streets, and Mexicans in sombreros and serapes; in those days, however, such paintings were unique. American artists had not yet discovered Mexico; that would not happen until the 1930s and 1940s when colonies of artists began to appear. In 1895, not even Mexican artists were painting such scenes. In that sense, Boyer Gonzales's watercolors of late nineteenth-century Mexico are, indeed, special.

Regarding Mexico, comments must also be made about the family's ancestral connections with that country. Boyer Gonzales's Spanish-born grandfather, Victor, practiced medicine there for over twenty years; his father, Tomás González, was born in Tampico in 1829; and his uncle, Francisco, was born in Guanajuato a year earlier. Today, Boyer Gonzales can, without hesitation or question, be considered the first American of Mexican descent to become such a successful and respected artist, and today's Mexican-American community can and should take pride in that. In fact, there is no indication that the family ever thought of qualifying themselves as Mexican Americans.

As will be seen, both of Boyer Gonzales's grandparents were Spanish by birth; they found their way to Mexico by historical accident during Spain's attempt to crush Mexico's rebellion to gain its independence. Boyer's grandfather was a surgeon in the Spanish army. The family's immigration to the United States was directly related to problems Mexico was having with Texas in the 1830s. When Boyer's grandmother and her two sons arrived in New Orleans early in 1836, they responded as did the vast majority of immigrants of that period. Like the Germans, Irish, French, or British before them, immigrants from Mexico did what was expected of them in order to become Americans. Like other Mexicans, the Gonzalezes were obliged to forget their ancestral customs and attitudes and adopt the more Americanized Anglo-Saxon attitudes of the United States.

Society, in those times, and for the most part even today, expected all immigrants to cast off most of the cultural baggage that they brought with them, including their native language, in order to more easily assimilate into the American culture. History shows that children of immigrants always find it easier to do than their parents. So it is today with the children of Cuban, Asian, and Mexican immigrants.

And so it was with the three Gonzalezes when they arrived in the United States over a hundred fifty years ago. Boyer's grandmother evidently discovered that adapting was so difficult that she ultimately moved to Havana where she felt more comfortable in its Hispanic atmosphere and where she died. His father, however, easily acculturated. While Tomás González never forgot his native Spanish, he quickly learned English, felt quite at home being called Thomas Gonzales, later married an American from Philadelphia, left the Roman Catholic faith, and took on the Episcopal religion of his wife. Be that as it may, as he grew older, he learned quickly that his Mexican birth would benefit his cotton firms, as he often did business in Mexico. The same is true of his brother, Francis, who was appointed by the Mexican government to be the first Mexican consul in Galveston, with the offices of the consulate in his home on Broadway. It was a post he proudly held for thirty years, having the distinction of being the dean of the Consular Corps in the city at the time of his death.

However, the children of Thomas Gonzales, including, of course, Boyer, never seem to have given a second thought about their ancestral roots. They were born Americans; what Spanish they knew was rudimentary. Phrases such as "Quién sabe" are scattered throughout Boyer's diaries. But not learning the language of the ancestors was common among immigrants. Whereas today, many descendants of immigrants take pride in their ancestry and take great pains to seek out their cultural roots, in those days, immigrants, more often than not, did not strive to pass on their native language or customs. Many, regrettably by today's standards, made special efforts not to. Such was the case of the Gonzales family in the late nineteenth century.

Boyer Gonzales had a profound affection for Mexico, but when he traveled south of the border, as he did many times, he did so as an American, either, at first, as a businessman working for his father's cotton firm, or later, as a tourist always taking time out to paint the landscapes that fascinated him. Both Boyer and later his son are typical of the children and grandchildren of immigrants. They simply thought of themselves as Americans. Be that as it may, Boyer Gonzales retains the honor of being the first and foremost American artist of Mexican descent.

Finally, this work is more than the biography of a talented and critically acclaimed American painter. Boyer Gonzales's story brings to life the years during the Mexican Revolution of 1810 and the three decades of turmoil that followed as Mexico tried first to gain its independence and then to pull the country together. Those were the times of Gonzales's Spanish-born grandparents. The story of Boyer Gonzales's boyhood is also the story of Galveston and Texas during the last half of the nineteenth century, touching all the bases: social, political, and economic. Those were the times of Boyer Gonzales's parents and their friends, the Rosenbergs, the Kempners, the Moodys, and the Seinsheimers, names that ring throughout the history of the city.

The biography of Gonzales, however, also reveals much about life and culture in Europe during the end of the nineteenth century and the beginning of the twentieth. In addition, it opens a hitherto unknown door to reveal something new about the life and works of America's most famous painter, Winslow Homer, Gonzales's mentor and close friend. But central to the biography is the struggle of a man who had faith in himself and overcame any number of obstacles to do something that only he believed he could do: develop his artistic talents and become a painter of international note. Boyer Gonzales's story is a typical American story about a man who relentlessly attempts to turn his dreams into realities.

Writing about the life and times of the Gonzales family has been anything but dull. My work was made more pleasant by meeting and working with many helpful people, mostly librarians, throughout the United States and Europe, including Mattie Kelley, registrar at the Bowdoin College Museum of Art, which has the Winslow Homer archives. Special among them are those good friends at the Rosenberg: Nancy Milner Smith, the executive director of the Library, and Lisa Shippee Lambert, former head of Special Collections at the Galveston and Texas History Center, who is currently the archivist at the Research Center at the Panhandle Plains Historical Museum in Canyon, Texas. I would also like to give special thanks to Casey Greene, formerly the assistant archivist who so expertly catalogued the Gonzales family papers and who was appointed the head of Special Collections at the Rosenberg when Lisa Lambert departed. Others on the library's staff of experts who have been a part of this work include Shelly Henley, Anna Peebler, Judy Young, Pat McCall, Lois Ranck, Jessica Clarke, Julia Dunn, and Helen Campos. I would be remiss not to mention John Hyatt, formerly of the Rosenberg Library, who was the first to offer me the challenge of writing the biography of Boyer Gonzales. And then, of course, there are the active members of the Board of Directors of the Rosenberg who granted the funds for the publication of this book.

I would like to recognize my colleague Cecilia Steinfeldt of the Witte Memorial Museum in San Antonio, who has worked over the years in the Gonzales archives at the Rosenberg and who, in 1993, helped bring Boyer Gonzales back into the public eye by including some of his works in her book *Art for History's Sake: The Texas Collection of the Witte Museum.*

I should also like to thank the rector of the Universidad de las Americas-Puebla, Enrique Cárdenas, and the administration of this, the institution in Mexico where I have taught for over twenty years. For the last four years, they most generously provided me with grants that have helped me to travel and conduct the research to complete this work. Those grants accurately represent the sincere interest that the University has regarding faculty research.

My thanks also go to Drs. Stephen Curley and Donald Willett, two colleagues at the Galveston campus of Texas A&M University. During the spring of 1994, they gave me the opportunity to present an illustrated-lecture on Gonzales and his paintings as part of a seminar series titled "Texans Who Made a Difference." Two years later, in April of 1996, I gave another lecture on his father, Thomas, as part of their series "A Galveston Odyssey," offered in celebration of the 125th anniversary of the Galveston Historical Foundation.

There are those friends, old and new, both in the United States and Mexico who have always shown an interest in this effort, beginning with Ann and Bobby Moody, Karina Romero, Dessa Crawford, Richard Eisenhour, Carlos Germán Gutiérrez Lara, Miguel Sanchez Sandoval, Sue Yeatman, Carmen Lopez Blumenkron, and Aquiles S. Serdan. Finally, I would like to mention Sergio Campos and Juan Carlos Bolaños, two young scholars, one from Galveston and the other from a village in Michoacán, Mexico, both on their way into the academic stratosphere. Now they can all get to know the individual to whom I was addicted during the last four years.

In a special corner is Nonie Thompson, who most kindly is always there sitting in for my mentor, the late Arthur Graham, the individual who inspired me and so many others during our years at Ball High School in Galveston. I would also like to thank Margaret Schlankey, Don Willett, and Brian James Schmidly who critically read various versions of the manuscript and Craig Burrow who assisted me in transcribing and editing my conversations with Lise Darst that appear as the Afterword to this work. There is one other person very important to me, James Frederick Korth. Often, when times were strained and difficult, I could always count on a phone call and a question, "How's Boyer?"

Two others who became actively involved at the very end of the writing of this work are Merri Scheibe Edwards and Dorothy Tefft. Both of them have careful and critical eyes as well as active and accurate editorial pens. How fortunate it was for me to have them accept the tedious job at the eleventh hour of reading the manuscript as I readied it for publication by the Texas A&M University Press. Not enough thanks go to all of those at the Press.

Finally, I would like to mention someone essential to the writing of this biography: Elisabeth Darst of the Rosenberg Library. No one knows more about the works of Boyer Gonzales than Lise herself, an accomplished and award-winning artist as well as part-time peanut farmer. She actively participated from the beginning to, literally, the very end. During the summer of 1995, Lise took time to speak with me on several occasions specifically about the development of Gonzales as an artist and the role that Winslow Homer played in that development. Without her honest interest, devoted attention, and constant encouragement, this biography could never have been written. To Lise, my very special gratitude.

EDWARD SIMMEN

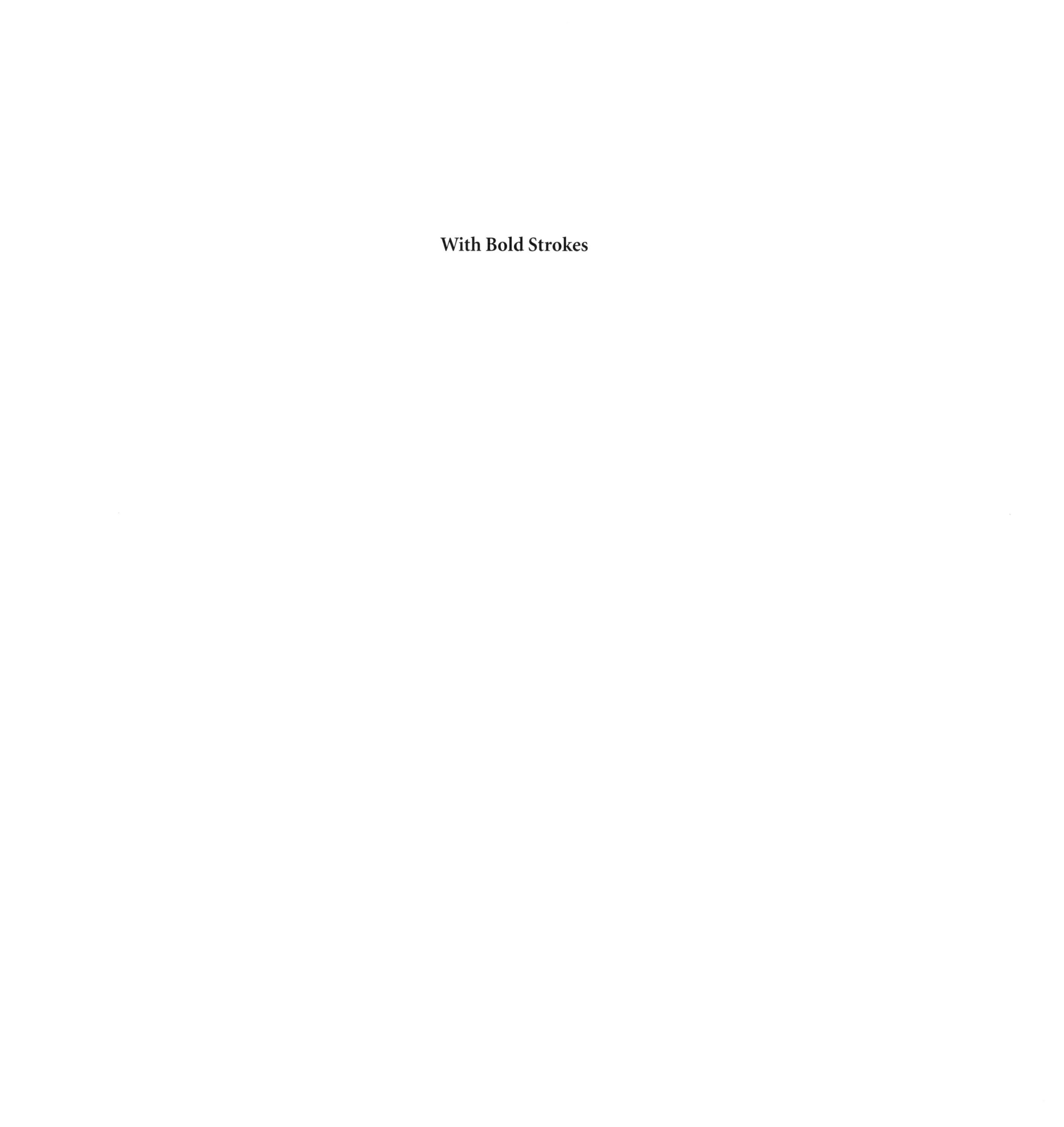

With Bold Strokes

Part 1

BOYER GONZALES'S LIFE

The Gonzales Family

Boyer Gonzales, a critically acclaimed marine and landscape painter from Galveston, Texas, died in his hometown on February 14, 1934. He was sixty-nine years old. Less than a year later, his biography and photograph appeared in volume XXIV of the prestigious publication *The National Cyclopaedia of American Biography*. Therein it was noted that "few artists have understood so intimately the moods of the sea and the ways of the seabirds [as did Gonzales]." And while he "painted the mountains around Taos and other landscapes elsewhere . . . his marines are the cream of his work." Gonzales was recognized as "a writer of talent [who] did several articles on wild life, bird habits, etc. on which he was considered an authority" and was praised as "a man of brilliant, vital mind and modest, retiring, lovable nature, a witty conversationalist, well-informed, kindly and courteous."[1]

The entry ended by listing some of the more important clubs and societies that he had been invited to join during his lifetime. These included: the National Arts Club, the American Watercolor Society, the New York Water Color Society, the Salmagundi Club of New York City, the Wash-ington [D.C.] Water Color Club, the Mississippi Art Association, the Texas Fine Arts Association, and the American Federation of Art. His paintings were to be found in the collections of the Rosenberg Library of Galveston, the Delgado Museum of New Orleans, the Houston Museum of Fine Arts, the Witte Memorial Museum of San Antonio, the municipal schools of Galveston, and in numerous private collections in the United States, Canada, and Europe.

The first time he exhibited outside of Texas was when an early work was shown in the Texas Pavilion at the St. Louis World's Fair in 1904, but his big break came in 1916 when he was fifty-two years old. His watercolor, *In a Texas Swamp*, was selected to be included in the Twenty-Eighth Annual Exhibition of Water Colors, Pastels and Miniatures by American Artists, sponsored by the Art Institute of Chicago. This particular exhibition was larger than usual in that it contained 612 works by 170 American artists. Gonzales's prize-winning work was then selected to go on an extended tour of museums in cities throughout the United States.[2]

By 1924, the name Boyer Gonzales was well-known in the art world. That year the Art Institute of Chicago presented its Fourth International Water Color Exhibition, with works by American artists displayed with those by artists from across the globe. For this exhibit, 515 works by 154 Americans were presented, including watercolors by George William Eggers, Lois Lenski, George Pearse Ennis, Joseph Pennell, Edward Hopper, and John Singer Sargent. This time, the jury selected five works by Boyer Gonzales: *The Hunter, The Lobsterman, Taking in Sail, The Beacon,* and *Nutting Time.*[3]

During his lifetime, he had innumerable one-man exhibitions in well-known art galleries and museums throughout the country. His name was closely linked with other highly respected artists of the day, including Winslow Homer, George Bellows, Birge Harrison, and William Whittemore, yet he was nearly forty-five years old before he decided to change the direction of his life in order to devote his entire time to his art.

Boyer Gonzales was a most unusual and complex man, and he led a most unusual and extraordinary life. However, to understand him, it is necessary to be acquainted with the lives and times of his fascinating ancestors, each of whom affected the artist profoundly and had much to do with shaping his life as well as his work.

Gonzales's father, Thomas, who was a native of Tampico, Mexico, arrived in Galveston from Port Isabel in 1853. Accompanied by his second wife, Edith, he wasted little time in setting himself up in business as a cotton exporter. He was only twenty-four years old but the city itself was even younger. It had been founded just fifteen years before in 1838, two years after Texas had gained its independence from Mexico.

Together Galveston and the Gonzales family grew and prospered, and, ironically, together they declined. Once the ancestors of Boyer Gonzales left Spain and landed in the new world, the Gonzales family lasted only four generations before it died out and disappeared. However, for over a century, until the death of the last Gonzales in 1980, the family carved a deep impression on all aspects of life in the city, commercial and cultural, a mark that was later to extend far beyond the limits of Galveston Island. The deepest roots of the family, however, are found in Spain and their history, as it is related to Texas, begins with events that took place in Mexico early in the nineteenth century.

The Mexican Revolution of 1910 and the Arrival of the Spanish Army

It was still very dark in the small Mexican pueblo of Dolores in the state of Guanajuato on the morning of September 16, 1810, when the priest of the village, Father Miguel Hidalgo, began ringing the church bell earlier than usual to call his parishioners—most of whom were poor, illiterate, and totally devoted Indian farmers—to morning prayers. On that morning, however, he had something else on his mind. Once he had them together, he raised his voice and began to incite them to unite and declare their independence from Spain. This plea—later to be called the *Grito,* or Cry, of Dolores—had been long in arriving. But once heard, the Mexican people responded in great masses and began a bloody insurgency that raged across the country for more than a decade, ripping Mexico apart.

From the very beginning of the revolt, the Spanish crown took every move it could to quell the uprising for independence. The first act was to send troops, and with each additional setback, they sent more troops.

With the additional troops, of course, came the need to increase the size of the medical corps. Among the soldiers was a young surgeon named Lt. Victor González, the grandfather of Boyer Gonzales. Very little is known about him. He was born around 1790 in Valladolid, the capital city of Castile, the son of Gen. Antonio González, a celebrated military surgeon. Victor González, at an early age, followed his father's example and joined the army. He became a junior officer under the command of Don Juan Samaniego, the surgeon general of the Spanish army, who was also from Valladolid and a close friend of the González family.

Another young doctor on General Samaniego's staff was Juan Justo de los Reyes. In Tarragona, Spain, early in 1814, he had married his commanding officer's daughter, Rita Samaniego, a lineal descendant of Ponce de Leon. On February 13, 1815, Rita gave birth to a daughter, Elena de los Reyes Samaniego.[4] Some months after the birth, Samaniego's regiment, including Victor González and Juan de los Reyes, was deployed to Mexico to help put down the ever increasing revolutionary activity.

With the capture and execution of José María Morelos later in 1815, the Spanish authorities felt that Mexico was safe enough for their soldiers to bring families from Spain, which is what Juan de los Reyes did. Rita Samaniego de los Reyes and her daughter left Spain and sailed for Veracruz.

The constant arrival of additional troops did little to put down the insurgents, especially in the provinces. Fierce fighting continued throughout the country for another five years. An uneasy peace came when a mestizo officer in the Spanish army, Agustín de Iturbide, published a declaration on February 24, 1821, proclaiming Mexico's independence from Spain. He placated the Roman Catholic episcopacy by establishing Roman Catholicism as the official religion of the country. Of special interest to the Spanish population, including Victor González, was Iturbide's proclamation granting citizenship and equal rights to all those living in Mexico, including Spaniards, Criollos, Mestizos, Indians, and Africans, who had been brought to New Spain as slaves.[5]

However, Iturbide chose not to leave well enough alone. To the general confusion of everyone, on July 21, 1822, Iturbide crowned himself Agustín the First, Emperor of Mexico. His reign was short, lasting only until March 19, 1823, when he abdicated and fled with his family to London.

Congress declared Iturbide a traitor and issued public orders to execute him if he returned to Mexico; this is exactly what happened when he arrived in the spring of 1824.

A degree of peace and harmony finally did come to the country later in 1824, when Congress wrote and ratified a constitution and elected Gen. Guadalupe Victoria the country's first president. He remained until the end of his term in 1828.

During the years following the overthrow of the Spanish rule, the Mexicans' hatred and distrust of Spaniards and, indeed, for anything Spanish, became legendary. There always loomed the threat—real or not—of an attempt by the crown to invade and reconquer the colony. Among the Spaniards, there was the ever-present fear that Mexicans would retaliate against the Spanish as Hidalgo's followers had done at the outset of the revolution. As a result, many of the Spaniards in Mexico fled the country—either to return to Spain or to live in friendlier territories or in colonies such as Cuba.

But many others remained, like Victor González and his fellow surgeon Juan Justo de los Reyes, who were determined to make Mexico their home. Then, sometime around 1825, de los Reyes died, leaving Rita a widow with a ten-year-old daughter, Elena. Whether out of love for the woman or a feeling of loyalty to his friend and colleague, González married Rita and, with Elena, moved first to the colonial city of Puebla and then to Guanajuato, where González settled into medical practice. In the fall of 1828, Rita gave birth to their first son, Francisco Alcibíades.[6]

Not long after Francisco's birth, Mexico began again to have serious political problems, problems that threatened its social stability. Its first president, Gen. Guadalupe Victoria, had managed to sustain a delicate balancing act and remained in office to serve out his four-year term. In the election that followed, Gen. Manuel Gómez Pedraza, a conservative, won by one electoral vote, defeating Vicente Guerrero, a liberal general. Guerrero's supporters, however, led by Gen. Antonio

Lopez de Santa Ana, forced Pedraza to resign before he could take office. That left Congress open to offer Guerrero the presidency. He accepted.

To add to the confusion, rumors resurfaced that Spain was going to try once again to reconquer the country. There were solid grounds for such fears. After all, the Spanish government, which had never officially recognized Mexico's independence, was well aware of the turmoil within and the instability of the Mexican government. In addition, the Spanish knew that there existed a strong pro-Spanish sentiment; there were many Spaniards living in Mexico who actively and vocally supported an invasion to overthrow the shaky Mexican government, annul its independence, and reclaim the land in the name of the Crown. Given the conditions of the time, such rumors were completely believable.

To counter such fears, the Mexican government, on the very day that Guerrero had been selected president, passed a law that would have forced Spaniards living in Mexico to leave the country, a great many of whom—exactly like Victor González—had been members of the Spanish military. González, with reason, was immediately suspect, and he was forced to act with dispatch. Together with his wife, who was two months pregnant, his infant son, and step-daughter, González left Guanajuato and traveled across Mexico to Tampico where everyone imagined the invading forces would land and where the González family could find refuge among fellow royalist sympathizers.

Regarding the rumors of a Spanish invasion, Spain was actually in no position to do anything overt to bring down the Mexican government and its legally installed president. Every move had to be executed in secret. Gen. Ignacio Barradas, the king's commanding officer in Cuba, received instructions from Spain to take a force of 2,700 troops, invade Mexico and begin to retake the colony.

On June 24, 1829, the Barradas expedition landed at Tampico, just as rumor had predicted. After the troops dis-embarked, the ships were ordered to return to Havana. González promptly offered his services as a military surgeon and joined the forces of General Barradas.

Barradas and his troops conquered the city with very little trouble and marched inland. They then readied themselves for an attack by Mexican forces under the command of Santa Ana, who had personally assembled a force from the state of Veracruz, commandeered a small fleet of sailing vessels, and embarked for Tampico. Upon landing, he began making his plans to attack, which he did on August 21, but the Spanish forces drove Santa Ana's troops into a temporary retreat. By mid-September, however, the Spanish army collapsed and surrendered, devastated by disease and a lack of supplies. In less than three weeks, Barradas lost 908 men, one-third of his troops, mostly to contaminated water and yellow fever, to which the Mexican troops from the tropics were immune.

The Mexican government promptly demanded that the Spanish troops, as well as any Mexican collaborators, among them Victor González, return to Cuba. However, there were no Spanish vessels available since the ships that had brought the army to Mexico had already returned to Havana. There was nothing left for Santa Ana to do but to allow his prisoners of war to remain at large in the region and to treat the injured prisoners in local military hospitals until a means of transport could be found. Quickly, arrangements were made with the government of the United States, acting under the terms of the Monroe Doctrine, to come to Mexico's aid and by October, the majority of Spaniards had been taken to New Orleans on American ships where they awaited the arrival of Spanish ships to transport them to its bases in Cuba.

Not all the Spaniards, however, were forced to leave Tampico. In the aftermath of the battles, Victor González helped treat the wounded Mexicans as well as the Spanish, and Santa Ana relented and permitted González and his family to stay. This was fortunate, as Rita, in the last months of pregnancy, was unable to travel. On November 10, 1829, less than a month after the Spaniards had left Mexico, she gave birth to their second son, Tomás.[7]

Even with the defeat of the Spanish invaders, Mexico could not be considered a sea of tranquillity. Political tension continued between the conservative and liberal factions. President Guerrero, who in 1829 ascended to the presidency by an act of Congress, was able to hold on to the reigns of government until 1830 when he, too, was overthrown by his vice president, Anastasio Bustamante. Bustamante served until 1831, when he followed his predecessors and resigned under pressure from a liberal faction led by the General Santa Ana. As Iturbide had done, Bustamante sought exile in London.

With Bustamante well out of the way, the Mexican Congress selected Santa Ana to be the next president, but the general pulled another surprise out of his bag of political tricks. After accepting the presidency, he promptly left Mexico City, retired to his hacienda near Jalapa, in the state of Veracruz, and let his vice president, Valentín Gómez Farías, serve as provisional president. For the next two years, Gómez Farías ruled the country with dictatorial strength, issuing drastic decrees directed at the army and the Roman Catholic Church. First, he moved to secularize the University of Mexico, whose faculty at the time was composed entirely of priests. Then his government declared that it, not the Church, would make clerical appointments. In addition, tithing to the Church was declared illegal, and finally, all members of the clergy were to renounce their vows.

Confusion was rife. The country once again shattered into several factions. In the past, Santa Ana had championed liberal causes. Now, the more conservative elements of the Church appealed to him to come to their aid. Hearing the call, he left his comfortable hacienda in 1833 and returned to Mexico City. In three quick moves, Santa Ana denounced Gómez Farías, displaced him from office, and took over the government. Then, to strengthen his hand, he not only canceled the Constitution of 1824, but he proceeded to nullify every reform that Gómez Farías had made. He also took drastic steps to transform the Mexican government—taking the rights and responsibilities of government away from the states and centralizing all power in the government in Mexico City.

His actions produced immediate effects, especially in Texas. At the time, non-Mexicans outnumbered Mexican nationals in Texas by five to one. The vast majority of the non-Mexicans were English-speaking Protestants from the southern United States, most of whom favored the more liberal Constitution of 1824 by which they had settled in the Mexican state of Coahuila and Texas. That constitution had given them many of the rights and privileges that they were accustomed to as American citizens. And these American settlers were not alone; many Mexicans, especially those in the northern states of the republic—such as Coahuila, Nuevo Leon, and Tamaulipas—also began to voice concern at Santa Ana's totalitarian acts and began to resist.

At the same time, significant changes were also taking place in the González family. In Matamoros, in 1832, Rita's seventeen-year-old daughter, Elena, married Richard D. Blossman, a prosperous cotton merchant from New Orleans who had business dealings and financial interests in Mexico. Blossman, born in 1799 in England, had immigrated to the United States, settling in Alton, Illinois, a small town on the Mississippi River about fifteen miles north of St. Louis. It was not long before he left to seek his fortune in New Orleans. During this period, great fortunes were easily made in the Crescent City as long as the individual was willing to forego pleasure and work long and hard. Blossman was such a young man. His business had expanded until, by the time of his marriage, he also had offices in Matamoros and Tampico, where, in February of 1833, Elena gave birth to the first of thirteen children. Soon, apprehensive at so much political turmoil in Mexico, the Blossmans packed their belongings and, late in 1834, sailed for New Orleans.[8]

Victor and Rita González remained in Tampico with their two children, though each day they worried more as they watched the relationship worsen between the Mexican government and the settlers in Texas. Increasing numbers of American settlers as well as native-born Mexicans in Texas began to be more and more vocal in their opposition to the changes and the reforms that the tightfisted, determined Santa Ana had imposed upon them.

González knew that he had to do something, so during the summer of 1835, he boarded the schooner *Felicia* bound for Cuba. His final destination was to have been Spain where he would arrange for the family's return, but unfortunately, somewhere between Tampico and Havana, the schooner sank and Victor González drowned, leaving Rita once again a widow. This time she was older, with two growing sons aged six and seven, and she tried to decide what to do as she watched the political situation deteriorate not only in Texas but in the region around Tampico.[9]

The problem with the settlers in Texas finally climaxed late in 1835 when Santa Ana and seven thousand troops began a march north across Mexico to put down the open rebellion. He began by laying siege to the Alamo which, after thirteen days of bloody battle, fell to his forces on March 6, 1836. Three weeks later, on direct orders of Santa Ana, Mexican riflemen at Goliad were ordered to kill some 340 rebel troops that had duly surrendered and were disarmed prisoners. Santa Ana was determined to destroy anyone who stood in the way of bringing the region back under his dictatorial control.

Three weeks later, on the afternoon of April 21, an army of about nine hundred rebels, led by Gen. Sam Houston, attacked the much larger but unsuspecting Mexican army bivouacked on the banks of the San Jacinto River near the settlement of Harrisburg. In a battle which lasted a mere eighteen minutes, Houston's forces decimated the Mexicans, killing an estimated 630 and taking prisoner not only 730 officers and men but the Mexican president as well.[10] In an attempt to bargain with General Houston for his life, General Santa Ana agreed to grant the rebellious settlers their independence from Mexico and ordered what forces he had left in Texas to retreat across the Río Bravo, as the Rio Grande was and is still called in Mexico, and to return to Mexico by way of Matamoros, to the north of the port of Tampico.

*The Escape to New Orleans
and a New Destiny*

All of this, however, was of little concern to Rita. Earlier in the spring of 1836, in the midst of the chaos, the enterprising widow, who had lived in Mexico for nearly twenty years, sought the help of friends and sailed with her two sons safely out of Tampico on a ship bound for New Orleans. There, in the home of her socially prominent and prosperous daughter and son-in-law, they found refuge, and her two Mexican sons, Francisco and Tomás, began completely new and vigorous lives,[11] living in the fashionable Creole section of New Orleans, in the heart of the Vieux Carré. At that time, New Orleans was a city divided into two parts: the Spanish and French Creoles lived in the old square section of the city, the Vieux Carré; the new immigrants from the eastern United States settled in the American section on the other side of Canal Street.[12]

The Blossman home was located in the 700 block of Esplanade, between Royal and Bourbon, and accurately reflected the good taste of a well-educated and extremely successful Southern cotton exporter. It was a structure typical of the early nineteenth-century mansions of the area: a two-story town house with a brick front, wooden sides, and

Greek Revival detailing. All told, by 1840, sixteen people made up the Blossman household: Richard, Elena, one son, four daughters, the three Gonzálezes, and six domestic slaves, two males and four females.[13]

Becoming Americans

Tomás and Francisco grew up in a bilingual atmosphere, usually speaking Spanish at home with their mother and English with their Blossman cousins. For the few years that they attended school, they did so along with the Blossman children and were tutored to become what were called "accomplished young gentlemen" as were other male children of the privileged class. Besides English, Latin, and French, they studied literature and mathematics and took classes in music, dancing, and fencing, as well.

In the summer, when yellow fever epidemics plagued the city of New Orleans, the two boys, ages eight and nine, were sent with the Blossman children to Alton, Illinois, where Blossman had first entered business after arriving from England and where he still had business connections and friends.[14] Together the children traveled on one of the many steam boats like the *Belle of the West,* the *Fashion,* the *Henry Clay,* or the famed *Grey Eagle,* known as a "floating palace."

When Francisco and Tómas were ten and eleven, Blossman saw to it that their education took a more practical turn. As with other immigrants, the González children were given lessons in the Protestant work ethic. Their brother-in-law found jobs for them in his cotton brokerage firm; his New Orleans offices were at 86 Bienville, between Royal and Bourbon Streets, just a ten-minute walk from their home. As his firm grew and he prospered, he moved his offices to 12 Conti Street, just off Decatur and one block away from the docks on the Mississippi River.[15] Blossman's prosperity was no accident; he was obsessed with his work, and he expected those who worked with him to be likewise. He obviously taught the two young González boys that success in America meant more than being an "accomplished young gentleman." To be successful meant learning a business, and the business they learned from the ground up was the cotton business. And the language of success in the United States was English.

The older they got, the more they changed, and the more they changed, as did other immigrants, the more American they became. It was not long before Francisco was called Francis by his teachers and Frank by his friends and Tomás was Thomas or Tom. The spelling of González was anglicized to Gonzales and the "a" was sounded as a short "a" as in "add" or "fat": Gon-zal-is. They were not the only ones in the family to become assimilated into the American culture. The census taken in 1850 recorded that even Elena Blossman decided to become known as Helen.

The two boys made one more journey. In 1842, when Francis was fourteen and Thomas had not yet turned thirteen, the boys were sent by their mother to Spain, where they still had relatives in Valladolid.[16] It was not a successful visit because they were unable to adapt to the European way of life. Indeed, even though they were Mexican by birth, they had become not just Americans; they had become "dyed in the *cotton*" Southerners. Only their mother, Rita, was never able to adapt to the American lifestyle. About the time that her two boys returned to Louisiana, she left for Havana, where she felt more comfortable.

When Thomas returned from Spain in the summer of 1845, he began working again in the office of his brother-in-law. Early the next year, Blossman sent the young man on his first trip to Texas to oversee his cotton-related interests in Port Lavaca. Thomas was sixteen; Texas was in its last months as a Republic, prior to being annexed to the United States on December 29, becoming the twenty-sixth state. That annexation led directly to the war between Mexico and the United States that erupted in mid-1846 when American troops, under the command of Gen. Zachary Taylor, invaded

Mexico from various points in Texas. The hostilities did not end until Mexico surrendered and the two countries signed the Treaty of Guadalupe Hidalgo on February 2, 1848.

It was a time of tension and concern for those in Texas like Thomas Gonzales and his brother-in-law, Richard Blossman. Their lives were directly intertwined with Mexico, both personally and financially. Much of their business was with firms in Mexico, and, of course, Thomas had a definite edge. He was a Mexican by birth, which he was always proud to admit. But he also had one other advantage over many other Texas businessmen with whom he was competing: he was perfectly bilingual, speaking both Spanish and English without a trace of a foreign accent. And as with the language, he often found it beneficial to assume two personalities. When he was in Mexico, he was Tomás González. When he was in Texas, he was Thomas Gonzales, cotton merchant.

It was at the height of the Mexican War when Thomas fell in love with Elizabeth Blair, the daughter of a Presbyterian minister. They were married in Port Lavaca on February 13, 1847, in a ceremony conducted by her father, the Reverend William C. Blair. Thomas was the first of the Gonzales family to marry outside of the Roman Catholic faith; this often happened with foreigners who had immigrated to the United States. Both Thomas and Elizabeth were seventeen years old.[17]

They made plans to settle in Port Lavaca, and on November 20, 1847, just ten days after his eighteenth birthday, Thomas surprised his bride with a gift. For $500, he had bought two lots on which they would build their first home. The happy times ended abruptly two months later in January when Elizabeth died, the victim of a cholera epidemic. She had not yet turned eighteen. A little over a month later, on February 28, 1848, Thomas gave his father-in-law power of attorney "to handle all the property I may possess in this state."[18] With that, the distraught young man returned to

New Orleans, three weeks after the signing of the Treaty of Guadalupe Hidalgo.

Thomas Gonzales and Edith Boyer of Philadelphia Wed

Once more in Louisiana, Thomas resumed working for Blossman and living with his family. Early in 1849, he helped them move to a new and even more grand house on the corner of Derbigny and Palmyra in the American section. It was then that he met Edith Boyer, a sixteen-year-old young lady from Philadelphia who was in the city visiting her brother, Pierre C. Boyer, a socially prominent and highly respected Charity Hospital physician who lived near the Blossmans. The Boyers were proud of being related by either marriage or blood to some of the most prominent families in the United States, including the Verplanks and Rumseys of New York, the Weathereds of Maryland, the Sykes of Missouri, and the Caverlys of Delaware.[19]

Two and a half years after the death of his first wife, Thomas and Edith were married on August 28, 1850, in St. Paul's Episcopal Church of New Orleans, the second permanent Episcopal congregation in Louisiana. The Reverend Charles W. Whitall, a chaplain at St. Peter's Chapel, officiated.[20] The bride was just seventeen and the groom was twenty.

Even though he was only twenty, Gonzales had learned the American value of working for himself. After his marriage, he parted company with his brother-in-law and moved with dispatch to be on his own. The couple soon left by boat for Port Isabel, near Matamoros, in Cameron County on the Texas-Mexico border. During the war with Mexico, Gen. Zachary Taylor had used Port Isabel, then Point Isabel, as a base to receive supplies for the American forces stationed at the fort in what is now the city of Brownsville. Beginning in 1849, Port Isabel became an official port of entry for those adventurers setting out for California in search of gold. By 1850, the port was a growing commercial center.

Aided by his Mexican origin and his ability to speak Spanish fluently, Gonzales made the necessary contacts and established a lighterage firm that loaded and unloaded goods coming from and going to ports in both the United States and Mexico. The business quickly prospered. At the same time, in order to become better known, he became active in local politics, serving for a short time as a commissioner of Cameron County.

Thomas was then joined in business by his brother, Francis, who, in 1851, had married Martha Rhea, the daughter of a customs broker in San Diego, Texas, on the Brazos River. Their first child, a son named Francis, Jr., was born later in the year, and a daughter, Mary, in 1854.

Both families intended to settle permanently in the region. In February, 1853, Thomas took the initial steps necessary to purchase five leagues or *sitios*—approximately twenty thousand acres of ranch land—which was carved out of a Spanish land grant called Ganado Mayor, originally belonging to Don Domingo de las Garza. The purchase was legalized on May 16, 1853.[21]

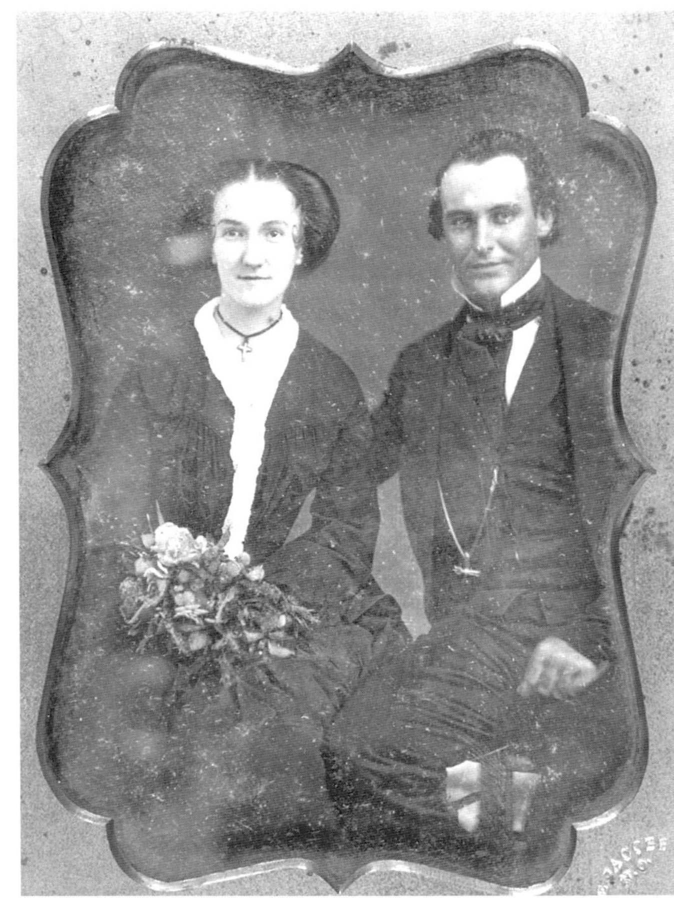

Boyer Gonzales's parents: Thomas and Edith Gonzales

Galveston and Gonzales: Cotton Capital and Cotton Merchant

After living in Port Isabel for three years and showing every intention of establishing themselves there, Thomas and Edith, several months pregnant with their first child, suddenly packed their bags and traveled north to Galveston. Thomas, while only twenty-four, had learned well during the many years he worked for his brother-in-law, and he had obviously developed a fine sense of business acumen, as shown by his successes in Port Isabel.

Galveston, although it had been founded only fifteen years before Gonzales arrived, already had a population of nearly seven thousand and had gained the reputation of a booming financial center, with cotton being the central commodity. During these early years, the island city attracted any number of those who used it as a base for building financial empires in cotton factoring, banking, and shipping. Among them were enterprising young men like George Ball who, at age twenty-two, had arrived in 1839 and Henry Rosenberg, who had emigrated from Switzerland in 1843 at the age of nineteen. Both John H. Hutchings, at age twenty-three, and John Sealy, at age twenty-four, landed in 1846.

Soon to follow Thomas Gonzales would be others like William L. Moody, a native Virginian who arrived following the Civil War in 1866, and Harris Kempner, a native of Russian Poland, who moved to Galveston in 1870 at the age of thirty-three and opened a wholesale grocery establishment with another Jewish immigrant from Prussia, Marx Marx. Three years later, Joseph Seinsheimer landed in the port.

Like the others, Gonzales wasted no time in establishing his business—a wholesale grocery and cotton factoring firm—on the Strand between Twenty-first and Twenty-second Streets. It was right in the heart of the banking and merchandising district. The couple moved into a home on the corner of Fourteenth Street and Avenue G and became communicants of Trinity Episcopal Church, whose rector was the Reverend Benjamin Eaton. Eaton had arrived in Galveston in January of 1841 and a year later had founded Trinity, where he served as rector until his death on March 19, 1871. The Gonzales family attended Sunday services regularly and Eaton paid an occasional social call at the Gonzales home as he did at other active members' homes.

Later in 1853, Edith Gonzales gave birth to their first child, who was christened Eva but called Daisy from the very beginning. Five years later, in 1858, their second child, Thomas Edward, was born and the Gonzales family moved to a larger house on Twenty-first Street. It was there that another daughter, Edith, was born in late 1860. That same year Thomas's mother, Rita Samaniego viuda de González, who was never able to assimilate into the American culture as did her sons, died at her home in Havana.

Thomas's older brother, Francis, soon arrived in Galveston with his wife and their two children. As he had done in South Texas, Francis joined his brother in business and moved into a house at Twenty-sixth and G. Unlike Thomas, however, Francis and his wife joined the congregation of St. Mary's Roman Catholic Cathedral. In addition to his work in the cotton business, he soon took on another responsi-bility: he was appointed to serve as the Mexican consul in Galveston. Of course, because many of the transactions conducted by the Gonzales brothers were between Mexico and the United States, serving as consul certainly did not hurt matters. It would often help to have the Mexican con-sul—Mexican by birth but American by adoption and as-similation—readily available to cut through whatever bureaucratic bottlenecks were created by customs officials in either country.

As proof of Galveston's growing importance as a port of entry, the city, by 1860, had consulates representing, among others, Great Britain, Prussia, France, Spain, Switzerland, Russia, Austria, Belgium, and Holland as well as Mexico. The Gonzales brothers prospered along with Galveston, whose population had nearly doubled from 4,177 in 1850 to 7,307 in 1860. Then, suddenly everything changed.

Lincoln and the Blockade of the Port of Galveston

Events happened quickly and decisively. Abraham Lincoln was elected president of the United States in the fall of 1860 on a platform that shook the Southern states into immediate action. On December 20, three months before Lincoln's inauguration, South Carolina declared its sovereignty as an independent republic. Alabama, Florida, Georgia, and Louisiana soon followed. Texas joined the ranks on February 1 when, over the protests of Governor Sam Houston, its secession convention voted 168 to 8 to join the Confederate States of America.

On February 23, that decision was ratified by a popular vote of 46,129 to 14,697, indicating that statewide, Texans voted 3 to 1 to secede. In Galveston, the vote to secede was drastically different. Actively led by merchants such as Thomas and Francis Gonzales, George Ball, George Sealy, and Henry Rosenberg, Galvestonians poured out in large numbers and voted an overwhelming 765 to 33 in favor.

While Texas as a state approved of secession 3 to 1, Galvestonians voted 13 to 1 to leave the Union.

Upon closer examination, the lopsided vote in Galveston was easily explained. The citizens of Galveston were voting with their pocketbooks. On February 16, just one week before the election, they had read in the *Galveston Weekly News* that once Lincoln was president, he "will attempt to retake the Southern ports now in possession of the seceding States." The newspaper also stated that "the blockade of Southern ports had been decided upon." If that were to happen, the port city of Galveston was doomed. The cotton merchants were quick to spread the word. And it worked.

When Governor Sam Houston refused to declare his allegiance to the Confederacy, he was removed from office and, on March 16, was replaced with Lt. Governor Edward Clark.

Lincoln took the oath of office on March 4, 1861, and on April 12, Confederate forces took the first violent step and attacked Fort Sumter in Charleston. Three days later, Lincoln retaliated and moved to mobilize the country and prepare for war.

As far as the business community of Galveston was concerned, especially those businesses involved in shipping like that of the Gonzales brothers, the crucial act occurred on April 19 when Lincoln, as he had promised during the bitter campaign, ordered the blockade of all Southern ports to begin on June 15. His intention was two-fold: first, to prevent the importation of manufactured goods from Europe—meaning guns and ammunition—to the South, and second, to stop the exportation of cotton to Europe, primarily to England, from southern ports.

Lincoln's strategy would in time strangle the South. Both sides realized that if the rebellion lasted for an extended period, the Southern cause would no doubt fail. Without being able to replenish guns and ammunition, the Confederacy could not fight for long, and if they could not export cotton to the textile industries of Europe, they would not be able to pay for the necessary weapons.

Of course, any successful blockade of the Gulf would be doubly destructive to the port cities that thrived on shipping. Not only would the Southern cause be killed, but also the ports would likewise be destroyed. No one knew that any better than the Galveston merchants.

Lincoln's plan had some unexpected results, however. It caused other Southern states which had not yet seceded from the Union, like Virginia and North Carolina, to join the Confederacy, and the proposed blockade brought forth a most unexpected and unwanted denouncement from around the world. The most vocal countries were Great Britain and France, which had textile industries that depended heavily on cotton imported from the South. These governments saw the blockade as a violation of international rights to conduct unrestricted commerce.

While no country ever officially recognized the Confederate States of America, many kept open their already existing consulates; any communication between a consulate and the foreign government was routed through Richmond, Virginia, the capital of the Confederacy. Of particular importance were the consular offices in port cities. One by one, the consulates in Baltimore, Mobile, Charleston, New Orleans, and Galveston withdrew their allegiance to the United States and aligned themselves with the Confederacy, vigorously condemning the intended blockade.

Dean of the Consular Corps in Galveston was the consul for Great Britain, Arthur Lynn, a cotton broker from England who had lived in the city for twenty years. In addition to Francis Gonzales for Mexico, the other designated diplomats were B. Theron for both France and Spain; Jacob C. Kuhn for Switzerland; Jules Frederich for Hanover and Oldenburg; Julius Jockusch for Prussia and Hamburg; Julius Kaufman for Russia, Austria, Belgium, and Holland; and Theodore Wagner for Electoral Hesse.[22]

It is little wonder that each one of the consuls threw their allegiance and sympathy to the Confederacy. Each one had a business that an effective blockade would affect, directly, as in the case of Gonzales, the cotton broker or, indirectly, as in the case of Julius Jockusch, a banker.

Early on, the Gonzales brothers decided to take a stand in support of the South. They were, of course, protecting their very livelihoods, but they also had sincere feelings for the South. To show his loyalty to the Confederacy, on January 1, 1862, Thomas purchased $3,000 worth of bonds issued by the Texas legislature. The bonds, with an interest rate of eight percent, were to be redeemable on July 1, 1877. Four months later, on April 30, he purchased additional bonds worth $1,800 issued by the Congress of the Confederate States of America, which likewise had an interest rate of eight percent and were to be redeemable on July 1, 1869.[23]

The Gonzales Light Battery and the Army of the Confederacy

The brothers agreed to serve the Confederacy in different ways: one at home and the other in the military. Francis remained on the island, acting both to protect their financial interests and to represent Mexico as its consul. During the spring of 1862, Thomas enlisted in the Army of the Confederacy as a lieutenant in the artillery. He then recruited a hundred fifty men from the counties surrounding Galveston, completely outfitted them with uniforms and weapons, and spent May and June forming them into what became the highly regarded Gonzales Light Battery. By mid-July of 1862, Lieutenant Gonzales, CSA, and his men were incorporated into the army of the District of Western Louisiana commanded by Maj. Gen. Richard "Dick" Taylor, the son of former U.S. president Zachary Taylor.[24]

From the beginning of the war, Galveston had been considered a prime target of the Union navy, under the command of Rear Adm. David G. Farragut. Although Lincoln had ordered the blockade to begin on June 15, 1861, it was not until July 2 that the first ship appeared, the USS *South Carolina,* a heavily armed cruiser-schooner commanded by Capt. James Alden. His first hostile acts were to raid the port and capture and press into service several small vessels, including a pilot boat, the *Sam Houston,* and a yacht, the *Dart,* that was hastily outfitted with a cannon. For the most part, the Union vessels did not provoke any attacks from the Confederate installations on the island, but everyone in the city soon realized that the blockade, although not completely effective, was making itself felt in the community.

Then, on November 7, 1861, two days after the inauguration of Francis Richard Lubbock as governor of the state, the USS *Santee,* the flagship of the Union blockade, sailed into Galveston harbor and sank a Confederate vessel, taking thirteen prisoners. It was now obvious to everyone that not only was the blockade taking effect but that the defense of Galveston was impossible. If the Union forces wanted to, they could invade and with little trouble take the city. Governor Lubbock responded immediately stating, "There is little doubt that the defense of Galveston . . . in the event of formidable attack, is a very difficult if not impossible matter. It is a cotton port, and if in the possession of the enemy would be a nucleus for the disaffected, of which there are, I am sorry to say, many in this state."[25] As a result, no efforts were made to fortify the island.

But the fears of invasion by the Union forces increased until, by December, the governor decided that plans must be made in case such an invasion were to take place. In a letter dated December 7, 1861, and addressed to the commandant in charge of the defense of Galveston, he stressed, "Every effort should be made to prevent the enemy from effecting a landing . . . and to drive them off entirely, or much crippled, in their attempt to land."[26] But from everything that he had heard and from every official document that he had read, he was not at all sure that this would be possible.

He continued, "If, however, it is impossible to prevent the enemy from taking possession of the island, then I would suggest, as a dernier resort, that the city of Galveston be entirely destroyed,—buildings and everything else which can afford them comfort, convenience, or shelter: every cistern both wood and brick should be entirely destroyed, the water turned out, and they be rendered wholly unfit for use. The stock, including horses, cattle and sheep, driven from the Island and every spear of grass burned." He reasoned, "If you should leave the city unharmed, the enemy will go into the most delightful winter quarters, with every comfort and convenience. They will require but a few men to hold the Island, against our best directed efforts, and the Fleet will go to the other points to operate. The buildings left standing will serve them for fire wood."[27]

For Lubbock, there was no other alternative for, as he concluded with graphic descriptions and explanations, "If you destroy the place, turning off the water from the cisterns, they will be exposed to the severe Northers and rains, that will soon be upon them, forced to drink salt or brackish water, or be compelled to abandon the point, or visit the main land for wood and water, where you will be enabled to cut them to pieces, and continually harassing them. Constant exposure and bad water would produce their results, and the whole force subject to disease and death."[28]

The effect of the fall of the city would be far-reaching and "the consequence would be the most gloomy; it would dispirit the people from one end of the state to the other; if there be reason hiding its head in the land, it will rear itself in our midst, ready to yield a willing obedience to the invaders, particularly so, if by so doing, their homes and property would be saved from destruction by the enemy."[29]

Even though the letter was meant to be confidential, it soon found its way into the Houston newspapers and spread throughout Texas.[30] The effect it had in Galveston was as devastating as the blockade. Then, to make matters worse, the number of ships in the blockade increased. By January, 1862, just a month after Lubbock's suggestion that Galveston be destroyed, the blockading forces included 5 warships, 80 guns and 7,000 men. In the face of these threats, people were fleeing in large numbers. Many businesses, including the *Galveston Daily News,* moved to Houston. The economy had all but collapsed as the city's population fell from 7,307 in 1860 to fewer than 3,500 just two years later.

The Union forces remained quiet but poised for attack throughout the spring of 1862 until finally on May 17, the commander of the squadron suddenly demanded that Galveston surrender. Realizing that they did not have sufficient forces or equipment to retaliate, the commander of the Confederate forces in the city began to make plans to turn over the city without a fight. Although some citizens protested, the orders were followed and nearly the entire population was evacuated to the mainland.

With that accomplished, it was obvious that all the Union commander had to do was to sail into the harbor with his five warships, debark his troops, and occupy the city. But he did nothing more than continue to remain idle off the coast and, as a result, the people began to return to the city.

Then, in October, the blockading squadron was joined by the warship *Harriet Lane.* Flying a white flag of truce, the *Harriet Lane* sailed into Galveston Bay, dropped anchor, and sent an envoy to the Confederate authorities requesting that representatives board the *Harriet Lane* for an interview. The envoy did not wait for them, however, but returned immediately to the *Harriet Lane* and reported what he had seen: Galveston was in no condition to defend itself. There was, he had observed, only one cannon at Fort Point on the easternmost end of the Island. Learning this, the captain of the *Harriet Lane* promptly sailed into the harbor and reissued the order demanding the city's surrender, granting the authorities four days to evacuate the people. Among those who fled to Houston were Edith Gonzales and her three children: Daisy, Thomas Edward, and Edith, not yet two years old.[31]

By October 10, the federal troops controlled the port city—now virtually empty—and held it without incident. They still made no real attempt to occupy the city by force; instead, the fleet tied up at the wharves and part of the 42nd Massachusetts Regiment was sent ashore. With quiet restored, Galvestonians once again began to return home. The Union forces wanted little to do with the civilian population. Their main concern was with the management of the port and shipping activities which, by now, had been stopped by the blockade. However, with victory in sight, the Union commanders made one grave tactical error. Instead of destroying the railroad bridge that connected the island with the mainland at Virginia Point, they left it intact, using it to bring food and supplies to the city's populace.

The Battle of Galveston: January 1, 1863

Life on the Island proceeded smoothly until November 29, when John Bankhead Magruder, a respected and successful Confederate general, assumed command of the forces in the Department of Texas. Prior to his taking command, plans to recapture Galveston began to take shape. In October, in preparation for the attack, Confederate Army Gen. P. O. Hébert ordered Lt. Thomas Gonzales, as an ordnance officer, to report to Lynchburg, near Houston, and to assume charge of all arms and ammunition in the area that would be used in the attack.[32]

The person Magruder needed in planning the attack was someone who knew the region to help him with intelligence matters. He was informed of the presence of Gonzales in nearby Lynchburg and immediately sent a communiqué ordering Gonzales and his battery of light artillery to proceed with dispatch to join his ranks and bring with them all the arms and ammunition in his charge. It was another

stroke of the military genius for which Magruder was known. Gonzales would be an invaluable addition; not only could he provide the strength of a hundred fifty seasoned soldiers, but more important to the success of any attack, Gonzales also would be valuable to Magruder in regard to matters of logistics. No one on either side could match the Galvestonian's intimate knowledge of the wharves or of the harbor where the attack would take place.

Gonzales would also be able to advise Magruder on the planning and handling of material and personnel as well as the facilities that were available in the area. For Magruder, Gonzales would be his surprise element. His presence and assistance would certainly do much to determine the success or failure of the battle plan.

On December 10, General Magruder issued the command that all citizens leave the city. Free transportation was provided; those who stayed were warned that they did so at their own risk.

A plan was devised for the Confederate forces to strike simultaneously by land and by water. The attack on the Federal fleet was to be made by two riverboat steamers—the *Bayou City,* a side-wheel vessel, and the *Neptune,* a sternwheeler—which were hastily but not very effectively converted into men-of-war. The main firepower consisted of one cannon aboard the *Bayou City.*

Magruder and his forces waited on the mainland ready to cross onto the island, using the railroad bridge that connected the island and the mainland. This was the bridge the Union forces had unwisely not destroyed. Magruder's troops would then proceed under the cover of darkness to the wharf area. But on Christmas morning, the Union commander gave orders that surprised the Confederates; three hundred Union soldiers made their way through the harbor in small craft, landed and barricaded themselves on Kuhn's wharf at the foot of Eighteenth Street. There they remained.

Neither side made a move until during the dark, early

morning hours of January 1, 1863, when General Magruder took personal command and ordered an attack on the forces that were occupying Kuhn's wharf. He also ordered an attack on the Union gunboats in the harbor to be made by the two converted riverboat steamers that, unbeknownst to the Union forces, had moved in during the night and lay waiting nearby. The battle was a short one; the Confederate forces quickly and decisively defeated the Federals, both on the island and in the bay.

Less than a week later, the British consul forwarded to the British Foreign Office the following enthusiastic and biased report regarding the "defeat and partial capture of the U.S. land and naval forces at Galveston [and] The Blockade of the port raised: My Lord, I have the honour to report that on the 24th of December last a force, consisting of about 250 Soldiers of the United States Army, arrived at this port and took possession of the city, and that in the morning of the 1st instant the forces of the Confederates, consisting of 2 small Bayou Steamers armed with 3 guns, accompanied by 2 unarmed tenders, and a land force of about 2,000 men with 20 pieces of artillery, 6, 12, and 18 pounders, attacked the United States Squadron of 4 heavily armed gun boats and 7 tenders. The engagement, commencing about 5 o'clock in the morning continued for 2 hours, resulting in the capture of the Soldiers of the United States, the gunboat 'Harriet Lane,' carried by boarding, two Barques, merchantmen, and one Schooner, and also in the destruction of the gunboat 'Westfield,' which was burned by the United States Capt. commanding. The remainder of the vessels hoisted the white flag, and after remaining in the harbor until 12 o'clock departed under the same flag. On the morning of the 2nd instant the United States Squadron had disappeared and the blockade of this port having been thus raised had not, at this date, been reestablished. I have the honor to be My Lord, your most obedient, Humble Servant Arthur T. Lynn."[33]

On the same day, January 6, Thomas Gonzales, who had been promoted to the rank of captain, made his report to his immediate commanding officer, Col. Xavier Blanchard Debray, stating, "I have the honor to report the part taken by my battery of light artillery, in the engagement, on this island, on the morning of the first . . . I received orders to proceed with my battery and to establish it in three sections on the Strand, as follows: One section, the left, at the foot of the brick wharf near the Hendley building; the center section at the foot of Kuhn's wharf near Parry's foundry; and on the right at the foot of Hutchins's wharf near what is known as 'The Iron Battery.' Major George R. Wilson commanded the left; Lieut. R. J. Hughes was in command of the center and the right was under my own command. The fire was opened up at about half-past three in the morning from my left section, [with] the Major-General [Magruder] commanding in person, firing the first gun. This being the signal to commence firing, the battery opened and the firing was continued until about daylight when orders were received to cease firing and to withdraw, the battery having fired 317 rounds."

The casualties Gonzales's soldiers received were minor. Two privates were recovering from slight head wounds and another, whose leg had been amputated, had since died. But in all, he reported, "The officers and men behaved well and though . . . very much exposed, handled their guns with coolness and did their work bravely." He ended the report, "I have the honor, Colonel, to be, very respectfully, your obedient servant, Thomas Gonzales, Captain. Light Artillery, C.S.A."[34]

In total, the Confederate forces suffered 26 dead and 117 wounded. One vessel, the *Neptune,* sank. Fifty Unionists were killed and 367 were taken prisoner, along with 500 tons of coal and 500 barrels of provisions. The Union navy lost its main gunboat, the *Harriet Lane.* And as the British consul noted, the flagship of the blockade squadron, the *Westfield,* went aground on Pelican Island and was scuttled by its commanding officer, who was killed in the explosion.

The remaining ships sailed out of the harbor flying white flags of surrender.

After the Battle of Galveston, however, everything was not well with Captain Gonzales. From Houston later that year, on September 2, he found it regrettable but necessary to write to his commanding officer, Capt. E. P. Turner, stating, "I most respectfully beg herewith to tender my resignation as Captain of Light Artillery in the C. S. Army. For upwards of two years, I have been laboring under a very painful chronic disease, which has at length assumed such a form, as to totally incapacitate me for the service, hence my resignation. I have the honor to be, Very Respectfully / Your Obt. Servt, T. Gonzales, Captn. Commanding Light Battery."[35]

The letter was accompanied by one from the surgeon in charge of the General Hospital in Houston, stating that he had "examined Captn. Gonzales . . . and find him unfitted for the performance of military duty in consequence of [illegible name of a disease]. This disease is evidently of long standing and at the present time, an aggravated and serious complaint sufficient so, in my opinion, to justify his resignation."[36]

In September, under orders from General Magruder, his aide-de-camp sent Gonzales the following letter: "My dear Captain, I am in receipt of your letter . . . accompanying your resignation. I regret extremely that the service is about to lose such an accomplished and efficient officer. I was not fully aware of the amount of your suffering until it was represented me. . . . Your resignation has been forwarded to Lt. General Smith, endorsed by Gen. Magruder who is equally distressed at losing an officer in whom he felt he could have such confidence."[37] The aide then wished him a speedy recovery.

Gonzales did not return to Galveston, which continued in the strangling throes of an economic depression caused by being cut off from commerce by the war. Instead, he left Houston with his wife and three small children and traveled overland across the border to Matamoros, a journey which was made, by one account, in an army ambulance. It was a time when Edith Gonzales showed "bravery and fortitude and endurance." It was later reported that "a worse and more dangerous trip was probably never made when the end was successful. The Indians were overrunning the whole country, murdering and pillaging and committing all sorts of depredations." Indeed, Thomas Gonzales "ran the gauntlet with his wife and children and escaped by a miracle. In one instance, the village in which they had stopped during the night was sacked by the Indians within a few hours after they left it. The roads were rough and dangerous, yet the little party made the trip to their destination in safety.[38]

By mid-1864, the Gonzales family was back in Houston, where, on September 22, Edith Gonzales gave birth to their fourth child, a son whom they christened Boyer.

Soon after the last of the Confederate forces surrendered on May 26, 1865, the family returned to their home in Galveston and Gonzales reestablished himself as a cotton broker on the Strand between Twenty-third and Twenty-fourth Streets, just three blocks west of where he and his men were stationed during the Battle of Galveston.

CHAPTER TWO

Thomas Gonzales, Cotton Merchant

It did not take long for the city to recover from the economic disaster caused by the blockade during the Civil War. Industries that depended on trade with foreign countries, such as Great Britain and France, which had suffered when trade with the Southern states all but disappeared, were quick to respond. As trade routes opened, shipping quickly grew to answer the demand, and the port cities of the South regained their economic equilibrium long before those inland. Businessmen, especially, were ready to accept the reality of defeat, take their losses, and get on with rebuilding their shattered fortunes.

Thomas Gonzales—now no longer in partnership with his brother—was soon thriving once again as a cotton buyer and commercial merchant. His personal life was filled with both sad and happy occasions. First, on August 17, 1867, his seven-year-old daughter, Edith, died of a stomach infection. But, then, on June 9, 1869, the last of his children, Julian

Caverly, nicknamed Alcie, was born. And the following year, Thomas moved his family into a large frame home he had built on property located on the northeast quarter of lot number 44, which would later be identified as the corner of Nineteenth and Avenue N. The residential sections of the city were moving both south and west.

Francis Gonzales followed his brother two years later, building a home on the northeast corner of Nineteenth and Broadway. A year later, he added Spain to his diplomatic duties and used his home for the consulates of Mexico and Spain.

In 1875, Thomas established a partnership with Horace T. Sloan of Philadelphia; they opened their own cotton factoring firm of Sloan and Gonzales with offices on the second floor of a building on the corner of Twenty-first and Strand. Edward, his eighteen-year-old son, employed as a clerk in the firm, had been working for his father since he was thirteen, exactly as Thomas had done for his brother-in-law in New Orleans. That same year, Sloan, as the senior partner, served as the firm's founding member on the Galveston Cotton Exchange and Board of Trade.[1]

The year 1877 proved to be memorable for the Gonzales family for reasons other than business. The eldest child, Daisy, was being courted by Francis Coolidge Stanwood, a young Bostonian who had been in Galveston since 1874. The Boston firm of E. L. Dorr and Company had sent him to serve as its agent in the city. He opened offices in the Hendley Building, but evidently the trade from Galveston was not as successful as was expected and the offices on the Strand were closed two years later. However, before he returned to Massachusetts, Stanwood and Daisy were married, taking out their license on July 13.[2] The ceremony took place on the following afternoon at the Gonzales home, as was the custom for summer weddings in Galveston. The Reverend Stephen Moylan Bird, the new rector of Trinity Church, officiated.[3] The bride and groom then set sail to make their home in Boston on Beacon Hill in a stately mansion at 34 Chestnut Street that Standwood's grandfather had built in 1824.[4]

The firm of Sloan and Gonzales continued to grow and prosper until Sloan moved with his family from Philadelphia to Galveston late in 1877 and began building a large home far out in the west end of the city at Thirty-third and Avenue K.

Also in 1877, Edward left Sloan and Gonzales to take a position with the Galveston firm of Stafford and Hawkins. The following year, he was hired as a cotton inspector for still another Galveston firm, Merchants Press. His father had obviously decided that Edward, as the oldest son, should have the experience of learning as many aspects of the cotton business as he could. By working for other companies, the young man would be learning methods and techniques other than those of his father who, always the business man,

certainly did not mind that his son was learning while on someone else's payroll. Then, in 1880, Sloan and Gonzales brought into their offices another clerk: Thomas's fifteen-year-old son, Boyer. Two years later, Boyer was named the company's bookkeeper. Meanwhile, Edward was learning yet another facet of the business as a cotton classer, at yet another firm.

The elder Gonzales continued to expand his business interests in Galveston when, in 1876, he and others became proprietors of the Taylor Cotton Press, on the northwest corner of Thirtieth and Postoffice. William F. Ladd served as president; Gustav Mayhoff, vice president; and Gonzales, secretary-treasurer. The Taylor Cotton Press was a new invention that was destined not only to revolutionize the cotton business but to make the investors in the invention a great deal of money.

In that same year, Gonzales became an active member of the Galveston Cotton Exchange and Board of Trade. Three years later, he was elected to serve the first of four terms as vice president. Col. William L. Moody was the president, and serving as members of the board of directors were business associates of Gonzales, including Francis W. Lammers, John O. Aymes, William F. Ladd, and Thomas J. Groce, who was also president of the Texas Banking and Insurance Company of Galveston, a bank that often made loans to Sloan and Gonzales. Gonzales stood shoulder to shoulder with every important businessman in Texas.

Thomas Gonzales was a busy man, and staying busy meant he was making more money. He served as vice president of the Cotton Exchange for the years 1885, 1886, and 1887, with George Sealy as treasurer. His position at the Exchange often sent him traveling, as it did in 1885 when, on April 13, he was in New York to represent the Exchange at the inauguration ceremonies of the new building of the New York Cotton Exchange.[5] Everything he did was in some way connected with a business that he had. Rarely did he do anything just for pleasure. He was intent on making his mark as an entrepreneur.

Late in 1885, all of Galveston suffered a major setback that made headlines throughout the world; tragedy struck early in the morning of Friday, November 13. A fire swept across the island, devastating the central part of the city from the bay to the beach between Sixteenth and Twentieth Streets, burning hundreds of homes and buildings and destroying many businesses in its path. Although several of its competitors were burned out, the firm of Sloan and Gonzales was saved. In total, the fire caused property losses estimated at $2 million. The headlines of the *Galveston Daily News* the following morning blared: "A GREAT HOLOCAUST: More Than 40 Blocks of Buildings Destroyed and 100 Acres in the Heart of the City Laid Bare." And while his business was not touched, his home and his brother's on Broadway were caught in the path and consumed.

The Move to the Mansion on Avenue O

For Gonzales, however, the loss of the home was simply a setback, an annoyance, nothing more. He treated the loss of his homestead as if it were just another obstacle—like the Civil War—to be faced and overcome. Instead of rebuilding on the lot at Nineteenth and Avenue N, Gonzales purchased the home of Alfred F. James, who had arrived in Galveston in 1839 and had been elected alderman the following year. James had quickly amassed a fortune by speculating in real estate on the island. When he built his home in 1847, it was the largest residence on the island, complete with servants' quarters behind the house, next to an immense underground concrete cistern. Located at Thirty-third and Avenue O, near the Michel B. Menard home, the James mansion had been for years the unrivaled show place of the city and the center of social festivities. The inside was finished in cherry wood and brilliantly illuminated by gas lights which were fueled with gas manufactured by a gas works on the grounds of the estate, the first gas works on the island.[6]

However, the family did not move into the home immediately. Gonzales went to the top and hired the highly regarded as well as expensive New York architecture firm of Palliser, Palliser, and Company to draw up plans to renovate the historic mansion completely. In mid-June of 1886, he received the plans and passed them on with his own suggestions to J. Lee Burton, a local contractor. The result, as it was modestly described at the time, was "a convenient and handsome residence" that showed "taste in design and skill in craftsmanship."[7]

The mansion was a typical tropical-style white, two-story frame residence with front porches, trimmed with gingerbread. There were the usual two parlors, one in front of the other; the back parlor was more formal and was used as a ballroom on very special occasions. On the ground floor were a library, a dining room, and a kitchen. Upstairs were six rooms, four of which were bedrooms; one of the remaining two served as a sewing room for the Gonzales women. Gonzales employed two servants—both Mexican women—who lived in the original quarters behind the house.

It was decorated like other mansions of the late Victorian period. Clutter was everywhere, the woodwork was dark, and the floors were made of brightly polished hardwood. The fireplace mantle in the front parlor was draped and fringed. In the corners of the room and against the walls were plant stands holding porcelain pots of leafy ferns. Portiers hung at the doorway ready to be untied and drawn together during the winter months to help keep the parlor warm. The furniture in the library and dining room was of the Eastlake design made of either walnut or oak. Leaning against the settee was a banjo—the family loved music.

The furniture in one upstairs bedroom, obviously occupied by Boyer's mother, was painted shimmering white.

The windows had valances and ruffled lace curtains. Her four-poster bed was draped with mosquito netting, which in coastal Galveston was absolutely necessary during the long, humid summers to help guarantee a restful night's sleep. Rosey-faced angelic cherubs were painted on the footboard. All the furniture was dressed in ruffles as was her oil lamp, and on the walls were hung mementos, photos, and paintings of more blushing cherubs. In the corner was a typical art nouveau dressing screen.

Downstairs, in the back parlor, the unadorned windows reflected the outside shutters. The furniture was wicker. Long narrow paintings depicting an idyllic shepherd cavorting in romantic fields with his shepherdess flanked the windows. Beneath the low windows were carefully scattered pillows. For parties and dances, the walls would be decorated with smilax and other ornamental lilylike plants and flowers, and gaily colored paper lanterns would be hung from the ceilings.[8]

Everything in the renovated mansion had to be the latest, most modern, most elegant, reflecting the taste and social status of the family that lived there. If Gonzales were to be in the same business clubs as Henry Rosenberg, George Ball, George Sealy, and Col. William Moody, he was also going to rival them in the social world. He had the contractor tear down all but two of the fireplaces and install in their place the newest oil stoves.

It seemed that the more he worked, the more he made. Every business Thomas Gonzales ventured into prospered, the center of his holdings being the firm of Sloan and Gonzales. In 1887, just two years after the great fire, his firm was listed in the publication *Industries of Galveston* as ranking "with the largest shippers from this port. To January 1st, they had handled about 15,000 bales, with 2500 more in hand, indicating a business for the season of 1886–1887 rising 25,000 bales. These were purchases both here and in the interior, for foreign as well as coastwise shipment. The house is an old one, one of the oldest in the trade. It was estab-

lished something like twenty years ago, and has a continuous and unsullied record to commend it. Personally, Messrs. Sloan and Gonzales are much esteemed for substantial business and social qualities."[9]

In addition, the Taylor Compress Company, of which Gonzales was not only secretary and treasurer but a major stockholder as well, was growing and prospering. It was obvious that Gonzales and his associates were progressive in their willingness to spend freely in order to keep their company technologically advanced in every way. The owners wanted the Taylor Compress Company at the forefront of the industry, ready to cut down the competition, and they were doing it.

Industries of Galveston noted:

In the erection of this press . . . the cotton buyers and merchants of Galveston were chiefly interested, for an improvement in the method of handling cotton at this port was then being agitated. That was in 1876. The machinery adopted— the Taylor patent compress—afterward gave to the company its name. The Taylor press added twenty-five percent to the carrying capacity of vessels, and forced the other concerns engaged in the compressing industry to follow suit with new equipment. The Taylor was the first hydraulic and steam press put in service here. The original Taylor press . . . was replaced from time to time, by improved machinery with increased power, until an improvement from 1000 to 1100 tons pressure was gained and capacity acquired to compress over 1000 bales every ten hours. The company is now putting in a Miller press of still greater power and effectiveness. In a single season, this press has compressed 130,000 bales and in one of their yards (covering the entire area of a full city block) has handled 80,000 bales in one season. The company has yards under cover extending over two blocks, and storage capacity for 25,000 bales of the staple. They have 75 to 90 hands, and a thorough fire service consisting of water-supply, hydrants, hose, etc., and men thoroughly disciplined to their duty in case of such contingency.[10]

One year following the publication of those reports, drastic changes began to take place. First, Gonzales's partner, Horace T. Sloan, decided to resign from the firm, leave Galveston, and return to Philadelphia. Before this happened, however, Sloan's son, H. P. Sloan, borrowed—in the name of the firm of Sloan and Gonzales—$6,000 from the Texas Banking and Insurance Company of Galveston. On June 15, 1888, Sloan's son, as a resident of Philadelphia, signed three promissory notes, one for $2,298.48 and two others for a total of $2,298.49, due two, three, and four years after each respective date.[11] The notes were endorsed and transferred to Thomas J. Groce, president of the company. The promissory note stated further: "Should this note be placed in the hands of an attorney for collection, I agree to pay all costs of collection, including ten percent of principal and interest then due, as attorney's fees."[12]

The transaction took place without the knowledge of Thomas Gonzales, who, in good faith and as a partner of the firm, would have had to co-sign the promissory note. But by the end of 1888, Sloan and his family—including H. P. Sloan—left Galveston for Pennsylvania, and the firm of Sloan and Gonzales was dissolved. Unfortunately for Gonzales, Sloan never met the payments on the loan. But those problems would not surface until several years later.

The Death of Francis Gonzales

The Gonzales family was shaken when on January 16, 1890, Thomas's older brother, Francis, died in his home; he was sixty-four. The following day his obituary in the *Galveston Daily News* headlined: "Death of Consul Gonzales: A Well Known Citizen." It noted that "flags upon the various consular offices throughout the city were flying at half mast yesterday out of respect to the memory of Mr. Gonzales . . . the Mexican consul, a position he had held for thirty years, and was hence the oldest consul by tenure of office in Galveston." At the time of his death, fourteen countries had consulates in the city and as dean of the consular corps, Gonzales held a respected position.

The obituary provided some family history and noted that Martha Rhea, his wife, the granddaughter of a governor and daughter of Galveston judge, "died many years ago, leaving him the sole protector of several small children. He never married again, but devoted his life to raising his children, for whom he seemed to live exclusively, and his paternal devotion was the subject of unusual commendation. He was a man of strong impulses and was as sincere and faithful a friend as he was a devoted father. He leaves three daughters and one son."[13]

The funeral took place at St. Mary's cathedral. The prominent businessmen who were pallbearers gave some indication of the role the Gonzales brothers had played during their three decades in Galveston: George Sealy, John C. League, Charles Fowler, J. M. Odin Menard, Adrien F. Drouilhet, John Z. H. Scott, James D. Skinner, and Bertrand Adoue, consul for Sweden and Norway, representing the Corps of Consuls.

The Establishment of Thomas Gonzales and Sons

With the departure of Horace Sloan from Galveston and the dissolution of the firm of Sloan and Gonzales, Gonzales formed his own company, Thomas Gonzales and Sons, which opened its offices on the second floor at 2020 Strand early in 1888.

Of the two junior partners, Thomas had always relied more on and given more responsibilities to Edward than he had given to Boyer. Edward, who was thirty when the firm was established, was not only six years older than Boyer; he had much more experience in the cotton business and had always, unlike his brother, displayed a keen interest in the business. The two young men were diametrically different. While Edward was outgoing, personable, and hardworking, Boyer was withdrawn, shy, and sensitive. Likewise, while Edward was robust, Boyer was often physically sick, suffering from occasional attacks that affected his breathing to such an extent that he was unable to hold down his responsibilities at the firm, which included keeping the books.

Thomas Gonzales was well aware of those differences, and as a result, it was Edward and not Boyer who had been groomed by their father to take charge of the family's business interests one day. It was a logical move as Edward, from the time he was fourteen, had worked actively and untiringly for several different firms, including his father's, at jobs always related to the cotton business. He definitely inherited not only his father's entrepreneurial talents, but also Thomas's obsession and enthusiasm for work. He had begun young, starting as a bookkeeper and in just a few years had learned a great deal about the cotton business, working as a clerk, cotton inspector, and cotton classer. He had traveled as a cotton broker throughout the United States alone and with his father on trips related to the family business, including several visits beginning in 1888 to Seattle.

Everything went well for the Gonzales family, and in particular, Edward. On December 28, 1887, at the height of the Christmas festivities, Edward and Ella Forbes were married in the front parlor of the Gonzales mansion with the Reverend Stephen M. Bird officiating. Three months later, on March 17, Ella was christened at Trinity, where a year later at a mid-Lenten Sunday service, she was confirmed by the Right Reverend Alexander Gregg, Bishop of the Diocese of Texas.[14]

It was time for Edward to begin to take the reins of the business. It was he who began to look seriously to the northwest with the intention of expanding the family holdings beyond Galveston. At the time, Seattle, on Puget Sound, had a population of 20,000 and the entire Washington Territory only 250,000, but the future of the region was outstanding. As was reported in an a long article that appeared on May 4, 1888, in the New York newspaper the *Daily Graphic:* "The commercial relations of Puget Sound are diversified. There are only two ports in the United States that exceed Port Townsend, the port of entry for this district, in American ocean steam vessels for foreign trade, to wit, San Francisco and New York. There is hardly a quarter of the world that is not represented in this harbor. During the past year, vessels have cleared for British Columbia, England, Australia, Hawaiian Islands, Mexico, China, Fiji Islands, Japan, Ireland, Central America and Peru. An important factor in the premises is a coastwise trade with California".[15]

Edward found the port ripe for investment and his father agreed. They both liked what they saw and read about the region. In 1889 and 1890, the firm bought property in Seattle.

Then death struck again and the Gonzales's plans quickly began to unravel. On February 19, 1892, the lives of every member of the family were devastated by the sudden and untimely death of Edward. The future keystone of the Gonzales cotton empire was dead at the age of thirty-four.

Boyer Gonzales: "My Pleasant, Happy Youth"

The person most affected by the tragic death of Edward was his younger brother, Boyer, who at the age of twenty-seven, was immediately thrust into the most unlikely, unexpected, and completely unwanted position of authority and responsibility with regard to the financial interests of the Gonzales family.

Boyer Gonzales had other plans, however. For some time, he had wanted to break away from the business and study art. As a child, he had shown a natural talent for sketching and painting, a talent that was never taken seriously, much less fostered by anyone, certainly not his father. It had always been Boyer's custom, as with most artists of this time, to carry a small three by five inch sketch book and draw when the occasion prompted it. This he did even later when he took business trips for the firm, such as the one to Seattle that he made with his father and brother in 1889.

Thomas Gonzales usually was accompanied by Edward on these trips, but on this occasion Boyer was included. Sensitive as he was to all surroundings, the second son found life in and about Puget Sound excitingly different but not in the same way as his father and older brother. While Thomas and Edward were busy investigating the possibilities of investing in the region, Boyer wandered off on his own and got lost in his sketching, something that his father seemed not especially to discourage, merely to tolerate. On this trip, the aspiring young artist made more than twenty-five drawings and water colors of lakes and the surrounding snow-capped mountains, tugboats, sailboats and side-wheelers, and a canoe with two Eskimos, which he identified as "Alaskan Indians" and a large "Salmon taken [in] Puget Sound."[16]

Boyer's interest in drawing was, as noted, never encouraged by the family. It was an activity that Thomas Gonzales acknowledged and permitted only as long as it did not interfere with his office duties and responsibilities. Boyer had never been allowed the opportunity to study art formally. Still, he always held secret the intention that one day soon he would leave the company to study on his own and paint. Now, with Edward's death, Boyer Gonzales knew that his plan was completely out of the realm of possibility. It went without saying that Boyer would take the place of his older brother at Thomas Gonzales and Sons. His father was sixty-three years old, and he freely gave the second son more and more responsibilities.

Little in Boyer's life had prepared this man of intense sensibilities for the hard and generally impersonal world of finance and commerce. It was something he would never be able to accept or reconcile himself to. No one knew this better than Boyer himself: he was being forced to enter a world in which he neither could, nor would, fit.

That he had always understood well that he would never fit was made evident in the entry in his diary dated November 14, 1899. It was dark—seven-thirty on a winter's night at the end of the century. He was thirty-five years old. Unlike his brothers, he had never married. By 1899, his mother, father, and older brother were all dead. His only sister was in Boston; his younger brother, Alcie, lived with his family elsewhere in Galveston.

Boyer Gonzales was alone, living in the big house on Avenue O. On this night he was especially lonely; his mood was melancholy. "I am at home. A norther is rattling my window shutters and moaning around the house corners. As I write these lines, the dying away cry of a flock of geese is borne to me on the wind. With their cry comes a flood of reminiscences of my past life, a great many are recorded in the pages of this book. I have just looked at the last entry— November 16th. 1883—Sixteen years ago! Many changes have come to Alcie and me in that time. The musical honk of those aerial wanderers has revived my pleasant, happy youth."[17]

His youth spent in Galveston had, indeed, been happy and pleasant, comfortable and uncomplicated. Those were the years between 1875 and 1883—wonderful times for the successful and socially prominent Gonzales family of Texas. The beautiful Daisy, Boyer's sister, had married in 1877 and was envied by all as she led the leisurely life of a much sought-after Boston socialite. With a home on Beacon Hill, she regularly took tea with the other ladies of patrician families listed in the social register. The Gonzales boys were also seen as greatly blessed. Still at home with their parents in the house on Nineteenth and Avenue N were Boyer and his two brothers, Edward and Alcie.

At the time he began writing in his diary in 1883, Boyer was about to celebrate his nineteenth birthday; he had already been working for Sloan and Gonzales for three years. Edward, twenty-five and still a bachelor, also worked for the company. Alcie had turned fourteen during the summer.

On the first page of the diary, entitled Season 83–84, is a pen and ink sketch of a male mallard. On the page following is written a sentimental ode, typical of the Victorian period, that Boyer had penned for the occasion, the arrival of autumn:

September—our greeting, success to our meeting;
Farewell to old August we'll bid with a rhyme
Like a bright dream of gladness unbroken by sadness
I liken thy coming oh sweet autumn time.

Soft wind of September, how well I remember,
The whispering cadence in years that have flown;
I know by their sighing that summer is dying
And with her bright beauties she soon will be gone.

How soon will be fading thine exquisite shading
Of warmest of crimson and brightest of gold?
I hear the leaves saying as gently they're swaying
That slowly but surely the year's growing old.

The entries proper during the three-month period in which he wrote regularly in the diary paint a cheerful portrait of three brothers and their friends whose leisure hours revolved around their favorite pastime: bird hunting down the west end of the island. It was September. Autumn was fast coming, and with it would come blue, wet northers that would carry with them numerous varieties of ducks and geese. Since

he was ten years old, Boyer had kept a list of the first sightings of the birds he had seen flying over Galveston as they migrated to their winter homes in the South. He knew well the markings and the movements, as well as the cries that each made, and could readily distinguish one from the other.

During September and October, the small lakes and bayous that dotted the island swarmed with redheads, mallards, canvasbacks, baldpates, sprigs, bluebills, blue-winged and green-winged teals, buffleheads, and spoonbills. And there were Canada geese, brant and snow geese as well as flocks of egrets and other herons. Early in the diary, Boyer mentioned that his brother "Ed saw a sparrow hawk this morning on Center [Twenty-first] St.—saw him distinctly as he was perched on a telegraph wire." Later he noted, "Will Bryan says that there are a few teal around Dollar point, and geese are at the head of East Bay. We had a rain of twenty minutes today, the heaviest while it lasted for six months." At another time he wrote, "Jim Kulch says he heard geese this morning while chopping wood." Alcie was also included: "Alcie says he saw two teal this morning; I think, though, it is a little too early for their arrival. There is no telling however. The signals are up for a norther, and they might have come down before it. If we do get a norther within the next day, I will be convinced that we are to have an early winter."

September 22, was special for young Boyer: "My birthday! [His nineteenth] Heavier clothing is in demand today, the weather being really chilly. On my way to the office this morning, I was really surprised to see quite a number of blue wing teal in market. It gave me a most pleasant feeling and I must say that numerous visions of duck shooting constantly rose before me in pictures vivid enough to be natural."

Even at this age, his artistic sensibility and sensitivity as well as his ability to express himself in a fluid prose style are evident in almost every entry. He shows occasionally that he is quite adept at spinning a yarn, telling a story, and having a good laugh, usually on himself. In each of these, he shows his ability to weave his words with colors and conflicts to create a series of pictures that reveal much about what life was like on the island in the early 1880s.

"The weather," he wrote on October 2, "has turned very warm again, and the ducks that arrived during the cool spell have disappeared; seemingly to seek 'greener fields and pastures new.'[18] Today is stifling, and the change from last week is remarkable. There is a storm above us moving this way that will very likely terminate in what we call a norther. If it does, game of all kinds will be quite abundant, particularly ducks, such as teal, pintails, bluebills and widgeon. Canvasbacks, red heads, and Mallards will hardly arrive before the first of November."

The feelings of a sensitive, young conservationist are also evident as he wrote: "Within the last few days, I have noticed quite a number of live quail in market. The abominable practice of trapping them in nets and shipping them to points where they command a good price, is carried on to an unlimited extent by unscrupulous persons. This method is so universally known that a description of it is unnecessary. The net when once set does terrible execution, very few of the covey escaping. I am afraid that it will be many years before these poor little fellows receive proper protection. They seem to have few friends in this State."

During these days, Galveston was changing drastically. There was always some new invention to gather a crowd. One such was the Galveston-Western Rail Road that opened during the summer of 1883. It was the object of everyone's interest. The thirteen-mile, narrow-gauge train began at Twelfth Street and Avenue N, running east and west down the island, passing just in front of the Gonzales home at Nineteenth and N. The tracks took a turn between Forty-second and Forty-third Streets to Avenue Q and then continued down the western end of the island, hugging the seashore and passing Green's Bayou and Sweetwater Lake, ending at Lafitte's Grove.

That railroad, too, became part of the lives of the Gonzales boys. On September 1, 1883, Boyer wrote, "I took a trip to the extremity of the Narrow Gauge road yesterday, my object being to see what I could in the way of the same. Plover are more numerous than ever; the prairies being resorted to by them, in great numbers. As I had heard the rumored arrival of teal, I went more for the purpose of seeing if I could see any of them, than anything else. It is needless to say that I saw none although Alcie saw two, and Jack [Spencer, a good friend], four spoon-bills in Market St. At Middlegges [a family whose farm was located near the seven mile post on the West end of the island], the train flushed a covey of partridges, the second I have seen on this Island. Both Ed and Alcie have seen sparrow-hawks, but I haven't. Today, however, I have seen twenty or more, sailing gracefully over the city; they seem to be in pairs. Their early arrival with the ducks in market, convince me more than ever that we are to have an early fall season. Weather cool and pleasant. Frost all over the north last night."

On occasion, life on the island could offer an experience somewhat more exciting than anxiously awaiting a norther that never arrived. Sometimes, one did! On September 21 he wrote, "About 4 o'clock yesterday, the wind shifted to the north, blowing with just force enough to cause a rustling in the prairie grass, gradually increasing til by 5 o'clock a first class norther—the first one of the season—was blowing. Ed and I concluded that it would be a good time to take a trip of observation down the Island. Our intentions were to go down the narrow-gauge road, but finding that on account of the threatening weather the accustomed evening train would not be run. We hired a horse and buggy from Levy.[19] We left the stable at about 5:15 and arrived at the Lake some hours after, without seeing a duck, plover, or anything else worth mentioning. One good thing; the result of yesterday's rain is that every pond from the most diminutive to the largest is filled to overflowing with pure fresh water. This, however, cannot be said of the ponds west of Green's Bayou. The rain did not seem to extend so far, and our fly and the ponds around it only wet and soggy. Say Pompey to me and I'll _____! I never saw a horse that had so many bad qualities combined: stubbornness, laziness, hard mouthed, in fact everything with stupidity predominating. A walk was fast enough for him and no persuasive power could make him go faster. You couldn't guide him; he knew the road better than we, and so he did, for by jingo if we didn't get lost. Quite a pleasant experience for two boys, born and raised on the Island, to get lost on it; facts are facts though. At one time, I could have sworn that we were going round and round in a circle. After going about half mile in a direction we didn't know, we had a council and determined to turn back and look for the bridge. This we did and had no difficulty in finding it. How we ever missed it is a problem, as it looked white and spectre like in the gloom and mist, and twice its size. Our way home was not very cheerful; pelted by rain and serenaded by the fierce wind howling in our ears. But it was a novel September experience."

That was not the only time the Gonzales boys had a hard time with a horse and buggy rented from Joe and Ben Levy's livery stable, located downtown near the Tremont Hotel. In Boyer's entry for November 1, the young hunter lamented: "I seem to be followed by a shadow in everything I do this season. I started upon my first shoot of this season with everything to indicate success. But what do indications go for; nothing! After going everywhere and seeing nothing, Ed and I became disgusted and turned our faces homeward where we arrived, disgusted and weary. We had the horse in the yard and were in the act of taking the guns, etc. out of the buggy when a locomotive came panting and puffing along. The horse was first uneasy but finally became unmanageable breaking away and rushing around in the yard, carrying the buggy over the wood pile. In frenzied fright, he rushed everywhere and over everything, upsetting the buggy and running over Ed, fortunately not hurting him more than a black eye. He finally got clear of the buggy and actually tried to jump a 6 ft. fence knocking the whole thing down. As I was on top at the time, I was in a pickle but managed to crawl from under the debris none the worse for my adventure. What a sequel to an already unfortunate expedition. Upon examination, the buggy was found to be pretty bad off for its experiences; while along the road we found small pieces of harness. We killed two snipe and our trip cost viz.:

> *Hire of horse* *$3*
> *Repair of buggy* *$25*
> *Repair of harness* *$7*
> *Total* *$35*

The whole thing was disastrous; particularly for our pockets."[20]

Expensive though the event was, it was the kind of happening that must have brought forth many laughs when it was later told and retold and, as Boyer Gonzales was known to do, embellished. Everyone in the family loved reliving the day when Joe Levy's horse went berserk in the backyard of the Gonzales home at Nineteenth and N. The most sensitive member of the family certainly had a finely honed sense of humor and knew how to make the most of a good story.

He wrote the last entry on November 16: "Alcie and I tried our hands again yesterday morning. It was bitter, bitter cold and raining. We didn't mind it one bit as we thought it gave us more chance for a bag; but pshaw! with the exception of a pair of sprigs and about twenty-five snipe, our bag was poor. I think hereafter I'll turn my attention to snipe if they be thick or ducks if they are in the majority."

But it is the final thoughts that reveal the depth of feeling of this reflective nineteen-year old: "It is a wonder I don't become disgusted and quit shooting, I've had such poor luck. Yet it is not only for game I go; on the contrary, the drive alone repays me for my trouble. I enjoy hearing a norther howling about my ears; or if only a gentle breeze is blowing, the sighing it causes in the prairie grass has a peculiar charm for me. I don't know of anything I enjoy more than to listen to the always musical cry of wild geese, particularly in the early morning. It has a soothing influence over me, yet it always causes me to grow sad; still I like to listen to it."

He evidently put the diary away and forgot about it until he found and read it sixteen years later as he listened to another norther "rattling [the] window shutters and moaning around the house corners" and thought about his "pleasant, happy youth" in Galveston when the Gonzales family was in its prime and the world belonged to Boyer.

The First Trips to New England: 1883–88

The boy's world, however, was in no way confined to the narrow little barrier island. Early on, he began making trips throughout New York state and into New England where he would stay with his older sister Daisy and her husband in Boston. Once he had begun working, his vacations were generally taken during the fall and winter months, periods when there was little activity in the cotton business. Sometimes, he would go with the entire family, but more often than not, he went alone.

These vacations, which always lasted from three to four months, afforded him endless hours that he could spend with the other pastime that thrilled him: wandering alone on deserted seashores or in the countryside, walking down country roads that led nowhere in particular, and stopping occasionally to draw in his pocket-size sketch books, recording scenes that he would later transfer to larger watercolors.

The first of his books contain sketches—pencil, pen and ink, and watercolor—that he made during trips taken between the years 1883 and 1888.[21] He had just celebrated his

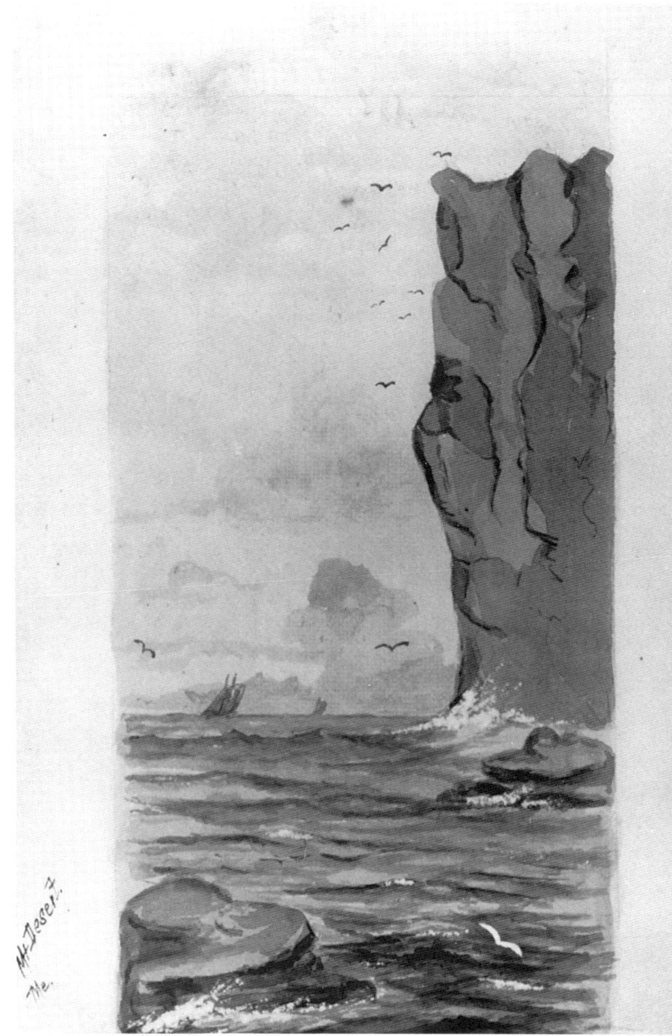

Mt. Desert, Maine

nineteenth birthday and had no formal art education, but the sketches clearly reveal his natural artistic talents as well as his definite drawing ability.[22] His first drawing, dated December 16, 1883, is a pen and ink sketch of a forty-foot, gaff-rigged catboat, a sailboat similar to an oyster sloop, sailing into a brisk wind in choppy waters. Included also is a formation of five ducks flying close to the water. In the distance is land. At the foot of the page, Gonzales scribbled, "Last glimpse of Galveston Bay."

That day, he was alone and on his way to Massachusetts via Key West, Florida. By December 30, he was in Franklin, which was then a village about ten miles southwest of Boston. He stayed there throughout January sketching winding country roads and farmhouses during a snowstorm and a Main Street intersection in the village. In February, he was out on the road to Wentham drawing an "Old Tavern" during a blizzard when the temperature dipped to ten degrees below zero. Then, early in the spring, Gonzales returned to Galveston, again by ship.

In July, 1886, he was off to Boston again. En route, the steamer stopped, as was usual, at Key West. There Gonzales drew four sketches: the Customs House, Fort Key West, "a glimpse of Key West," and a large, steam tugboat in the harbor of the Florida port. August found him sketching a "dandy" with a top hat and cane, prancing along the Boston Common. Several weeks following, he captured two lovers canoeing on the river in Newton, near Cambridge. Later in the summer, he journeyed to Stockbridge, in western Massachusetts. While there, he crossed over into New York

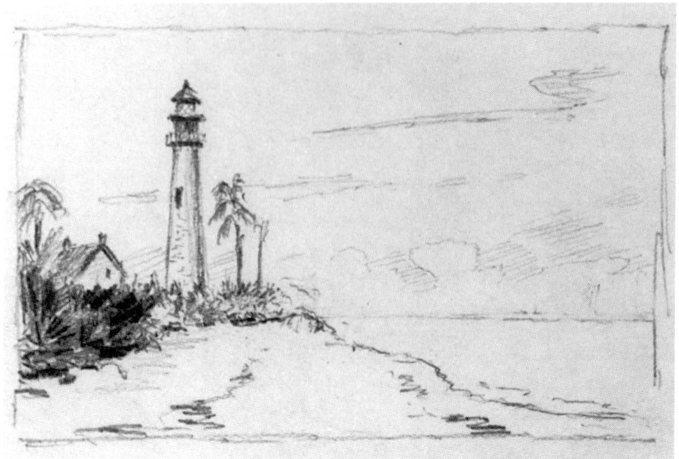

Key West, October 2, 1886

and spent some time in the Catskills, crossing the Hudson, getting as far as Tannersville, where he made an effort to draw "Haine's Falls." On his return to Boston in October, he paused long enough in Becket to draw some tavern signs that dated from the Revolutionary War.

Meeting His Mentor

Before the vacation ended, just as he had done in 1883, he planned one more short trip north to take in, as he later wrote, "the stern rocky coast of Maine, where the great surges of the Atlantic roll in, unbroken from the far off Azores."[23] This time, he was headed directly for Scarborough, a village with little more than a post office and train station for the railroad that ran between Boston and Portland. Nearby was Prout's Neck, where the internationally recognized American artist Winslow Homer lived and painted.

Gonzales knew one of Homer's brothers, Arthur, who lived in Galveston and was the proprietor of a rope factory. Not only were Arthur Homer and Thomas Gonzales business associates; the two families were the very best of friends,

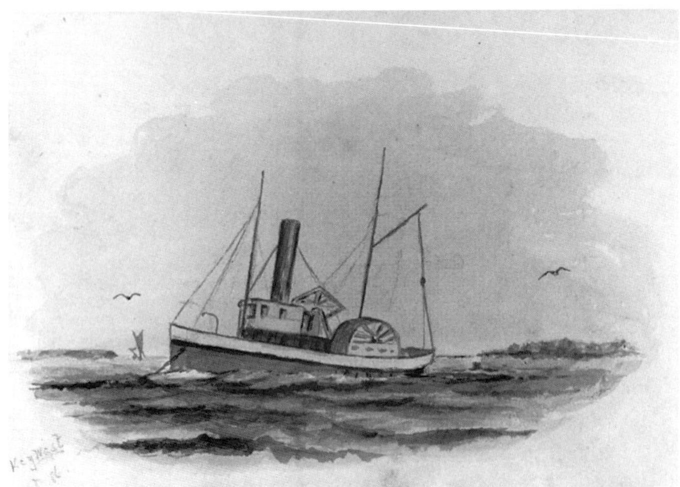

Key West, October, 1886

often seen together socially at the Garten Verein as well as at Trinity Church on Sundays. But being so shy, Gonzales did not have the nerve to present himself at Homer's studio. It was well known throughout the area that Homer openly detested visits from anyone, including his family, especially when he was painting. He rarely opened his door, much less his life, to anyone.

Even though Gonzales returned to Maine each year, it was not until his trip in 1887 that he got up the nerve to meet Homer. Then, he was better prepared. Arthur Homer had written a letter to his brother formerly introducing the twenty-two-year-old aspiring artist. How the private and reclusive Winslow Homer would react to Boyer Gonzales was entirely another matter. Arthur Homer could guarantee nothing.

To the surprise of everyone, especially Homer's immediate family who lived nearby, Homer and Gonzales got along famously. It was a friendship that took off immediately. While the two were quite different in personality, they had very much in common, especially their mutual love for the sea and the ever-present seabirds that swooped, glided, and perched on the rocks beneath Homer's studio. Both could spend hours in solitude sketching and painting. And when they were not painting, Homer was talking and the quiet Gonzales was listening, taking in everything he heard. Homer talked incessantly about how he had painted one work or another, explaining with great animation how he

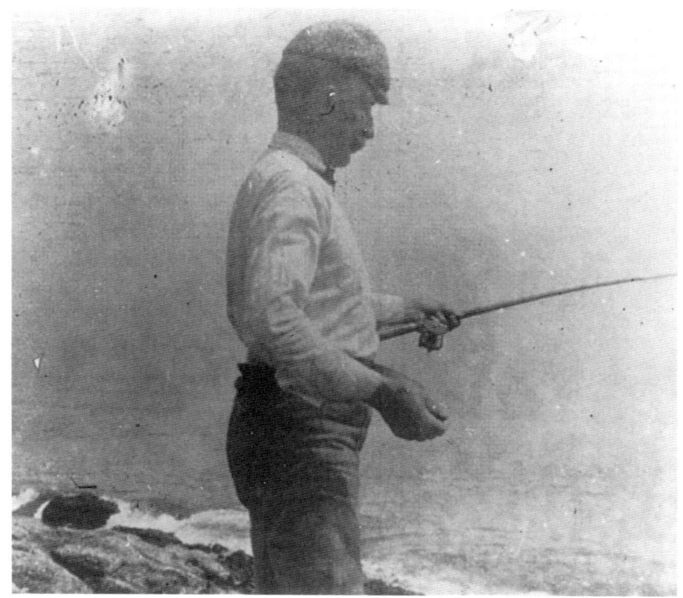

Winslow Homer

had overcome certain difficulties in a particular work. But there was something else they held in common: both Homer and Gonzales were avid fishermen. And what they caught, together they cleaned, cooked, and ate.

For six years, from 1887 until his brother's death early in 1893, Gonzales would somehow coerce his father to let him off from work to escape to Prout's Neck to spend a few days with Homer, painting, talking, and fishing. During these years the relationship grew closer, with Homer assuming the role of mentor and Gonzales becoming his protégé.

CHAPTER THREE

The Grand Tour of Europe

The first major problem that Boyer Gonzales faced after his brother's death surfaced soon thereafter: Thomas Gonzales and Son was threatened with a lawsuit of considerable proportions. It involved Gonzales's former partner Horace T. Sloan and the $6,000 that H. P. Sloan borrowed, without telling anyone, in the name of Sloan and Gonzales from Thomas J. Groce at the Texas Banking and Insurance Company. The first of the promissory notes came due on June 15, 1890. Gonzales's partner, the elder Sloan, died shortly after returning to Philadelphia in 1888 and no one seemed to know the whereabouts of his son. Upon inquiry, the only news anyone had was that sometime after his father's death, the son had declared bankruptcy and disappeared.

That left banker Groce holding a worthless note, worthless unless he could collect it from Gonzales. Groce had been searching for Sloan since 1890 when the first payment came due. Finally, in desperation, he gave up and took another approach to get his loan paid. He went directly to Thomas Gonzales.

No one could explain why Groce had waited two years to confront Gonzales. He knew the Gonzales family quite well, both professionally and socially. He had served with Thomas Gonzales on the Galveston Cotton Exchange. Gonzales, likewise, was a good friend of many members of the bank's board of directors, including Col. W. L. Moody and Harris Kempner. Gonzales and Sons, in fact, had conducted business dealings with Texas Banking, which had made several loans to Gonzales. Also, both families were parishioners of Trinity Church.

The elder Gonzales was in no condition emotionally to deal with the Sloan matter. Added to the death of his son was the fact that his wife was ailing and he needed to spend more time with her. The matter fell to the attention of Boyer, who did not have the slightest idea of how to cope with it. As a result, he simply did nothing.

It was with these added responsibilities and stress that a recurring respiratory ailment, from which he had suffered as a boy, began to magnify; the attacks became increasingly and progressively more serious. There were periods throughout his life when he could not control his breathing. Sometimes the condition was a mild wheezing, but at other times the tightness in his chest was so severe that he literally could not breathe. The hyperventilation was so intense, the heartburn so strong, and headaches so severe that he was unable to function normally, and he could no longer work. Sometimes, the attacks lasted only a short time, perhaps only thirty minutes; other times, the attacks lasted for days. During these periods, he experienced periods of deep depression.

The condition was similar to that of asthma but not the type that results from a sensitivity to specific allergens. Boyer did not seem to have been allergic to pollen, mold, or dust, nor did time, place, or temperature have anything to do with the attacks. They could happen anywhere. One thing was certain: the attacks seemed to always happen during times of great anxiety, stress, and tension. In particular, they seem to have occurred when he was forced to cope with situations which he would rather have avoided. Over the years, at the family's insistence, he had consulted various physicians, but neither explanation nor remedy could be found.

Father and Son: Worlds Apart

There could have been numerous ways to explain the reason for Boyer's problem. One of the most obvious concerned the son's habit of comparing himself to his father and his more robust older brother. Boyer was a slightly built man with a fair complexion who stood just less than five feet six inches, short compared to his father, who was closer to five feet ten. His father cut a dignified figure, with a long, flowing beard, and was always remembered as one of the great heroes of the Battle of Galveston—the man who had formed his own battery of soldiers and fought beside the legendary Confederate hero, J. B. Magruder. By the time he was twenty-eight, Thomas had been married, widowed, and married again. He was a financial success with a socially prominent wife, two children, and a large home with two servants.

How different, in so many other ways, were the father and son. When Boyer was twenty-eight, he had done nothing to compare with his father's great successes, nor did it seem that he could ever achieve any of these goals. He was looked upon by his family as merely a sensitive, boyish-looking young man who was always closer to his mother than his father; who kept a diary; who loved most to paint, draw, and travel; and who was happiest when he was alone with his thoughts, diary, sketchbook, and paintbrush.

Still, from the time he was a boy, his father did what he could to help Boyer alleviate his physical problems, as he did in 1881 when Boyer was sixteen. Gonzales took the family to Atlanta to attend the International Cotton Exposition, a fair that was sponsored by a group of progressive Georgians who were eager to break with the past and create the image of a "New South." The event did, indeed, spur the rapid growth of the textile industry in the state, and, of course, Gonzales, as a cotton broker, wanted to be on the inside of such activities. In an attempt to help Boyer, the family spent several enjoyable days at a fashionable hotel and popular health spa in the town of Powder Springs, just outside Atlanta, where Boyer could take the cure and drink the waters.

Eleven years later, in 1892, Boyer was a man shouldering major responsibilities at the firm, which was now known officially as Gonzales and Son. Thomas Gonzales decided that it would benefit the company if Boyer took an extensive trip to the east coast and Europe to meet personally the officials of companies with which they did business. He would travel first to Boston and then continue on to New York where he would take a steamer to Europe and meet their clients in England, Germany, and the Netherlands and try to establish new contacts.

At that time, he was in no physical condition to travel, suffering as he was with the respiratory ailment. He was especially upset by the death of his brother and by the realization of his parents' declining health. He had new and serious responsibilities. In addition, there was the lawsuit over the

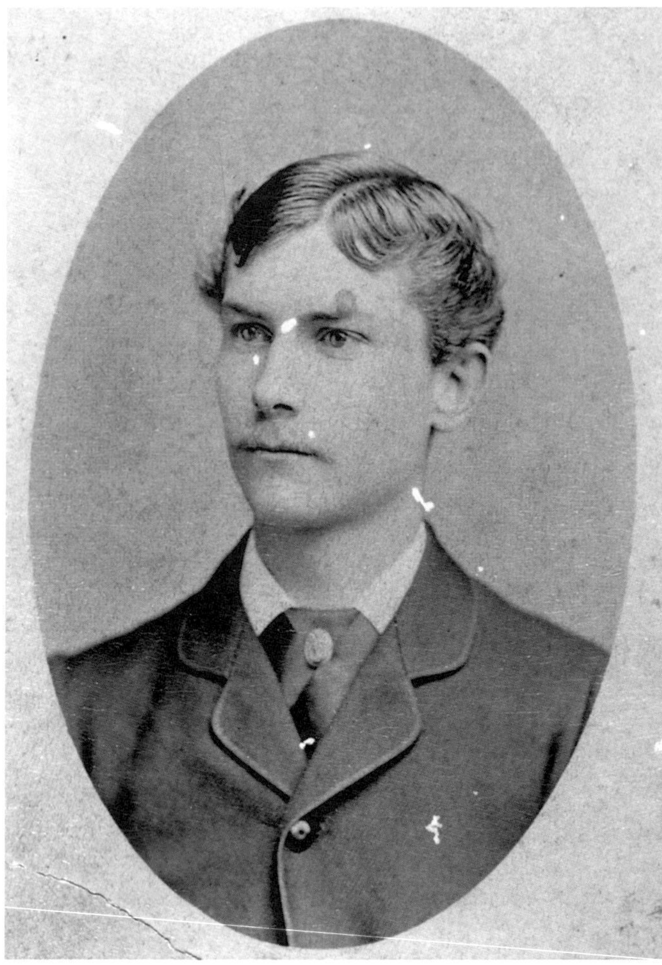

Boyer Gonzales, 1890–94

money that had been borrowed by H. P. Sloan. By the time Boyer reached New York, he was seriously ill. He later wrote in his diary that he "had been in wretched health for some time." He did not waste any time: "I consulted one of the most able physicians in New York who examined me thoroughly, after which he stroked his chin, mused a moment and remarked, 'Hum . . . nothing organic, slight digestive derangement, neurasthenia.'"[1]

The doctor's prescription changed Boyer Gonzales's life:

"A course [at a fashionable health spa] in Schwalbach [Germany]." He added, ". . . a month drinking the iron water and taking the baths will make a new man of you. Yes, I shall order you to Europe." Gonzales remarked wryly, "All of this with as much composure as if he had ordered me to change my diet. How he realized I was a millionaire in disguise remains an unsolved mystery."

On June 11, 1892, less than five months after Edward's death, he sailed from New York on the SS *Britannic,* taking with him not only his diary but, as he had always done, a new sketch book, purchased for the occasion. He arrived in Liverpool on June 24 and was met by one of their agents, the owner of M. Frost and Company, who invited him to dine with the family. With the invitation came the opportunity for him to see "for the first time the machinery of home life, amongst the English." He noted, "I can't say that I altogether like it. The children are made to occupy a position too far in the background, and look upon a father and mother in awe and up to a certain age, apparently not one of the family—but belong in school, in bed, or in the nursery. Under the circumstances, I should think they would be reared with not enough vim."

He also reacted adversely to other formalities of Victorian life: "The English dinner, while it is nice, I don't like for the simple fact that it is interminable, one thing at a time being served, and when the women leave, rum is served as libation—and the talk becomes general. A fast compliment to the ladies. For certainly, it seems, that while they wait for an hour or more in the drawing room, the dining table is the liveliest than when they were here."

Three days later, he left by train for London and checked into the first class Charing Cross Hotel on the embankment of the Thames. It was a delightful sunny, Sunday morning. Someone suggested that he stroll through Hyde Park, a pastime every Londoner enjoyed. And he, too, was instantly thrilled as he later wrote: "I saw London there—not the nobility, but the middle class whose lives are cleaner and who interest me more than the nobility!" There he found "an endless chain of humans passing and repassing, and a study of the human race was there. I drank it all in, and was much amused." He also commented that "during the season, Hyde Park is the place to see the nobility display itself, from eleven to 1. Horseback, drays, victorias, and coaching—the latter is just the thing. With all their doings, it is my conviction that their happiness is but on the surface [and] that all is done for display." Later that evening, he walked about Picadilly Circus, where he "was accosted by 187 women in two hundred yards."

The following day, the aspiring artist "thoroughly did the Art Galleries," beginning with the annual summer exhibition at the Royal Academy of Art, just down the street from Picadilly. Later, he confessed "that the old Masters have little interest for me save for the age that each picture possesses. Neither can I see art in Turner's composition in muddy colorings. Only when Landseer is reached, do you see Art: the perfection of technique I also visited the exhibition of the Royal English School of Watercolor painters.[2] Here again, I was not much impressed for, with but a few exceptions, there was with watercolor as a medium, every indication of an oil technique. There was not that freshness, broadness, or purity that is seen in either the French or American school. The Gallery on New Bond Street of French works, on the contrary, pleased me very much. There was nothing there but what was good, original, and well-painted. Mostly by modern French painters."

Time was passing and he had to move on but he vowed: "On my return to London, I will do art more thoroughly."

It is obvious that his mind was not primarily on the business of Thomas Gonzales and Son; he was simply enjoying being a tourist. The following morning he "did nothing but ride up and down, on top of the bus, studying the people." In the afternoon, he visited the Houses of Parliament and then Westminster Abbey of which he waxed eloquent: "Ah!! There is nothing in Europe that can possess the interest it does." There, before leaving, "I attended divine service . . . and even now I can hear reverberating through the arches, and around the tombs of the English illustrious dead, some of whom have been sleeping for nearly ten centuries, the soft chant of the choir or the melancholy mutterings of the priest. Nothing ever impressed me more, and it will ever remain with me as one of the events of my European trip." Indeed, it had been a most unusual day for the young cotton merchant. That night he "went to the theater and saw a wonderful ballet."

In London, he was definitely not suffering from any severe respiratory ailment or depression.

On July 1, he arrived at Dover to cross the English Channel to the Belgian port of Oostende "where for the first time, I realized that I was in a foreign land by the gabble of French and Flemish heard on all sides." After passing through customs, he boarded a train for a thirty-minute ride to Brughes. He had been away from Galveston since June 11, and for the first time, he took out his sketchbook and drew "the famous Belfry that Longfellow writes about," with the clock in the steeple showing five o'clock. He took special note of the wooden shoes "clattering over the pavement." Reluctantly, he left "quaint Brughes, perhaps forever," and continued on to Ghent and Brussels, arriving at 8:30 in the evening at the Hotel de la Porte where he beheld for the "first time, an insight into continental hotel life. I was ushered into a nice little room, and saw with awe the little candle you have to pay for. I got a good supper and then wandered amongst the people drinking beer in the open air."

He was alone, but he never seems to have been lonely. He was on the move. He did not want to miss anything. He noted in his diary: "To visit Brussels and not visit the famous battlefield!" So he took a short side trip to Waterloo. Once back in Brussels, he left for Antwerp, where he spent "most of the day wandering around looking at the quaint gabled buildings and the many shops that are placed over the doors. What a grand building the cathedral is and how massive."

The following day, he was in Amsterdam where, as he had done in Liverpool, he presented himself to a firm with which Thomas Gonzales and Son did business, the Dutch company of D. H. Joosten. While there, they drew up a contract to renew their connections and Boyer cabled his father and asked to have him confirm the agreement by return cable. His father had given him certain responsibilities, but when it came to all financial matters, Thomas Gonzales still had the last word.

However, as was evident from the earlier diary entries, Gonzales's thoughts were not entirely on cotton exports. He took time to see the city, which seems to have whetted his fine sense of humor. He saw Amsterdam as a "veritable Venice and a Dutch Venice—full of quaint buildings, quaint people, quainter canals and quainter boats." London, it was not. "Quaint windows and quaint gables abound. I arrived in the evening and seeing my porter, a small man with a cap ten sizes too large, I handed him my baggage, and got the odd little three windowed bus that was soon rattling over cobbles toward the hotel. Winding in and out alongside the Canal and crossing and recrossing numerous bridges, I noticed at about equidistant between bridges—say a distance of about 600 yards—the most peculiarly constructed ferry flat with gaudy canopy imaginable. It appeared to never be idle after dinner and being late I wandered about and for a little time watched, from my position on the bridge, the shadows deepen over the City of Amsterdam. The twilight seemed loath to depart. A tender light lingered in the Western sky and long after, the East was night."

While there, he made friends with a young Dutchman about his own age, and one evening, they took a skiff and rowed seven miles up the Amstel River: "We soon passed

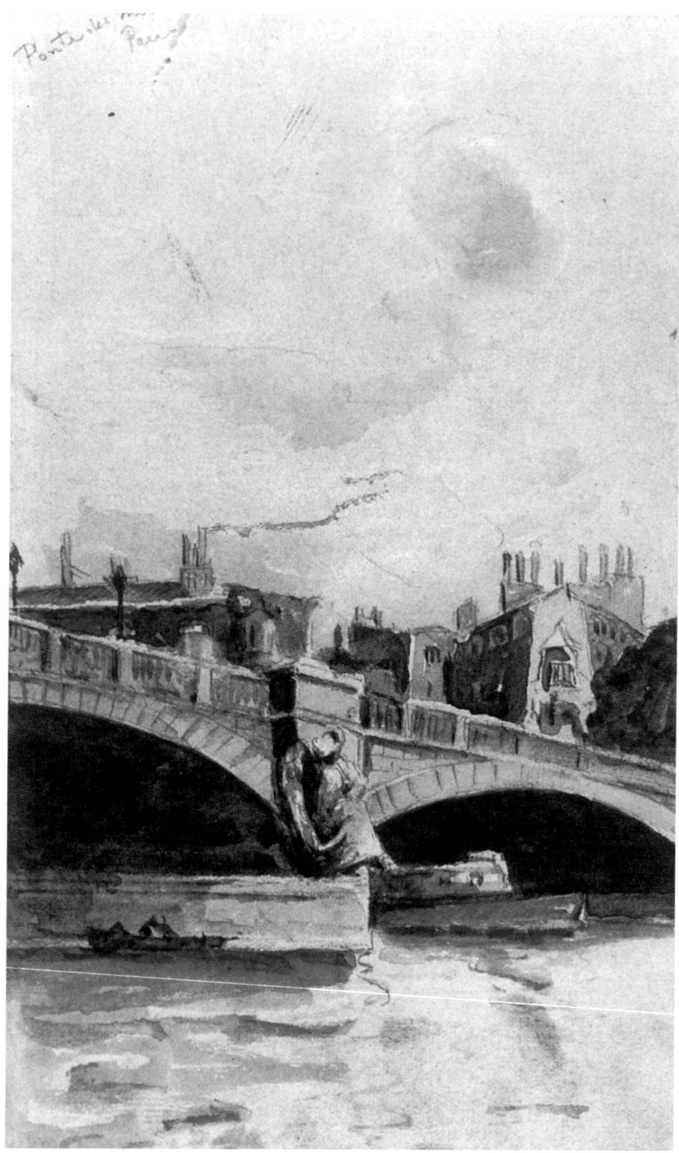

Paris, Pointe des Invalides

out of the city and the green banks began to slide by. Once we made a sudden turn in the river and disturbed and put to flight a flock of wild ducks. They lent an additional charm. We rowed two hours in a bewitching twilight—soft, balmy, tropical and hard to realize that just beyond the green meadow was the North Sea. On the way back, it gradually grew dark. At 10 o'clock, it was quite dark, and the river bank looked somber. We passed a windmill—a real dutch windmill. It was moving and caused an odd sensation down my back. It looked for the world like a great ghost with arms outstretched to grab us." He wrote that it was that short trip that he "enjoyed most and which made an indelible impression on me."

On July 6, he departed the Netherlands for one of Germany's great sea ports, Bremen, where he advised his father that he was happy to report that he had made two new connections for their firm. As usual, he asked for his approval of the new contracts. But there was little else about Bremen and the surrounding countryside that he found very attractive. The region was accorded only six words in his diary, not enough to even merit a verb: "Uninteresting country—hay-making chief occupation."

With that, he was off by train to the fabled city of Cologne. After seeing the cathedral and the match market and "having difficulty in purchasing soaps," he boarded one of the many paddle boats that steamed up and down the Rhine stopping at the many villages on either side of the river. He was finally sailing down the Rhine on his way to his destination: the spa at Schwalbach.

For the most part, the trip was quite uninspiring until they left the neat and orderly village of Bonn, with its tree-lined avenues. Then, suddenly, "the hills began to assume the proportions of mountains growing at every revolution of the paddles, more picturesque, more interesting." Then, they appeared—the legendary castles on the Rhine, more magnificent than he had ever imagined: "Castles in varying states of decay and preservation . . . glided by and I felt, as I noted each, a yearning to visit each, learn its history more thoroughly than related in the guide books, and fill the locality with romances of my mind."

For the first time in any letter or diary entry, the image of a very special young lady appears to him and his entry becomes quite personal and touching but ever so brief: "Thoughts of 'that' girl on the other side of the Atlantic crept in my mind, mingling with my impressions of the Rhine, making a most agreeable combination, and I smiled to myself at the intermingling of the two. I'll bet a mark (Yes, a mark, I'm in Germany) however, she hasn't given me a thought." That, for the time being, was all he would say, but for years later, she would appear again and again: the first and only—for now nameless—love of his life.

He returned to reflect once more on the river: "The Rhine as a stream is not much but the surrounding country is charming, being a continuation of our own Hudson and Columbia; with mountains resembling more and more, the Catskills." Braubach, his port of debarkation, "came all too fast." Just one week had passed since he sailed from Dover bound for the continent.

From Braubach, he traveled overland to Schwalbach where he registered at the Hotel Metropole, which boasted not only two hydraulic lifts but "the latest sanitary improvements" as well. The first entries in his diary reveal that Boyer Gonzales's first impressions were anything but favorable. Nothing seemed to agree with him, and he criticized almost everything. He found, for example, the village of Schwalback "upish. The Americans toady to the dukes and duchesses of Europe and are afraid to speak one to the other, fearing that they will be thought natives of the land of the brave, the home of the free. Lord, it makes me sick—DAMN—yes, damn, the German national air, this little German band regales me with it every morning, and it is worse to me than rubbing velvet. The tennis courts and drinking houses afford me much amusement. The nationalities, national peculiarities, and costumes are all represented, and I love to study them! I hate the English as a race. They are the vainest, most bigoted, narrow-minded, small people I ever met."

Never had the young man revealed himself in his diary

in such a miserable mood, so disgruntled and so critical of almost everything and everyone. But his negative attitude seemed to derive primarily from the feeling of rejection by the young lady back in Galveston whom he fancied, "'that' girl on the other side of the Atlantic," whom he now referred to as "Miss Mary." In fact, she was Mary Davis, the second child of a wealthy and prominent Galveston business man, Waters S. Davis, and his wife, Sarah.

What a disappointment! Boyer had been away from the United States for at least six weeks, and he had written faithfully to everyone, including, of course, Miss Mary. He had sent them his Schwalbach address and upon his arrival at the spa, he expected to have mail waiting for him from his family and friends, especially Miss Mary. When he arrived, he noted in his diary that indeed he did have letters "but the one I expected most of all—was not there. Miss Mary, you are a friend and are trifling with the best friend you ever had." He then confided, "I do believe she's engaged, which causes her silence. I'll have patience," he promised.

That patience was short-lived. The following day he wrote his deepest thoughts regarding his attitude toward his relationship with Mary, in particular, and with women, in general. He had never had much success with the opposite sex. There seemed always to be a bridge between him and any young lady, a bridge that he had always been incapable of crossing. Here he was in his twenty-eighth year vowing in a most immature manner: "Have written Miss Mary my last letter. Must accept her silence, as it is intended. I wonder where my pride, usually so rampant, has been. It never took a brick wall to fall on me before. And yet, in spite of it all, I feel I'd be more willing to render her a service than ever. As Lulu Hurt remarked, 'Man is so silly!' And I guess I'm in the swim."

Boyer perhaps never realized or wanted to admit that he was more comfortable keeping women at a safe Victorian distance rather than becoming actively and physically involved. He admitted, "Many and many [a] time I have thought with indescribable pleasure that I occupied a very high position in her regard, but like building castles in the air, such pleasing thoughts came tumbling down. Women are so peculiar. So hard to understand. Probably it will be a difficult thing to accomplish but now my pride and feelings will be set to one side, cost what it may." But he was still hounded by "the ghosts of many [a] delightful evening." He continued to fantasize about Mary Davis as his thoughts "all come stealing back and bring my better nature to the surface, and I can but think of them. So I'll let the future take care of itself, and try to take things as they come in good grace."

Not all of Boyer Gonzales's thoughts regarding women were quite so lofty. He was not always in mental anguish over his relationships with females. Later, in the same entry he wrote: "Got a letter from L. [a male friend] describing Miss Paine's bathing costume. Something like this: 'She not only fills the Gulf with her charming presence, but her bathing suit with her charming figure.'" Gonzales was either the epitome of a Victorian gentleman or a man in his late-twenties with somewhat overactive sexual inhibitions. His reaction to L's comment about Miss Paine's physical comeliness was, "I have noticed nothing of the kind, never having an opportunity, but," the artist in him did admit to his diary that "some bathing dresses do offer means of studying female anatomy."

Those thoughts and comments are his last entry before he, along with twenty other vacationers, began taking his "course" at the baths. At the same time, for the most part, he stopped writing in his diary and started taking long walks in hills and sketching various views of the village of Schwalbach and the surrounding countryside.

That the baths had an obvious beneficial effect, at least on his mental attitude, is made evident in a letter he wrote to his father just four days after his arrival. His mood had changed entirely. No longer was he disgruntled, unhappy, perplexed, disturbed, and quite so hypercritical of others. On the contrary, he was glowing with his usual enthusiasm: "Dear Dad, Here I am settled I hope for at least a month, and without any exception, I have dropped in on one of the most lovely places I ever saw, and such a climate. Soft, bracing, delightful. The place is situated in the German mountains, very much like Powder Springs and is something like the Georgia resort [which the family had visited when he was sixteen], but that everything is far more beautiful, and the climate—well, I thought Seattle magnificent, but Schwalback is perfection."[3]

As far as the "water" went, to him it seemed "to taste like strong seltzer with iron and other properties throughout."

He then told his father of the other guests—how noticeably different from the comments he recorded on his first day at the spa! "There are visiting the place about 2700 peoples, including some of Europe's nobility: The Grand Duke Michael of Russia, and the Grand Duke of Hesse, and several countesses. There are a number of Americans also. I have spoken to very few people, all seeming to hold themselves aloof, one from the other, because they are either great personages or nobodies. Generally, the latter. Snobbery."

Boyer's quick studies of people were generally right on the mark, but how completely different are his second impressions. Unlike his diary entry of the first day, in his letter there is not a cross word about the "toady" Americans or even those vain, bigoted, small people, the English, that he hated. And as to those "damned" Germans, he writes to his father: "I find the nicest people, those more agreeable, are invariably the Germans and my regard for them has risen wonderfully."

Gonzales then turns to matters of business, mentioning the firm in Amsterdam that he had contacted and adds: "In Bremen, Mr. August Block desired to open a business with us, but on specific terms, which he has written [to you].

I think that he very probably controls quite a large business. Messrs. Finke and Weinley [of Bremen] also desire to do business with us *after first assuring themselves that we are alright.* They, too, I understood do a large speculative and spinners business. I think it advisable to learn something about them through their references." Boyer was certainly careful to give his father the impression that he was attending to the matter at hand: spending some of this time making contacts for Thomas Gonzales and Son.

One other matter had been disturbing him: the lawsuit against his father regarding the loan Groce had made to the son of Gonzales's former partner: "I am daily expecting to get a cable, informing me that the old affair—as far as you were concerned—has been settled and that everything but the memory of the Sloans has been wiped out."

He concludes the letter explaining his plans for the remainder of his stay in Europe. His month at the spa would end around the middle of August, giving him two more weeks to travel: "My idea after leaving Schwalbach is Frankfurt, Leipzig, Reichenbach, Vienna, Venice, Verona, Milan, Italian Lakes, [Zurich,] Switzerland, Paris, London, Liverpool," where he would debark for New York on August 31 aboard the SS *Britannic.*

The last entry in his diary was written on July 8, the day he arrived, and he discovered that Miss Mary had not written to him. He did not return to the diary until August 10: "Three more days here and I will have to leave this charming place. I have really become attached to it, and have met some charming people and have had some delightful walks and drives to Frankfurt, Wiesbaden, along the banks of the Rhine, and always with Mrs. and Miss L. The latter is quite pretty and they have so literally spoiled me, that I ought to fall in love with Miss L. I never had anybody show, without flattery, that they liked me."

But all was not Victorian sweetness and light in Schwalbach. Around the corner, women of another sort were lurking in the shadows with different designs on the young man. He confessed: "Two nights ago, I had a strange experience. I met a fellow near the depot who accosted me with a broad, insinuating grin and asked me if I did not want to see a sight. Of course, I wanted to see a sight! So I followed him to a little theater—that I never knew existed—where I saw two very handsome Hungarian girls kick higher, disclose more leg, and do more other unladylike things than I care to record. Parisians would have 'encored' but after five minutes I went home in disgust. Every time I see anything of the kind, my respect for woman decreases."

He had to admit, however, that at another time and with a little less self-control, his reaction might have been quite different: "To think that I never knew anything about [the place] before! And I'm glad of it, for I know many a time when out of sorts I'd have drifted there." He could have added: "Who knows what might have happened?"

Finally, on August 13, the day before he was to leave, it happened: "'All things come to those who wait,' and for the first time in my life it has been proven. I have actually, after waiting since the 11th of June, got a letter from Miss Mary! Yes, sir, actually have received a letter and the pleasure it has given me cannot be expressed. I feel much better because she says she has written before, and if she says so, it's so! All the mean, queer, bitter things have gone out of me, disappeared like the snow before the sun and I feel much better."

As he read on, he learned the news was not necessarily good news. He soon found that as far as Mary Davis was concerned, he had little reason to rejoice: "Miss Mary says she is positively engaged to Von Harten!"

At first he was shocked. She was engaged to marry none other than Edward Gonzales's good friend William Von Harten, who worked for the Galveston, Colorado, and Santa Fe Railroad. Von Harten was the son of a socially prominent family who resided in the family home at 2327 Broadway, just two blocks away from the Davis home at 2322

Avenue L. His father, Maj. Edwin Von Harten, had been a successful grocery commissions merchant with offices on the Strand when on January 17, 1874, he was robbed and murdered, and his body was thrown underneath the New Wharf. The incident caused much commotion in the city. Young Gonzales remembered the event.

He had a difficult time believing that his own beloved Miss Mary would marry William Von Harten! At thirty-eight years old, Von Harten was two years older than Edward and nearly twice as old as Miss Mary. Gonzales may have been confounded and even appalled by the announcement, but the more he thought about it, the more he had to admit that he was not all that surprised: "This I expected for six months and attributed her silence to his desire that she should not write to me. And yet I think, too, that no man can influence her so, but Quien Sabe." He pushed the matter aside and vowed: "Until I learn it definitely, I'll try not to think it so."

His broken heart, however, mended quickly enough and that evening he "took a long walk with Miss Russell [another American vacationing at the spa] down towards Slanenbad. A most romantic road, over hung with trees, with here and there beautiful vistas of charming scenery. She is rather pretty and from her actions, I soon learned that she was becoming more and more romantically inclined and would consider it 'comme il faut' if a certain blonde young man from Texas would make violent love to her. And certainly after learning this, it would have been a shame to have disappointed her. . . . What a poor opinion she would have had of the South."

What actually happened remains unknown. All he could confess was "As it is *****!" Evidently, there were some things that the romantic young American would not even tell his diary, except to add, "She is from Boston and I have found them all alike."

The following day, August 13, he left for nearby Frankfurt where it was "hot as the Devil." To cool off, he passed the better part of the day being a "Bohemian rambler" and spending "most of the time in a shady garden drinking good Munich beer, listening to a Tyrolean band and thinking."

That was the last entry in this diary. The remainder of his trip is recorded in a sketchbook. By August 20, he was in Vienna leaving that day for Venice, where he spent four days sketching canals, gondolas, bridges, and buildings. After that, he went to Lake Como, Lucerne and, as he had promised his father, Zurich, leaving in time to return to London and then to Liverpool, where he was scheduled to leave for New York on the SS *Britannic.*

He had made his Grand Tour in less than two weeks: from Germany to Austria, through Italy, Switzerland, and France, across the English Channel to London, and then to Liverpool. He had precious little time for sketching and none for any serious painting or studying with any artist. By the end of September, Gonzales was home in Galveston ready to resume his role as partner of Thomas Gonzales and Son.

Immediately upon his return, he learned it was completely true that Miss Mary planned to marry William Von Harten. The wedding never took place, though. On the evening of November 5, 1892, Dr. Edward Randall was called to the Von Harten residence on Broadway. William was gravely ill. In a matter of hours, he was dead. Dr. Randall attributed his death to multiple neuritis. The following day, in the presence of his family and Miss Mary, William Von Harten was laid to rest in the Old City Yard cemetery.

It is not recorded whether or not Boyer Gonzales attended the funeral, but customs of the day would have suggested that he stay away and, for at least a respectable period of time, keep his distance from the bereaved fiancée. That he did.

CHAPTER FOUR

Chicago's Columbian Exposition of 1893

During the first six months of 1893, Boyer Gonzales was primarily occupied with his duties at Thomas Gonzales and Son. Then, in mid-July, he and several friends traveled to Manitou Springs, Colorado, where he climbed Pikes Peak, taking time to capture the scenery in sketches and watercolors. He then continued on to Chicago, which was the center of attention that year as it opened the World's Columbian Exposition to celebrate the 400th anniversary of Christopher Columbus's discovery of America. In 1889, Congress had selected the bustling, midwestern city over New York, St. Louis, and Washington to host the celebration. Chicago responded by pledging to spend an unheard-of $10 million to put on an unforgettable show designed to let the rest of the world, especially Europe, know that the United States had come of age as a cultural as well as an industrial power and was no longer to be regarded as merely a nation of manufacturers and salesmen.

President Grover Cleveland was there on May 1, 1893, to throw the switch that turned on the most spectacular display of electricity that had ever been seen. The Westinghouse Company had joined with the newly formed General Electric Company to light up the Chicago skies: 127,000 electric lights and 1,650 incandescent lamps and searchlights of such intensity that their rays could been seen eighty-five miles away. On display was Thomas A. Edison's kinescope, described at the time as a "specially constructed camera and phonograph working in perfect unison. The camera produces forty-six pictures a second. By thus rapidly photographing figures in action upon a sensitive film and adapting the phonograph to catch any sounds emanating from them, both sound and motion are reproduced."[1] Crowds flocked to see the first motion pictures. Exhibits from every state in the union as well as from nearly every country in the world filled the exhibition halls.

Another attraction that drew crowds was "Little Egypt" and her friends, who caused a sensation with the *danse du ventre*. Little Egypt, a Syrian dancer named Fahreda Mahzar, appeared at the Algerian Village and began to draw attention as soon as the word got around that *danse du ventre* translated as "belly dance." Not everyone was impressed with the dancers, however; some were scandalized. The *Illustrated American* found them "Shockingly unpicturesque, unromantic, and vulgar. . . . Their kinky hair, dirty-butter complexions, bad features, stained teeth, and tendency to embonpoint are dreadfully disillusioning, and their voices are of a timbre that would drive an American cat in disgrace from any well-regulated neighborhood." Be that as it may, the fact that Little Egypt and her troop performed daily to packed houses indicates that the majority of the visitors to the fair did not share that critic's view.

Little Egypt's stiffest competition came in the form of the first Ferris wheel, which "was both an entertainment and a demonstration of advanced mechanical engineering to modern living."[2] Its inventor, the American engineer George Washington Gale Ferris, intended it to rival the Eiffel Tower in Paris. The wheel was two hundred fifty feet in diameter and had thirty-six passenger cars. The ride captivated hundreds of thousands of fascinated and fearless visitors who dared to take the risk of being swooped high into the skies above the city.

For Boyer Gonzales, however, the high point of the Fair was the exhibition of painting and sculpture at the Palace of Fine Arts. Other visitors may have been thrilled by the rides on the Ferris wheel or captivated by the gyrations of Little Egypt. For the aspiring young artist, however, there was no experience that could compare with going each day to the Palace of Fine Arts to see what the world's finest artists had to offer. The exhibit had taken years to assemble. The Fair's Department of Fine Arts had invited countries to send the works of their outstanding contemporary painters, with the requirement that all had to have been painted since the 1876 Centennial Exhibition that had been held in Philadelphia. France responded by sending the latest paintings by its finest artists, including Degas, Delacroix, and Manet. Altogether, the Fair put on display more than ten thousand works of art by American and foreign artists.

The collection that drew the most attention and was accorded almost unanimous praise by critics from all over the world was the exhibit of works by American painters. Visitors were invited to see the largest and most carefully selected exhibition of American art that had ever been placed on display. The committee had invited 3,800 American artists, living both in the United States and abroad, to submit works. From those, juries selected 1,024 paintings and 160 sculptures by 521 American artists. American art was no longer disregarded as being provincial. In one single exhibit, the World's Columbian Exhibition had elevated art in America to a new international importance and stature.

It was obvious that Boyer was captivated by the works of America's most talented contemporary painters. He reportedly returned again and again to the Palace of Fine Arts to admire and study paintings that would soon be recognized as masterpieces, paintings such as John Singer Sargent's life-size *Study of an Egyptian Girl,* Thomas Eakins's *Portrait of Dr. Gross,* and Thomas Hovenden's *Breaking the Home Ties.* Outstanding was James McNeill Whistler's *Portrait of Ellen Terry as Lady Macbeth.* It was an endless stream of one masterpiece after another, including Abbott Handerson Thayer's *Virgin Enthroned,* Carl Marr's *The Flagellants,* Robert Koehler's *The Strike,* and George deForest Brush's *Mother and Child,* as well as canvases by Eastman Johnson, Guy Rose, William Merritt Chase, and George Inness.

Finding the Works of an Old Friend

Most thrilling for Gonzales, however, was to see works by his good friend of ten years Winslow Homer. Homer was especially honored; he had a grand total of fifteen works prominently displayed, more than any other artist. Young Gonzales saw paintings that he had heard Homer talk about during his visits to Prout's Neck over the last five years, works such as *The Two Guides* [1876], *The Camp Fire* [1880], *The Herring Net* [1885], and *Eight Bells* [1886]. Also on exhibit were works that were later to become some of Homer's most highly respected oils—one which Gonzales had watched him paint, *The Gale* [1893].

The painting that must have interested Gonzales the most was, however, *The Fog Warning*. He could have told anyone exactly how Homer had painted the work, how he had staged the scene by positioning the dory and the model for the fisherman. Later in his life, some year's after Homer's death, Gonzales would begin to write an essay about the times the mentor and his protégé had spent together in the artist's studio in Prout's Neck leisurely passing the time talking, and painting together.

Vicariously, Boyer Gonzales was basking in Homer's fame. A critic wrote, "Reaping reward among the critics who championed a homegrown American art was Winslow Homer, who was repeatedly complimented for merging technique with American subject matter." Homer was praised as an artist "who affiliates with no particular group in the home school, but is a law unto himself in technical methods and individuality of expression." His scenes of New England coastal life generated adulation for their "unyielding individuality" and "homely poetry." Homer was seen as "a painter of strength whose works command attention [because] they are American without preface or apology. They breathe of the soil and the sea, tell of their place of origin, give the American point of view."[3]

Homer had been at the opening of the Fair and later received a medal from the Fair's officials in special recognition for his work *The Gale*. He later said that the exhibition "was the best-hung collection of paintings he has ever seen in this country and it impresses everyone in the same way."

Boyer Gonzales would neither forget the Fair nor the way that Homer's works were received both by the public and the critics. They left a lasting impression. It was more obvious to him than ever: somehow he would find the time and space to pursue his one desire—to paint.

After leaving Chicago, he continued north into the isolated beauty of Wisconsin's lake district. As he always did, he wrote letters and cards to his friends and parents, who were vacationing in Colorado, staying at the same hotel Boyer had stayed at in July, the fashionable Cliff House in Manitou Springs. From Wisconsin, he continued on to Boston to visit Daisy. While there, he received a letter from his father sent from Colorado. Evidently, Galveston had been unusually hot that summer.

Thomas wrote: "My dear Bo, I have received your letter from the 'Thousand Islands' and at the same time, your mother received one dated 'Oconomowoc'—What a name! —Wisconsin. I have been timing our stay here so that we may have a week in Chicago and get home about the 7th October. And I think by that time there will be no longer a question of heat at home which I particularly wish Ma to avoid. We will probably go to Denver and from there to Chicago."

Unlike Boyer, who sought out the fair, Thomas Gonzales did not relish the vacation: "I have not much desire to see the Fair as I am well satisfied that the trouble and inconvenience of getting to Chicago and the drawbacks to see the Fair will be much greater than any enjoyment to be had there after arrival. But your mother seems to have a wish to see it and I do not care to say anything to discourage this fancy and so intend going accordingly, aiming to be there on, if not before, the 1st of October. She has had no ailing of any kind though she gets tired soon and cannot walk a great deal with comfort as her feet hurt her. . . . Affectionately yours, Papa."[4]

Thomas Gonzales did take his wife to the fair. It was to be their last trip together. He only planned to stay three or four days before leaving in time to be in Galveston by October 7. He certainly did not enjoy the visit. Even more certain, Thomas Gonzales never set foot in the Palace of Fine Arts or spent hours upon hours marveling at the works of America's foremost painters. It was as if Thomas Gonzales and Son had been to two different places.

Boyer had planned to travel again to Prout's Neck and visit Homer. Indeed, having been to the fair and seen Homer's most famous and recent paintings, the visit would have been an extra special one. But his plans changed after he received his father's letter telling him that they planned to arrive in Galveston on October 7. He felt that he was obliged to be there. He left Boston immediately by steamer, stopping, as usual, in Key West where he took time to do a proper water color of the lighthouse. By mid-October, the family was back in place, with Boyer at Thomas Gonzales and Son and Julian at the other family enterprise, the Taylor Compress Company.

News from Prout's Neck: "My Dear Gonzales"

It seems that sometime after his return to Texas, Boyer wrote to Winslow Homer at his home in Maine telling him of being at the Fair in Chicago, recounting his trips to Colorado and Wisconsin, and telling especially how thrilled he had been to see Homer's paintings displayed in the Palace of Fine Arts.

He waited for an answer and waited. Finally, a few days after Christmas, Boyer received a most enthusiastic and chatty response from his mentor and friend, mailed on December 20 from Prout's Neck: "My Dear Gonzales, I received your interesting letter long ago, but have waited until I had written to my brother Arthur before I could reply to you as I owed him many letters. Now I find on referring to your letter that I have written across the back of it, 'Well, Old Gonzales is a brick & a poet.' I think that with your nice observations of things & your power of description you could make a very profitable—and interesting to you as well as others—connection with some newspaper. And after a short time be able to go anywhere with perfect independence with only a pen and brush for baggage."[5]

Indeed, "perfect independence" and time to travel were what Gonzales wanted. It was also a compliment to have someone like Winslow Homer feel that one was good enough not only to write but to draw the sketches to accompany feature articles or releases. But writing for a newspaper or magazine was not what Boyer Gonzales had in mind.

Homer then turned to "news about myself. I like this life here, so long as my father is alive & I wish him to live long. I am handy to him & near enough. He is in Boston." Of his work, Homer said: "I have painted one or two very good things this year. & that is saying much." Indeed, 1893 had been for Homer his very best year as an artist. The critics raved when his painting *The Fox Hunt* was first exhibited in March and *The Gale* had won the gold medal at the Fair in Chicago. However, something had happened in Chicago that he was not happy with. He confided to Gonzales, "I shall not bring [my new works] out until times get better. They would only pave the way for others to do better & not benefit me. This sounds very selfish but I simply must take advantage of my experience." As Homer's biographer Philip Beam has written, during the summer of 1893, "Thomas B. Clarke purchased [the gold medal winner] for a ridiculously low $750."[6] Five years earlier, in 1888, Clarke had also bought *Eight Bells* for only $400. Beam notes that other collectors were paying very low sums for Homer's paintings and selling them a short time later for greater profits. It is no wonder that the artist decided to wait for better times when he could demand more money for his work.

From the tone of the letter, it is obvious Homer felt quite

relaxed in the company of Boyer Gonzales. He wrote of his studio: "I have improved my place & have more room & I am in what is known as a flourishing condition so if you should happen to be up here when I am home, I should be happy to see you again." He ended, "Wishing you a happy new year!" and signed it "Yours very truly, Winslow Homer."

Watercolors with Whittemore

The letter was obviously enough to inspire Gonzales to think of another trip East. Such a trip would include the usual visit to the various firms with which Thomas Gonzales and Son did business. His father would certainly agree to that. This time, however, the trip would be somewhat different. He wanted to take part of the time on the trip to devote to his art.

With the help of his sister in Boston, he arranged to spend the last part of the summer of 1894 at an artist colony in Annisquam, Massachusetts, where he would be able to study with William J. Whittemore, a New York watercolorist with a growing reputation.

Studying with Whittemore would be decidedly different from painting with Homer. He would be paying for the lessons and, in return, he could expect not only Whittemore's criticism but professional direction as well, something he did not feel free to ask from Homer. Although during those visits to Homer when he painted with the world famous artist and listened to him talk about painting, he did not feel as if he could intrude and ask for advice. During his formative years as an artist, the more Gonzales was with Homer, the more Homer became not just his friend but his mentor and model to imitate and emulate. When they painted together, Gonzales carefully watched Homer's every move and when he was away from him, unbeknownst to Homer, he would copy Homer's oils and watercolors over and over as he did with Homer's pictures of ducks. Whittemore would become something he had never had: his teacher.

Before he left for Boston, however, he became quite ill again with his ever persistent malady, a constant case of indigestion that would not subside. Although he would never have admitted it, the indigestion was most surely brought about by the tension and stress that he had been under since he had taken on so much responsibility in the family business.

He left Galveston aboard the SS *Leona* at daybreak on July 11, 1894. He wrote in his diary: "Crossed Galveston bar at 7 A.M. in quite a jumping sea. [The pilot] Capt. Billy, after going off in a small boat would be entirely invisible … [with] the waves apparently mountain high. There are people ashore who think that in the vicinity of Galveston, the sea is never particularly ugly! Galveston disappeared below the horizon. Finally, there was left only a film of smoke to indicate where it lay."[7]

This was a difficult time for Gonzales, who always seemed to sense and feel more than he admitted to others. His feelings and thoughts were deep as he began to analyze his trip: "What was I going for?" he asked himself. In answering, it is evident that he had not only the trip but his life all very well planned. He began with thoughts of his father, who during the last two years had suffered greatly with the deaths of, first, his brother Francis, in January, 1890; his son Edward, two years later; and then, his half-sister Elena Blossman, who had died the following year in New Orleans. And Boyer's mother was not well, another constant worry for Thomas.

He wrote, "First, Dad is arriving at an age when his business is getting to be a secondary consideration with him. He does not devote his old time [and] energy to it that he did in years gone. Then, too, the general demoralization of values has so disheartened him. My first object then is to get the reins stronger around the business."

And although he did not enjoy admitting the inevitable, he did: "Probably, I will have to make many personal sacrifices, but if good results follow and I can get Dad in his old time mood or prevent trouble from settling on his shoulders, who is there to say that I will not be amply repaid."

Then he wrote: "My second object will be to try to get rid of this d—m indigestion . . . or whatever the deuce it is that checks my natural, general good naturedness." Finally, he turned to himself and the one thing that was never very far from his thoughts: his art. He wrote that he would "try and learn more about watercolors," but the trip was not going to be all work: "Naturally, I like pleasure sufficiently well to throw in a little and get out of the way of none."

The first days of the voyage were uneventful. Gonzales spent most of his time playing poker and visiting with several young ladies on board. On July 14, the third day at sea, the calm was interrupted: "[We] had about as exciting a time yesterday a.m. as anyone wants to have on shipboard. About 4:30 A.M. the ship's cook, who in Galveston, had been on a protracted spree, [and] had kept it up, fell overboard and for the space of twenty minutes, the ship—as far as the passengers were concerned—was in an uproar. The discipline of the crew was excellent. In very short order, the quarter boat was manned and ready. We were twenty-seven minutes in getting round. The Captain was on the bridge, keeping a sharp lookout. And I was looking out and rather sick. I thought it a useless search, but soon I saw the captain throw his hands up and about a second after, I saw the poor wretch, on his back feebly raising his hands. The quarter boat was soon launched and away it went and we all had the satisfaction of seeing the poor soul hauled in. A very short time elapsed before he was alongside—unconscious. And then conflicting [directions as to how to handle the victim] were given by the ladies assembled—mostly en dishabille—was astonishing. After getting the man on board, the ladies seemed to recognize, all at once, that they presented a rather *showy* appearance, and fled. I thought and wondered what the poor half drowned fellow's thoughts must have been

when he saw the ship apparently leaving him. In falling, he had injured the ligaments of his spine and we left him at Key West—a conclusion of an interesting chapter in a man's life and a ship's log."

Gonzales took the opportunity to mail a letter he had written to the Miss M. Mary Davis was back in his life. Nearly two years had passed since the death of her fiancé and Gonzales had, once again, been courting her, taking her to dances at the Garten Verein and elsewhere. But she had not changed. She still continued to reject his advances.

Obviously this was a one-sided courtship: "I have wondered often," he wrote in his diary after mailing the letter, "how often she thought of me lately, and place it as a small weight on the scales. I enjoy yet last week's dance at the Focke's. Four consecutive dances. A red letter occasion! What an influence she has over me. I cannot understand it at all with her utter indifference. I never knew a woman like her. I wonder what it would be if she were not so indifferent. More like other girls. Quien sabe."

The journey by sea continued: on July 17, he wrote: "Got in the most 'exquisite' thunderstorm off Hatteras [North Carolina] I ever witnessed. Such flashes of lightning. For a second the Ocean for miles would be illuminated, brighter than by sunlight then would succeed black darkness that [was] almost as terrifying. Then a clap of thunder that would shake the ship from keel to trunk. After one thunderclap particularly the air was strongly impregnated with sulphuric odor. On the night previous, I witnessed something that is worthy of record. Just as the sun went down, a ball of red, subdued fire, the moon rose. The two globes were suspended, one on the Eastern—the other on the Western horizon at the same time. One red and glowing, the other silvery. As the sun went down, a bark drifted idly across the face of the moon. That night we assembled aft, on the hurricane deck. There we, all bathed in the most delightful moonlight, sang songs told stories and danced until midnight."

For several days, he did not make any entries, explaining later: "[I] met two school marms from Laredo. One is quite pretty and if I were particularly wicked and flirty, I could have oodles of fun. As it is, I have not lost all."

Gonzales was obviously being quite faithful to his word: "Naturally, I like pleasure sufficiently well to throw in a little and get out of the way of none."

After docking in New York, he contacted his business associates and had little difficulty in mixing business with pleasure. He was "greeted warmly" and everything was done to make his visit "pleasant." First, he was taken to the Koster and Biols theater to see the latest rage in New York: "living pictures." These were tableaus, generally of famous paintings or historical events, in which women were clad in skin colored tights. The presentation—considered by many as scandalous for the times—attracted enthusiastic audiences of men, in many cases visiting firemen like Boyer Gonzales. And he admittedly was fascinated! They were, he found, "beautiful, and as for anything vulgar is concerned in their presentation, well, 'honi soit qui mal y pense' [evil be to him who evil thinks]. Nothing is thought of looking at 'Psyche at the Spring' in a picture, and can't see why a beautifully formed woman, clad only in flesh tights, and butterfly wings should be less interesting. On the contrary, I think the living, breathing women should be the more interesting. [Presentations of] Aurora, Diana . . . and above all Diana at the Chase were greeted with storms of applause. The latter picture is wonderful. Fully twenty tights-clad, handsomely formed women posed exactly to represent the celebrated picture. I must confess that I saw nothing, immoral, indelicate, or vulgar at [the] performance." He was later taken to the Roof Garden where "it seemed as if every painted beauty in New York had turned herself loose in fine apparel. They are less bold than their sisters in Paris or London, but they were helping men spend their money, rather freely. On the following night we went to the Imperial Music Hall where again we saw the Living Pictures." What a difference in performances! "Here art was set to one side, and absolute sordid vulgarity held sway. . . . I'd had enough and thereafter turned my attention to legitimate plays."

He had been there only three days when his chronic indigestion once again became quite critical. He was bothered that he had not heard from Miss Mary since his departure from Galveston. He continued to be disturbed by her indifference to his obvious affection. An acquaintance suggested that he seek out a Dr. Pepper, who had a clinic on Long Island. He went to see him "with bitter feelings for a certain young woman in far away Texas who, no doubt, has almost forgotten that I exist. I had fully made up my mind not to write until I had heard from her. I saw Dr. Pepper and then wandered down to the bathing beach. Salt water, surf and ships always soothe me."

Thoughts of ladies were never far from his mind. "I was wandering along noticing the immodest costumes of Newport belles and their decidedly more immodest costumes when I inadvertently hauled a paper out of my coat pocket. It was a program of the Garten Verein. The last concert I had taken her [Miss Mary] to. Ye Gods. What a sensation I experienced. Inspite of her shabby treatment of me, there was nothing but the purest tenderest feeling within me for her. All my pique vanished & I did what I could not help doing. [I took] a piece of paper and wrote her a letter and having more trouble than ever in concealing my feelings for her. There's no use. She had bound me to her without knowing it with something that is stronger than steel fetters. . . . I've tried to break them, but I can't. They are just as strong when she is absent as when we are together. They are something superhuman."

On July 23, he arrived at Annisquam, Massachusetts, to begin a three week course "to learn more of water colors." He was immediately taken with the village: "This is certainly a quaint place. A rocky shore and rugged country. Exceedingly picturesque. And I scarcely wonder that it is resorted to by so many artists. White umbrellas are plentiful. Everywhere there are plenty of artists at work, getting together Winter material. The place is enveloped in an atmosphere of art and is very agreeable."

He met his teacher, William J. Whittemore (1860–1955), a native New Yorker who had studied with the American painter W. M. Hart as well as at the Academie Julian in Paris with Constant and Lefebre. Recognition came for his watercolors, and in 1890 he had been elected to the exclusive New York Water Color Club and the American Water Color Society. Gonzales "found at once that he was an enthusiastic artist, as much in love with his art, (almost) as with his sweetheart. I soon learned that he had a sweetheart by the way he used to haunt the P.O. at the same hour every day and the regularity with which his letters arrived daily made me sick. It seemed as if no one cared to write to me."

He added in desperation, "Finally I commenced to get mad and devoted my self to my watercolors and Yankee women with a vim that was astonishing. I met all the girls, took them bathing, boating. [I] danced with them, flirted with them, saying to myself, all the time that I did not care. But," he adds, "I did." He persevered: "I am meeting everyone at Annisquam. Females in large numbers. There are two handsome, plump girls—one from Springfield, the other from New York—who would take me off bodily if I would allow them. I have engagements with each for a week. Of course, this being spoiled by fine looking women is nice and I suppose I'd be but a poor man if I did not enjoy it."

Gonzales could not help but make comparisons between the behavior in the North and the South: "We do lots of unconventional things, but if you go to Rome, do as the Romans do. For instance, at home, it would not be considered the *thing* for a young man and a young woman to go off alone in a boat donned only in their bathing suits for about a mile, play and bathe on the sand and in the water for half an hour and return dripping wet, & this a mile from anyone. And while returning have the young lady remove her stockings and spread them on the seat to dry and then let down her hair also to dry. I soon got used to this order of things. But must say that the girls possess little or no modesty. The full exposure of their legs seems to daunt for nothing. Why a Southern girl would have a duck fit! But," he admits with a combination of some pride and perplexity, "I've had experience and seen them fall into customs, like those, in short order. I don't know what the world is coming to."

The following day, his world opened even wider: "Today in the water with Miss Pate and Miss Sims, new girls, we were diving off the raft and swimming. I was kept in much against my will because the water was cold but I staid. I was swimming overhand, when one of the girls tried it, but something impeded her. Whereupon she jumped on the raft and removed her skirt and stood forth a veritable living picture in black tights. I was so astounded that I swallowed a lot of water. She was soon followed by her friend & they deported in this comfortable garb for some little time. Hereafter I won't be surprised a bit, if they go in, in nature's garments. The women, these women! I wonder if they are shorn of all modesty."

There was more to amaze him. At one party he attended, one of the ladies, "a plump, pretty, matronly woman of about 35, gathered her skirts, jumped on the table, which was solid oak, and then grasping her skirts in each hand exposing two well rounded legs, two yellow garters and mysterious lace flounces, danced a perfect fandango, cancan. A photograph of myself, at that moment, would have been invaluable." On another occasion, "two of the ladies lit cigarettes, and as the other men did not appear in the least surprised, I did not either, but I was!"

Through it all, his thoughts seemed always to return to Miss Mary in Galveston. Finally, she wrote, but the two letters again were indifferent, written "in a very guarded manner, as if the writer was afraid that I might lose them and other eyes read them." And he thought of the way "that sweet pretty girl has me tied to her. I am fast becoming an Idolater for certainly I worship her, think her the most beautiful, the gentlest & most refined of all women. I find it mighty hard work to keep from writing, from verbally saying so. But I must—! Why? Because I think it would make her unhappy. I am all muddled. My heart says one thing. My reason says another. Better left to itself. Fate will unwind the skein."

He focused his attention on his work. He seems to have been quite pleased with Whittemore and his first formal instruction in painting, accomplishing what he had set out to do, "to learn more of water colors." He enthusiastically wrote in his diary: "I am doing wonderfully well with my sketches and see a great improvement in my work. Probably the greatest difficulty I have to overcome is timidity where color is concerned. 'Pitch right in. Slap it on.' Mr. Whittemore says, and I find where I observe his formula, my sketches are more and more successful."

Then, just as he was completing his third week in Annisquam, he received a letter from Miss Mary in which she apparently took exception to a phrase he had used in a letter to her. Mary's letter devastated him: "A brick falling from a height and striking one in the temple will at once render into insensibility the unfortunate individual struck. Never did weight strike one harder, in falling, than the receipt of a letter hit me. I was not rendered insensible: on the contrary, a two edged knife ran through my heart; twisted, and again inserted could not have caused the hurt that these few cold bitter lines in black and white did. I was stunned, but sensible to the acute hurt. And simply caused by a little playful expression—'Bonfiel Lady.' [Most Faithful Lady] So little consistency is displayed that I do not understand it. All last summer I, at intervals, did the same. And

[there was] no bitter response. Then why should I be so misunderstood. If I had never shown anything but care for her welfare, absolute respect, blind worship, and reverence, I could understand it, but I have never known a woman . . . so aloof. I don't think she has a throb of the heart, a bit of womanly sentiment or tenderness. If she had, she would certainly see my true character—understand that my greatest pleasure is serving her. But I've finished. My patience is exhausted and my pride stung to that degree that hereafter she will have no cause for complaint. My letters will be as cold as hers."

The receipt of the letter changed everything. "[It] has made me ill and I am going to Boston for a day or two and I don't care what I do after I get there."

With that, Boyer Gonzales, who was in no emotional condition to continue with Whittemore, left Annisquam on August 13, a week before the course was to have ended. But being in Boston was of little help. "After two days 'seeing Boston,' I have concluded that I better go out to Poland Springs, Maine, and be quiet. I've had a great time in Boston. What I saw and what I did, I guess I had better not write. I am sick. Scarcely an idea of my own. Every drop of blood in my veins seems to be in my head, and I am running down both in mental and physical condition, very rapidly."

Gonzales's sister had arranged for her brother to stay at the fashionable resort hotel in Poland Springs, Maine— twenty-five miles north of Portland, near Lewiston. The hotel catered mostly to older guests, but there were activities to keep him occupied. It seemed the best place for her brother, who had arrived in Boston "all unstrung," to rest, relax, and recover. There, he could "be quiet."

He left Boston on the 2:30 P.M. train which he had taken at other times before on his way to visit Homer. In his diary he wrote, "We passed Pine Point and I gazed across Old Orchard Bay to Prout's Neck. There was Checkly House and to the right of it Mr. Winslow Homer's studio. My mind ran back to the summer of 1890 and the pleasant times Mr. Homer and I had had together. How well I remember our last breakfast. Cooked by Mr. Winslow. My sole occupation, before enjoying the meal being to 'Watch the Kettle.' Breakfast consisted of Broiled Cod fish, fresh and crisp greenpeas, fresh from the garden. Bread, Butter, and coffee. I enjoyed every mouthful although a little out of the ordinary run. [The meal] was followed by no evil consequences. Mr. Homer's tongue got loose, and he was charming, telling me of his life just after the [Civil] war 'paintin' niggers in the Carolinas'—then his narrow escape from a celebrated outlaw. Then he drifted to the Cornish coast and back to tropical Bermuda, then we went to Cuba, thence across the Atlantic once more. His has been a very interesting life but I can't fathom or learn by any strategy why he has such an antipathy to women. (I believe I am getting that way, however.)" After what he had been through with Miss Mary, his comment is clear and understandable.

Arriving at Poland Springs, he went directly to the hotel in a "magnificent tally ho drawn by four grand horses." They started "down a very bad and dusty road [and] instead of getting better, the road got worse. Finally we got into a grand stretch of wood, spruce and white pine and the air was so delightful and fragrant with the odor of pine that I forgot all about the dust."

He tried to learn more about the resort from his driver and was told that "there were 526 guests, 75% being old, corpulent women." But he was pleased to learn "the hotel supported two baseball clubs, semi-professional & there were two games a week. Besides this, there were rowing, tenpins, billiards and pool. A grand concert everyday by the Boston symphony concert troupe, and dancing every night with a full dress ball on Saturday. Certainly a gentle sufficiency."

His final arrival was not the most friendly or warm: "I was gazed at, in a curious way, by four or five girls, sixty or seventy of the before mentioned fat women, and about twenty elderly men. Their stares quite embarrassed me." However, he found the hotel, itself, "charmingly situated in the foothills of the White Mountains—Mt. Washington & Mt. Kearsarge can be distinctly seen, while the rest of the range runs along until lost in a purple haze. The atmosphere is charming but so changeable. . . . the place strongly reminds me of Schwalbach, Germany."

It was not long before he had met everyone and had tried his hand at fishing. He had heard the lakes teemed with black bass, but all he caught one day were "two pickerel, about the size of your thumb. The lake and the shore, however, are very pretty and I enjoyed the scenery. Night Hawks were moving South in large bodies and I could not help thinking of Miss M. Somehow the more I attempt to think of some other girl, the stronger she asserts her presence & am certain she cares nothing." More perplexing was the fact that her letters began arriving with regularity: "All nice and interesting, but guardedly expressed. Sometimes she sees no gratification or pleasure in writing to me but simply does so because she said she would and these thoughts open the wound made by the receipt of the letter before I left Annisquam. Then I get in a mood which these people, who don't know me, must think cranky and avoid them." At those times, Gonzales took long walks alone or he got into a rowboat and pulled "like one possessed."

The result of this exercise was another seizure of indigestion. He wrote: "I never knew what indigestion was before. I've had it ten days. . . . If I thought I'd have it the rest of my life, I'd rather be dead. It is changing my whole disposition." The other guests helped very little. "There are three old women who make my life a burden. Whist! Don't mention it. I am beginning to hate the word. As soon as my breakfast is over they all chase me to play, 'Either now or this afternoon or tonight.' Patience and good nature is ceasing to be a virtue and I think they are at last becoming sensible of the fact that I'd like to do something else occasionally and I avoid them. So far there is very little difference, however."

Finally, he met someone more to his liking: "A Miss Gage from Rochester. Sweet, gentle, dignified, and *modest*. The latter must be emphasized. And she is an entertaining young lady & we spent very pleasant times together. A few days ago, on the lake, she very accidentally displayed about three inches of stocking above her shoe top. I could not help but seeing & her confusion and general embarrassment was as painful to me as to her. How different from the others whom I've met this summer. They as soon as they saw the exposure would have exposed a great deal more and laughed at what to them would be a joke." No matter, he feared that he was "very much down in Miss Gage's good graces. I will not dance! Have not taken a step. It seems to anger her. . . . Her mother has stopped our going rowing and I am speculating why. Does she think I am falling in love with her daughter or that I will elope with her. She is old and foolish!"

All was not quite so banal as rowing on the lake or playing whist morning, noon, and night. One evening, he was writing a letter to Miss M—"Somehow I am always writing to or thinking about that unappreciative young woman"—when he noticed the odor of burning grass, followed by the scream: "My God, the stable's on fire!"

"I forgoed my letter, for the time being, bolted to the fire leaving the letter on the desk. Men were scarce, but there were fortunately about six stablemen on duty & four asleep. I joined them, and our united efforts got all the horses out from the basement stalls—about twenty seven. Then we turned our attention to those upstairs. The stable was a tinder box and there were stored in it seventy tons of hay and by the time we got up stairs we were enveloped in flames on all sides but one. In the centre there was a perfect circle of burning cinders. The heat drove us back from the horses and we could only untie a certain number & they tore panic stricken around. Some turned their attention to saving the

carriages etc. [One being brought out] in the blinding smoke collided with me and knocked me in about eight feet. I think I was momentarily unconscious because I was burned quite badly on the right leg and did not realize it. I came out finally on my hands and knees as the smoke was suffocating. When struck, I did not think of burning up, but I remember thinking of mother and Miss Mary. I was not missed and could have burned & none been the wiser, til they removed the debris. . . . Just as I got out a beautiful horse came tearing to the door with mane and tail on fire, but did not come out. He stopped, turned and fell and burned and me unable to help the poor creature. What hurts me is the fact that poor Nero, the St. Bernard dog which I had grown so fond of, burned locked in a room whose door I could have opened a dozen times had I known the poor creature was there. Twenty five or thirty horses were burned to a crisp and I never want to see such sights again."

He never fully recovered after that experience. He noted: "I must have been injured internally when I was knocked down. I have been feeling wretchedly since and have been losing weight steadily. I'm nervous and don't appear to be much account physically."

On September 8, soon after the fire, he left Poland Springs; he was there three weeks. He went directly to his "old stomping grounds": Prout's Neck. But being there did not help: "The place is deserted. There are no gaily dressed summer girls on the rocks. No games of tennis going on. No dory races. Only the wind & sea keep accompaniment apparently wailing for the summer just gone. Mr. Winslow Homer is not here much to my regret but I have seen Mrs. [Martha] Homer and her husband [Charles]. Have an invitation to tea tomorrow . . . which I will accept." He went and "passed an agreeable time . . . after tea we sat around a dying log fire and told ghost stories amidst tuneful wails from the wind and sea."

Two days later, he was back in Boston visiting his sister

and celebrating his birthday on September 22. That morning he received ". . . the most appreciative present I ever received in my life. Without being asked, Miss M sent me for my birthday one of her pictures. The fact of her remembering that I had a birthday flattered me beyond measure, but her sending a photograph unasked was the sweetest, most gracious act I ever received. I was always more than willing to serve her, and now I am at a loss for adjectives and language strong enough to describe my feeling and appreciation. I have been feeling badly since I was knocked down but the receipt of that pretty souvenir has made a different man of me. The picture is pretty but not so beautiful as she."

By Sunday, September 30, he was again aboard ship bound for home. He arrived to find that earlier in September, during his voyage home, his mother had suffered a stroke which had affected her right side. Even though she recovered somewhat, she was never able to leave the house again. Two weeks later, she had a second stroke.

On December 21, Thomas Gonzales wrote to Daisy: "My Darling daughter, We are again in great misery and our joy has been changed into the greatest anxiety. I wrote to you giving you a daily account of your Mother's condition up to the 19th inst. And everything was favorable and hopeful, each day adding brightness to the situation and we were cheered to see how very great her improvement had been and how very surely if not rapidly she was recuperating.[8]

"When I left home on the 19th, I found your Mother talking to Alcie. She was sitting up in a chair, where she had been for some hours and which she enjoyed very much. As cheerful and chatty as she is by nature and so like her old self, even the impediment in her speech being much improved and we spent a delightful and very happy time with her, returning to her room after dinner when she had gone back to bed and she and we and all enjoyed the occasion more than I can express and were happy indeed in the present and were radiant in hopefulness for the future.

"The next day, the twentieth, was her birthday and I had been joking and making merry with her as to how I intended to 'dress up' for the occasion, and how I should present myself to her 'fixed up' in honor of the important day and in the gayest spirits on both sides I left her for the night (as she was getting sleepy) very comfortable and in the best of spirits. She passed a good night and all seemed well until after seven in the morning when without premonition of any kind and being the only one in the family up, Ella [the widow of Edward Gonzales who continued for a time to live in the Gonzales home] came to me and asked me to go for the Doctor as your Mother had become unconscious. This on the opening of the morning of her birthday which I had planned to have a joyful time and to make everything around her as merry and as cheerful as possible to enliven her spirits and to make her feel as happy as her ailing condition would admit.

"I have little more to tell you. This was a second relapse and on both occasions, they came on after the very highest improvement and the most perfect day. Bo told me that she was singing on the 19th she was feeling so well and her spirits were so cheerful.

"The Doctor says that it was the rupture of a small blood vessel in the head and that it is not in a part where serious consequences are to be apprehended and that nothing can be done for her but good nursing and perfect quiet. She has the best of nurses, a trained nurse, and fortunately your Mother has taken a great fancy to her and is really quite fond of her which is reciprocated on the part of the Nurse. I am plunged at once from the heights of hope and cheerful anticipations to misery of doubt and anxiety beyond expression. God bless you, my Daughter. Papa."

In a postscript he added: "I wrote this yesterday evening and being too late for the mail held it hoping to be able to give you more favorable information later. Today, the Doctor speaks hopefully of your Mother's condition and she has given evidence of returning consciousness. God bless her."

Then, on Christmas day, Edith Gonzales had the final attack which left her totally paralyzed. She died at home on January 2, with her husband and her two sons, Boyer and Alcie, at her bedside.

The obituary in the *News* was descriptive and detailed, giving an account of her ancestry as well as the important events in her life and that of her husband. She was remembered as being a "bright and vivacious woman, full of laughter and life and was often the center of an admiring group, every member of which had learned to love her for her kindly heart and pleasant ways . . . [She] was very charitable, but was retiring and unostentatious. She never let her left hand know what her right hand did. If there was a hungry man or woman at her door she never let them go away hungry. If there was ever a family in distress and she knew of it, she was the first to relieve them. In the course of her life she had done great good and few knew of it. There are many who have to thank her for many kindly deeds by which they have benefited."[9]

Edith Boyer Gonzales was buried next to her son Edward in the Episcopal cemetery on Broadway, with the Reverend R. J. Carter from Grace Episcopal Church officiating.

Though he continued to go daily to the office, Boyer's father never recovered from the death of his wife. In keeping with the custom of the time, each Sunday he would walk from his home to the cemetery nearby and spend some time sitting beside the grave of his wife. Occasionally, he was joined by one of his two sons.

His bereavement was interrupted briefly when, in February, John Henry Brown wrote informing him that he had been contracted by an Austin publisher, L. E. Daniell, to publish a collection of biographies entitled *Indian Wars and Pioneers of Texas.* Thomas Gonzales was invited to be in-

cluded. All Brown wanted was a biography of some two thousand words and a recent photograph of Gonzales. An engraving was to be made by the firm of H and C Koevoets of New York and a copy included in the book. Gonzales agreed to pay $250 for making the steel plate. In addition to the plate, the publisher agreed to send Gonzales twenty-five prints of the portrait once the book was published. Thomas signed the agreement on February 15, 1895. Also to be included in the volume was a biography of his brother, who would be listed as Francisco de Paul Gonzales.

The biography was written but without much concern for details. It contains numerous errors and some startling omissions, some of which were more than likely committed or omitted on purpose, perhaps by Brown in order to add interest to the prose. Working on the piece, however, gave Gonzales the opportunity to search his files for documents related to his activities during the Battle of Galveston when he organized the Gonzales Light Brigade and helped defeat the Union naval forces that occupied the island. It also gave him a chance to define his political beliefs and preferences. The biography declared Gonzales to be "a conservative Democrat, believing in the fundamental principles of the Democratic party and, within the bounds of reason and common sense, in party organization; but opposes bossism and blind partisanship and all less inconsistent with individual liberty and the purity of the ballot box."[10]

He also took the opportunity to recall his recently deceased wife; one-fourth of the work is devoted to Edith Gonzales, who is remembered as "an accomplished young lady who, though accustomed to all the comforts and luxuries of wealth, cheerfully came to this new country to help her husband make a home and win a fortune," and who, when she died, was "sincerely mourned by her family and a large circle of friends, to whom she had endeared herself by her kindness, charity, fortitude and other womanly virtues."

CHAPTER FIVE

Gonzales and Mexico: A Burst of Color

In the meantime, Thomas Gonzales helped his son prepare for a trip to Mexico. Boyer was quite familiar with the northern state of Nuevo Leon as the family had vacationed in Monterrey on several occasions. This time, however, he would be traveling into the interior as well. While he was not totally fluent in Spanish, he knew enough of the language to get along. Certainly his Spanish was better than his German, Italian, or French, and he had had little trouble making his way successfully throughout Europe three years earlier, so he expected to encounter no difficulties.

The trip, as always, would have a dual purpose. He would be expected to combine business with pleasure, with the pleasure aspect being time out to sketch and paint.

Like most travelers to Mexico in those days, Gonzales went to San Antonio and took the train to Laredo where he crossed the bridge into Mexico and boarded the Aztec Eagle after first going through customs and changing his dollars for silver pesos. The route of the train took him to Monterrey, over the mountains to Saltillo, south through the desert, past San Luis Potosi and Queretaro before climbing the mountains near Toluca, and finally into the valley of Mexico, where he arrived at Mexico City. The trip took only two days.[1]

Before he left on March 28, his father wrote for a him a letter of introduction to an old friend, Gen. Don Enrique Mejía, who lived in Mexico City:

> My dear Don Enrique, This will be handed to you by my son Boyer Gonzales, who visits your city on a pleasure trip.
>
> You knew him, as he knew you, in the long ago when he was much younger, but naturally he will have [illegible].
>
> He will tell you of our great and irreparable

loss very recently, which I have not the heart to more than mention.

Any civilities, which you may be pleased to extend to my Boy for the sake of old memories and acquaintances will be much appreciated. Your old friend, Thomas Gonzales.[2]

Boyer wrote often to his father during that trip. After he arrived in Mexico City, where he was staying with a family friend and business connection, Howard Carnes, he made several business calls. Soon he began making brief, one-day trips into the countryside. He wanted to search out the picturesque scenes of villages beside lakes and rivers, of the natives and their dress.

He chose Tizapan, an Indian village about ten miles southwest of Mexico City, on the road to Cuernavaca. In 1895, Mexico City had a sizable population of nearly three hundred thousand. It was, however, still limited in size, and visitors staying at the Hotel Iturbide had to take a day's excursion to visit Chapultepec and the castle of Maxmilian and Carlota.

Tizapan was known for its mild climate, lush growth, and delicious fruit: mangos, bananas, oranges, papayas, and strawberries. It was spring and for the first time in his life, Gonzales took time to stop, rest, and produce a series of watercolors—scenes of the village, the Indian men in straw sombreros, dressed in white peasant clothes with bright red serapes draped over their shoulders. He captured the simple men and women walking unhurriedly down dusty streets or standing in doorways of cantinas or huts or seated sleeping against adobe walls. All were painted with backgrounds of mountains and cloudy, blue skies with brilliant green banana and palm trees and other vegetation in the foreground.

He then decided that on April 10 he would leave Mexico City and the nearby villages and begin his travels north to Monterrey and told his father so. Thomas Gonzales re-

sponded: "I did not think your stay in the City of Mexico would be so short as it will be if you leave on the 10th as suggested in your letter. Do not be in a hurry to leave. Enjoy yourself all you can. It is a very interesting place and cannot well be seen in so short a time. It is a very interesting trip you are having and no doubt will leave agreeable recollections and connections."[3]

Mail traveled surprisingly fast in those days. It generally took no more than two days from Galveston to Monterrey, sometimes less, and usually no more than four days to Mexico City. It was on April 10, the time when he expected to leave for Monterrey, that Boyer received a letter from his father, dated April 7, that must have disturbed him greatly. It was a friendly, quite uneventful letter—to a point.

Using stationery with the letterhead of the long since defunct firm of Sloan and Gonzales, Thomas Gonzales began, "I have received your several letters including that of the 2nd [of April], and am much pleased, indeed, to see from them that you are enjoying yourself so well. I thought that you would enjoy it, as all you would see would be new to you."

Boyer had written to his father that he had been frequenting the many clubs in Mexico City such as the American Club in the Hotel Iturbide, once the Palace of the Emperor Iturbide, which was near the *zocalo* or main square, and the site of both the National Palace and the Cathedral. The clubs catered to the large English-speaking community made up of wealthy American and British businessmen and engineers who had settled in Mexico City. These had come to oversee their interests in a variety of businesses, mainly oil, coal, rail, and agriculture. One of the primary industries that had attracted foreign money was the making of textiles. And of course the states of Veracruz and Puebla were known as producers of cotton, much of which they exported, using American firms such as Thomas Gonzales and Son. Gonzales saw this as his son's primary reason for making the trip.

As a rule, the foreigners—even those who were business partners of Mexican nationals—did not mingle with the Mexicans, preferring to stay to themselves. They lived lives of elegance and ease, passing their leisure hours in their clubs and favorite restaurants. Here they ate and drank highballs or Manhattans made by exiled American bartenders. Here they could gamble with cards or dice. Thomas Gonzales had never been attracted to the life of the idle rich. He was a worker and taught his sons to be likewise. He advised his son, "I am afraid that the club life you mention may not be as enjoyable as a less exciting life might be. But you have sense enough and strength enough of will and purpose to avoid what is not desirable."

He continued: "I have delayed writing to you, wishing to find a card of a Mexican gentleman, a manufacturer living in Puebla near the city of Mexico, which he gave me while here some years since. You ought to go to Puebla; my mother lived there in her young days, I believe, and I have always heard it spoken of as being beautiful beyond description. Its name would seem to carry out this idea for it is Puebla de los Angeles, City of the Angels. I have found his card, at last, and hand it to you herewith. Ignacio Morales y Benitez, of the firm of Manuel M. Conde, Puebla, Mexico. Mr. Benitez married a daughter of Don Manuel Conde, a large manufacturer in Puebla, and bought a good deal of cotton. He knew me as vice-president of the Cotton Exchange here, which I was at the time. I forget who, but some one brought him up to the office and introduced him to me. We might buy some cotton for him in the interior. He tried to do something with Ladd and Co and had $10,000 in their hands to pay for cotton; but I believe they never bought any from him."

He reminded his son to not forget "to ask about Mariana's History of Spain. As everything in Mexico, being on a silver basis, if to be had, this work, might be bought there, for much less, than anywhere else."

Then came the news that must have shaken his son. Gonzales regretted that he had nothing very pleasant to write, "but something quite the contrary: Groce has brought suit against me for the Old Sloan Matter! And the first intimation I had of it was from the paper *The Tribune* which went into very full and small details."

He clipped the item from the newspaper and included it in his letter so as not to have to repeat the matter himself. Obviously, Groce was trying to recapture the $6,000 that his bank had lent to H.T. Sloan's son, who for one reason or another could not or would not pay. Groce was suing Thomas Gonzales not only for the $6,000 but for an additional $10,000 for damages as well as interest on the original loan, attorney's fees, protest fees and the costs of the suit.

This was the second time that the issue had surfaced; the first time was in 1892, prior to Boyer's leaving for Europe. This time, however, the matter was much more serious. Gonzales was being taken to court. He wrote: "I have had no notice of the suit from the plaintiff, but presume that I will be duly notified in time." He had seen his attorney but did not know as yet what "the defense will be nor how to be conducted." He was angry: "I will fight them to the last gasp, if there is any way to do so. The war shall be to the knife and the knife to the hilt in Spanish fashion. If they get anything by this course, they will have to be much more able to get *than I am able to prevent* them from getting. I have a good deal of confidence in my own ability to take care of my own interests. They may annoy me which I think is all they expect to hope to do. But they will get nothing more solid."

He ended the letter: "Give my kindest regards to Howard. I have always had a soft spot in my heart for him. God bless you, my boy. Affectionately yours, Papa."

The alarming news caused the return of Boyer's chronic indigestion. He went immediately by train to Monterrey and checked into the Hotel Hidalgo. That same day, he made arrangements to make regular visits to a spa, just north of the city: Topo Chico, known for its mineral water and health cures.

On April 17, Thomas wrote to his son another letter that stirred dual emotions. Once again came the struggle between the family business and his own art. His father described the very serious times Thomas Gonzales and Son was having within the cotton business: "Cotton has gone out of sight and continues to advance every day. Spots her 6.1-4 quoted and 6.3-8 paid. I closed out the futures as I wrote to you at a loss of over $700 and if they had been held until today there would have been an additional loss of $700, more to be added. I could have made a good deal, of course, by buying futures, but I was afraid to follow such a heavy advance. Since [then] it has been getting worse, in that respect, all the time. They are all Bulls here and expect an advance of 2 to 3 cents. There has been a cent and a quarter advance already."[4]

At times such as these, Boyer Gonzales must have felt it was his duty to be at home to cope with such matters. Then there was his art: When would come the time when he would be able to devote time to that desire?

Regarding his painting, his father had good news. Boyer Gonzales had sold his first painting. William Ladd, his business associate at the Taylor Cotton Compress, had bought one of his works for $50.00. His father wrote: "I thought that a very good commencement in your revenue from Art." To his father, his son's art was only as good as the money it could bring. What was more important to Boyer, however, was the fact that this was the first painting he had ever sold.

Later, Thomas Gonzales wrote again to his son in Monterrey: "I am much pleased that you went to Topo Chico Springs and more pleased that you found the place so lovely and the waters so beneficial. I think that you had better stay there a week longer or longer still if the place is so wonderful in the way of a cure for indigestion and other ailings through the medium of the curative qualities of its mineral waters. For certainly, the surroundings there must be much more pleasant and attractive than those of Sour Lake where you thought of going for a week. And if you can get sure benefit in Topo Chico, it is much better to secure it there than to go to Sour Lake hoping for the same result."[5]

He then turned to the business: "I have been so busy trying to lose as little as possible on the futures that I have not the courage to settle everything and go on the other side for fear of making things worse. . . . The opportunity was there to make a year's expenses but fear and prudence kept me back although I thought I saw the way pretty clear for a heavy advance. Having cotton on hand, our conservative course was to keep covered by futures to prevent loss. But this time this took the profits and did not work in our favor. It may not be too late yet, however, as the prospects for the new crop have never been so poor and getting worse every day. The 100 bales we took back from Nichols have not been sold yet and there should be a cent, at least, on that lot which should pay Frank all we owe him and leave something besides. I hope so." Boyer Gonzales quickly returned to take over the reins of the business; his father could no longer act in any strong administrative capacity.

By June, the lawsuit was ready to go to court. The case of *Groce v. Gonzales* regarding the Sloan promissory notes came before the district court on the first Monday in June of 1895. Gonzales hired the firm of Wheeler and Rhodes of Galveston as his defense attorneys. They argued that H. P. Sloan had never been a partner of the defendant and that he was never connected in business with Sloan. Likewise, they argued that Sloan was "a necessary party to this suit and the same should not proceed with until the said H. P. Sloan has been duly cited and required to answer here to."[6] That ended the suit and it evidently was settled out of court. The case of *Groce v. Gonzales* sank permanently out of sight.

The change in the cotton market and the lawsuit took its toll on Thomas Gonzales. His health had been declining since the death of his wife in January of 1895. Following the Sloan matter, that decline increased rapidly. By July of 1896, his heart condition worsened and in August, his son Boyer took him to Tate Springs, Tennessee, for treatment. From there, they went to another spa in Hot Springs, North Carolina. In October, he was moved to a clinic in Philadelphia where he seemed to improve to the point that several weeks later Boyer was able to take his father to Boston to be with Daisy.

Homer's The Lookout: 'All's well.'

Boyer took the opportunity to escape to Prout's Neck to visit Winslow Homer. The visit was brief but, as were so many of his visits to Maine, an especially unforgettable one. He later recalled one moonlit night watching Homer paint a model clothed in yellow foul-weather gear. The artist had his canvas inside the studio. "The figure was posed outdoors in the moonlight. Mr. Homer would rush out, look intently, rush back, and work on the impression. He worked rapidly. There was a big card party going on at the Burdit cottage directly opposite Mr. Homer's studio, and he asked me if in my opinion the people thought him crazy, as his actions suggested a hopping flea!"[7]

Hopping flea or no, what Gonzales was watching him work on that night was one of Homer's masterpieces: *The Lookout: 'All's Well'.*

Gonzales cherished those brief visits to Prout's Neck. Just being in the company of Winslow Homer revitalized him and somehow made more bearable his work with the cotton company. This time he returned to Boston to find Alcie who stayed with their sister while Boyer returned to Galveston.

The Death of Thomas Gonzales

Thomas Gonzales's condition worsened. Late in November he suffered a massive heart attack that proved fatal. He died in Boston on December 1 at the age of sixty-seven. Alcie immediately telegraphed the news to his brother and made arrangements to accompany the body back home by train.

Gonzales's lengthy and florid obituary appeared the following day in the *Galveston News*. The headlines proclaimed: "Thomas Gonzales / Death in Boston of a Prominent Citizen of the City of Galveston / A Brilliant War Record / Captain of the Battery in the Battle of Galveston—Death resulted From a Broken Heart."[8]

With his sons acting as administrators of his estate, an inventory was taken on December 28, 1896, showing his net worth as $34,416.50. The final inventory did not include any assessed value on the family business of Thomas Gonzales and Son. That, along with the home on Avenue O, was already in the pocket of Boyer Gonzales.

The Years with Homer

With the death of his father, Boyer Gonzales had to accept reality: he alone was in control of, and responsible for, the firm Thomas Gonzales and Son. He may have thought, since the death of his brother four years past, that he had accepted much of the responsibility. His father, however, was always there to guide him when he took his business trips. Now there would be no father to remain at home and take charge of any day-to-day crisis that invariably came up in the cotton industry and demanded immediate action. Alcie had his work with the other business in which the family had a large interest, the Taylor Cotton Compress, where he was paymaster and cotton clerk.

A Visit to the Kellogg Sanitarium in Battle Creek

Almost immediately after the death of Thomas Gonzales, William F. Ladd, president of the Taylor Cotton Compress, and its vice president, Gustav Mayhoff, decided that it was Boyer's familial duty to take over the position of secretary-treasurer of the company, a title his father had held since

1882. This Boyer did begrudgingly! And as he expected, the pressures of the added responsibilities took their toll and the periodic attacks of acute indigestion intensified. June of 1897 found Boyer in what was at the time the fashionable health resort in America, the Kellogg Sanitarium in Battle Creek, Michigan. While there, he wrote to Winslow Homer at Prout's Neck, indicating a desire to visit the artist again.

On July 2, Homer answered, "I shall be here from the 14th to the 24 of this month as you suggest this date. I shall be away for August & on. It gives me great pleasure to hear from you. I know several cures for indigestion & shall be very happy to see you."[9]

At some time during the spring, before he had gone to Battle Creek, Boyer Gonzales sent Homer a watercolor, to which Homer, harried but apologetic, responded: "I have your watercolor tacked on my door & can see it now from my desk & I did not answer your letter. Many other letters have been unanswered from different parts of the country but have often regretted that I did not reply to your last letter from the French Broad somewhere down in Georgia. At any rate, I will be glad to see you. Yours Truly, Winslow Homer." His regret at not responding to the gift of the painting was sincere.

Gonzales left Battle Creek and went directly to Maine. Once again, the visit was a memorable one, closely connected with Homer's painting of one of his great works. Gonzales wrote later that "during a drizzling, mid-summer nor'easter, we had wandered along the rocky coast to a point near the bathing beach. Retracing our steps, we entered the little wood that Prout's Neck boasts of, and at the foot of a pine tree, I noted many feathers which Mr. Homer explained were the feathers of wild geese. He had purchased them for his table that winter and after getting them to his studio had decided to paint them. His picture of wild geese resulted." Gonzales recalled that finishing the painting did not come easily. Homer "was bothered for a long time because he was undecided how the birds carried their legs in flight. Some

time after, near Elizabeth lights, a flock of geese flew directly over him, and the problem was solved."[10] Gonzales had watched Homer complete his *Wild Geese,* which was first titled *Flight of Wild Geese* [1897].

He returned to Galveston and was soon caught again between being the sole proprietor of Thomas Gonzales and Son as well as being secretary and treasurer of the Taylor Cotton Compress. Often, he would steal a few moments for himself, leave his office on the Strand, walk to the wharves a block away, and watch the vessels—steam and sail—tied up to the piers or anchored in the harbor. There were always multitudes of seagulls circling above or diving for food tossed to them by the sailors on the ships. In the evenings, he would take the street car to his home on Avenue O, where he continued to live quietly with his younger brother. The only real escape for Boyer was his art, which often took him down the island to West Beach where he could be quiet and alone with sketchbook and paints. Occasionally he would write to Homer, of course, never really knowing when or whether he would receive an answer. Early in October, he had mailed him a box of pecans that had fallen to the ground from the tree in his yard.

On December 14, 1897, Homer answered: "Your letter of October 5th at hand. I received it on my arrival home from Pittsburgh where I had been on a jury of awards & a thankless job it was—& I didn't feel like writing—I was very glad to hear from you & will be—I went to Canada last summer after you left here—I was for weeks at The Grand Discharge Lake—two weeks of it. I worked hard. I got 14 fine watercolors. It cost me $12 per day—but it paid. I had 2 men & canoe for the time I was there—The last two weeks my brother came up & we went fishing together & I taged [*sic*] him about sketching from him & his men on the fly without posing. I am very busy now preparing a small exhibition of twenty water colors—I received yesterday a box of pecan nuts or 'paughcon' as my Texans [his nephews, the sons of Arthur] call them. I thought my days of nut eating were over but I find that I can chew them very easy. They are so fresh & very fine. I thank you much. Yours very truly. Winslow Homer."[11]

He made use of the weekends and holidays to travel at short distances on the mainland, painting the birds, fish, and alligators that inhabited the bayous near Dickinson. Or he would return to familiar haunts down the western end of Galveston Island, places on or near the beach where he had gone hunting with his brothers and friends when he was growing up. Or he would wander down to the eastern-most tip of the island where he could sketch the pelicans, seagulls, and other sea birds or the many ships leaving and entering the Galveston Bay from the Gulf. Then, when he felt he could no longer bear the pain, he journeyed from one health resort to another in search of some relief from the almost constant indigestion and depression which continued to plague him.

Special were the moments he spent writing to and hearing from Homer. He always notified his friend when he planned to make a trip East. He wrote on May 20, and surprisingly he received a prompt response from Prout's Neck dated June 2, 1898. Homer, anxious to see him, was at his most cheerful: "I have been on hand in Scarboro all winter answering many letters. That is all I have done—& my entire years work is now at the Rhode Island School of Design in Providence R. I. They have fine galleries & I have loaned them for four months."

Then, he turned to a lighter topic, displaying some of his occasional wry wit: "I am now engaged in something with great pleasure & I hope with more profit than the painting business! (It appears to me that I wrote about the same thing to you last Spring. I have a memory! It sometimes bothers me & on rare occasions is of great service.) It is Planting. I have hired half an acre of land & I am raising corn on all of it—Indian Corn—I am doing it for the *pleasure* & profit to

my health, although I am very well. But I look forward to the time when I shall just cut off & sow my *wild oats*. If I have not cut off before you get here I shall be happy to see you. Let me know at the time. Yours truly, Winslow Homer."[12]

By mid-July, 1898, Gonzales wrote to Homer from the Queen of the Mountains health resort in Porter Springs, Georgia. Again, Homer's answer was sharp, quick, and uplifting. His door seemed to be always open to Gonzales. Dated July 25, 1898, it began, "Dear Mr. Gonzales, I have no doubt that I shall be in Prout's Neck about the time that you would like to make your stop here. & it will give me great pleasure to see you—many changes here that will interest you. Lots of new people here & most of the old ones that are still alive. Plenty of 'moonshine' and lemons! Yours truly, Winslow Homer."[13]

During these visits, Homer was always with Sam, "Mr. Homer's much loved, much spoilt Yorkshire terrier, possessing, as Mr. Homer said, the intelligence of a human, and in a way he proved it.[14] The great tides on that coast, as they recede leave delightful natural bath tubs, in the rocks, and on one occasion before he began to descend the cliffs, Mr. Homer suggested that we give Sam a bath. We went down, but when we looked for Sam we saw that little imp way up on the cliff wagging his stump tail. No bath for him that morning. How Mr. Homer chuckled. He realized that his suggestion had been made a little too loud!"[15]

Homer, Gonzales recalled, "painted when things were just right, but he fished always and a more successful fisherman, I have yet to meet. The tautog—the black bass of the sea—that lurked in the shadows of the rocks as the Atlantic's surged [*sic*] over them was his game. When the tide was out many delightful walks did we take in search of the little crabs that we used as bait."

Homer made a tremendous impression on Boyer Gonzales and he enjoyed reflecting on the artist: "Correspondence was most irksome to him. He put off and put off answering even his business letters so that at all times the accumulation of mail was appalling. But contrary to the accepted idea, he was hospitality itself, the most genial of hosts, and no one knocked at his door and was refused admittance, unless he was busy painting or realized that the knocker was some ungenuine, curious person, and of these he was bothered by legions."

Being with Homer on those trips was without a doubt therapy as was just getting away from Thomas Gonzales and Son. More and more, he found reasons to get away, either at a health spa or in Maine, painting and visiting Homer whenever the artist was in his Prout's Neck studio.

Life in early 1899 was not going well for Boyer in Galveston. The company had been showing increasing losses since his father's death. It was a great relief to receive a letter from Homer dated May 3, 1899: "Dear Gonzales, It gives me pleasure to hear from you—I will simply answer this letter briefly—& at some time write you a decent one—I have just written enough for one morning—a letter to a former sunday school teacher of mine in reference to 'something that will interest the present generation' on the occasion of the 80th anniversary of our sunday school——& it was the effort of my life! I will write to you as I say some other time—We will yet have that outing—Perhaps next winter—I spent the Winter in the Bahamas very hard at work. I do not mean to work much longer. It costs too much & the returns are too long in coming in—It cost me $500 per week all past winter—I give you this as a hint—that I will never go on any cheap trip. Your mention in your letter of the low price of S. Ships prompts me to write this. Yours very truly, Winslow Homer."[16]

Making the Ultimate Decision

The two had planned one day to return to England and the village of Tynemouth where Homer had spent the years 1881 and 1882. But trying to escape from his problems at home soon became a problem in itself, and he finally decided to make some decisions about the business.

The first decision was to sell the family interest in the Taylor Cotton Press. His father had owned ten bonds in the Press valued at $500 each. In addition, there were 168 shares of stock valued at $100 per share, for a total worth of $21,800. It was all sold and the name of the concern was changed to Merchants' and Planters' Compress. At last, Boyer Gonzales was divesting himself of burdens that he could not tolerate.

By June he was once again back at the Kellogg Sanitarium in Battle Creek, Michigan. Later that month, he heard from Homer again: "I ought to write to you & here goes to say that, after you get through with your numerous hospitals and Doctor's Shops—if you should show up at Prout's Neck sometime or any time in August I am quite sure to be at home. At any other time I am doubtful. I am not working! Yours truly, Winslow Homer."[17]

Unfortunatelly, Gonzales's grave condition prevented him from leaving the sanitarium until mid-August when he went to Boston to stay with Daisy. It is there that he received another hastily written letter from Homer dated August 30: "My dear Gonzales—I shall be here from now on to winter as I have now got through a long vacation & prepare doing some work—I shall be very glad to see you. The Texans are here all but the old man. They will doubtless be happy to show the social side of these afternoon teas—'The Willows' I am told keeps a fine table if you cannot get in at the Checkley—Yours truly, Winslow Homer."[18] Gonzales promptly accepted the invitation staying until mid-October, when he returned to Galveston.

On an evening late in November, Boyer Gonzales found by chance the diary that he had begun in 1883 when he was fifteen years old. After reading it, he was moved to write once more: "November 24 1899, 7:20. I am at home. A norther is rattling my window shutters and moaning around the house corners. As I write these lines, the dying away cry of a flock of geese is borne to me on the wind. With their cry comes a flood of dear reminiscences—of my past life—a great many are included in the pages of this book. I have just looked at the last entry—November 16th, 1883—Sixteen years ago. Many changes have come to Alcie and me in that time. The musical honks of those ariel wanderers have revived my pleasant happy youth."[19]

He wrote in the diary a month later on December 31: "The year 1899 will in a few moments be a thing of history. It is going rapidly. Whistles and midnight mass bells are welcoming the year 1900. It is here! 1899 is gone forever. May 1900 be a bright year with happiness for Alcie and me."

Boyer Gonzales was thirty-five years old, alone and desolate.

1900: "I Would Gladly Turn my Back on Galveston Forever!"

Beginning with 1900, Boyer Gonzales's life began to change, to take off in a new, very different direction. March found him once again in the north of Mexico, at Topo Chico, the spa near Monterrey. Not only did he go there to rest and take the curative mineral waters and baths, he also went there to paint. Undoubtedly it was there that he decided to keep the promise that he had made to himself on July 11, 1894, when he left Galveston bound for Boston. At that time, he wrote in his diary that he was determined "to try and learn more of water colors." That was the fall that he had studied with his first teacher William Whittemore at the art colony in Annisquam, Massachusetts. With the lessons, he had progressed. As Whittemore had told him, he had to relax, to become less timid: "Pitch right in. Slap it on!"

On returning to Galveston, he contacted his sister in Boston who introduced him to the respected marine painter from Maine, Walter F. Lansil. Arrangements were made for him to study with Lansil in his Boston studio. Born in Bangor in 1848, Lansil had studied first with the American painter J. P. Hardy before leaving for Paris where he enrolled in the Academie Julian. The painter to have the most profound effect on Lansil was the Dutch master of marine painting, Hendrik Willem Mesdag (1831–1915). In 1884, Lansil had sailed to the Hague to study with the early impressionist, who was one of the most influential painters of that style. Mesdag, then at the peak of his career, was represented with several works in the Rijksmuseum in Amsterdam. He had concentrated on fishing and harbor scenes as well as sailing ships at sea. That summer of 1900, Lansil passed on his own enthusiasm for Mesdag's monumental works to his pupil. Together they studied the techniques and style of the Dutch master. That indirect influence of Mesdag never left Gonzales, especially in the oils that later brought Gonzales to the attention of the critics, both in America and abroad.

He painted that entire summer with Lansil, ending with his usual trip to Maine to visit Homer in Prout's Neck. On the way, he stopped off to paint in village of Provincetown, at the very tip of Cape Cod. He was back in Boston in early September, ready to board a steamer bound for home, when he was shaken by the early reports of the hurricane that devastated Galveston when it struck on September 7. Reports of the disaster filled the newspapers of the world. Thousands were reported dead. The city had been destroyed by a massive tidal wave that washed away many of the city's homes and buildings. Dozens of ships from throughout the world lay sunk in the harbor. More than six thousand people had died; lists of the dead had begun appearing in newspapers.

Gonzales and his sister were finally able to get reliable word that, while the family home had suffered much damage, their only remaining relative in Galveston, brother Alcie, was safe.

As soon as telegraph and postal services were restored, wires and letters were exchanged. Alcie wrote, sending snapshots he had taken of their home as well as of the Ursuline Academy, seven blocks to the east. Boyer had also written to his good friend, Walter S. Beadles, a cotton broker who lived with his wife, the former Louise Hertford, in the corner house at 1503 Broadway. In return, he received a letter from Beadles's sister-in-law, Eleanor Hertford, whom everyone called Nell. She and Bo had occasionally attended parties and dances at the Garten Verein together—nothing constant or serious. He may have called her "Nell," but to her, he was still "Mr. Gonzales." There existed a polite, Victorian distance between them, a distance that satisfied Boyer Gonzales.

On September 17, Nell wrote: "Dear Mr. Gonzales, Bess [Walter Beadles] has just handed me your letter and we all appreciate it so much. How thankful you should be that you were many miles away from here on that memorable day of September 7. It would be impossible for anyone to describe the horror of the whole thing as they [*sic*] really were. To read the papers telling of it is like hearing children's prattle in comparison to the reality. I guess those away from here, who have been in suspense have really suffered more than the ones who were here to experience it all, for everyone here seems *stunned,* & you never see any emotion displayed of any kind, everyone is perfectly calm! We all seem to have gone through so much, that we seem beyond tears! At noon, when I saw people being brought in from the beach, I became very much frightened & excited & bid them all to leave this house and go to Mrs. [Walter] Gresham's [at 1400 Broadway] as the wind was coming from the north east & this house was rocking so terribly, but Mama and Bess wouldn't listen to me. The Bowens have been renting the Campbell house for the summer, so about 5 P.M. Mr. B[owen] came over and told us we were in danger as part of the roof was gone. We went out into the water which was to our waists but couldn't go against the wind then to Mrs. Greshams, so thinking of course that the Campbell house

was safer than ours, we went there. The same calm which is prevailing over the whole town took possession of me then and I was able to be of great assistance to the men in keeping the door from coming in. The whole roof came in on us, and 16 of us were huddled in the vestibule. I think we could not have stood it a half hour longer, for when the front door gave way we knew that we should only go out to be drowned, as 'twas moonlight and we could see how high the water was. We fully realized our danger and stayed as closely together as possible, so if we perished we would all four go. After the water receded, we went to Mrs. Lobit's house [at 1527 Broadway] which was damaged very slightly, & there we stayed for two nights, as this house is not habitable when it rains. But Mr. Gonzales I had so fully made up my mind that we were going to die that night that 'twas the longest time before I could fully realize that the storm was over and we [were] all safe. But the whole town is a perfect *wreck,* you can picture the *awfulness* of it all, & as for dead bodies, we couldn't sit on the galleries at all without seeing wagon loads of them going by. At first, people didn't realize that there would be so many and they were carried by one at a time on litters, but later they had to be carted away like so much debris. There were two wagons full taken from the wreck right there in front of us on the esplanade and the poor things had stiffened in the positions in which they had died, most of them with their hands clasped high in the air, in the attitude of prayer. The ones I saw will haunt me to my dying day! Louise [Nell's older sister] and I are begging Bess to go away from here to live[.] I would gladly turn my back on Galveston forever! but [of] course we have no plans made as yet.

"Alcie came to hunt us up the day after the storm & drops in every once in a while to cheer us all. Although he is one of the busiest men in town, he said he would probably come here and stay until your house could be fixed. He is now staying with Mrs. Brown [at Ashton Villa on Twenty-second and Broadway]. Well I think I had better wind up this grewsome [*sic*] letter, & I only wish I could have written a more cheerful account. We have all been sick, I think from the terrible odor, and living on canned goods and brackish water, but we are all right now. If I was selfish I would wish you were here to make us all feel better, but for your own sake I advise you not to come home if you can possibly help it. We all send our love to you and hope you will write often. Nell."[20]

Gonzales returned to Galveston the first week of October and commenced immediately to repair the house on Avenue O, which had suffered more damage than he had been told. Others, like Winslow Homer's brother, Arthur, had lost too much to stay. His house remained intact, but his business, the Galveston Rope and Twine Company, had simply and entirely been washed away. There was nothing to be recovered. Devastated and defeated by his financial ruin, Arthur Homer packed up his belongings and with his wife and his two sons—"The Texans"—left for Boston where he opened the same type of business in nearby Quincy.

Then, quite unexpectedly, Boyer Gonzales, also, made a decision, a decision not in keeping with his hesitant, deliberative nature. In 1901, just months after the storm, he divested himself of the firm of Thomas Gonzales and Son, selling it to John Rogers and J. A. Robertson, proprietors of John D. Rogers and Company. Founded in 1868, the firm was one of the oldest and largest of the cotton factors and commission merchants in the city. Gonzales agreed to stay on with Rogers as bookkeeper, but with the understanding that he wanted freedom to follow what had always been his primary interest—his art.

Life with fewer pressures and more leisure time to spend with his paints and brushes seems to have agreed with him. Winslow Homer certainly thought so. On December 29, 1902, he wrote a lively letter to Boyer in Galveston: "I am glad to see by your being at home that you are well—if you

were not, you would be at Battle Creek or Hot Springs." Then he mentioned the possibility of their meeting and being together: "I think some of going to Florida—Homospat— [Homosassa] or some such name on the west coast where there is good fishing & no *painting. If I go, I will let you know.*"[21] That, of course, meant that he was inviting Gonzales to join him.

Added inspiration came in the form of a photograph of Homer taken on December 2, 1902, showing the painter wearing a bowler and strolling jauntily with a cane in front of his home in Prout's Neck. It was inscribed in a bold script: "A Happy New Year to Boyer Gonzales from Winslow Homer."[22]

From that time on, Boyer Gonzales painted in earnest, traveling to the east coast. His paintings began to sell in galleries in Boston and Galveston, but to no great extent until 1904 when he received a letter that boosted his spirits considerably.

St. Louis was hosting its great world's fair that year and the state of Texas set up a commission to direct its participation, which was to prove considerable. Texas built its own building with rooms designated to display an exhibit of works by Texas artists. On May 31, Mrs. Thomas F. Taylor, chief of the Department of Art of the Commission in Austin, wrote to Boyer indicating that the exhibit would open on June 15. "It is not the aim of the art department to collect a large exhibit, but to show a few of the best works from each of the leading artists of Texas. Such a collection would of course be notably incomplete without something from your gifted brush."[23]

The exhibition may have been more regional or provincial than many artists would have aspired to, but it was the first time that Gonzales would show along with other painters that he knew and respected. He responded immediately.

He continued to work for Rogers but for the most part at his pleasure. He also continued his membership in the

Galveston Cotton Exchange and attended meetings when he was in residence. When he was at home, he generally found himself in the company of Nell Hertford, as on June 7, 1905, at the wedding of Elisabeth Focke and E. Maury Robertson at the Focke residence at 1228 Market. Nell was a bridesmaid, together with Emma Seinsheimer, Ethel Randall, Josephine Gresham, and two other friends.[24]

From that date, Bo Gonzales and Nell Hertford were always paired at dinner parties given by their young friends, the Robertsons, or her sister and brother-in-law, Louise and Bess Beadles, or at dances given by friends in their homes or at the Garten Verein.

During those years, the Gonzales family began to grow. Soon after the devastating hurricane of 1900, Alcie had married Emiline Davis, younger sister of Mary Davis, the same young lady who for several years had kept Boyer dangling by his nerve endings. On December 13, 1903, Emiline gave birth to a son, Julian Caverly, Jr. Boyer and his sister Daisy were among the godparents when the child was christened at Trinity Church in May of 1904; another child, Julia Boyer, was born on August 8, 1906.[25]

His brother's family was growing, but Boyer was feeling more and more alone. He continued to live by himself in the large family home. Loneliness often turned into periods of deep depression. This mood was not helped by the fact that in July of 1907, Nell had left Galveston to accompany her sister, Louise, on a leisurely trip that took them to the Catskills in New York. Accompanying them was her good friend and neighbor, Josephine Gresham. Nell wrote to him often, but her letters seemed not to help.

By the end of August, he made plans to register at the Kellogg Sanitarium in Battle Creek. He advised Nell what he was doing and she continued to write long, newsy letters to him every other day while he was in Battle Creek. He wrote her that his health was improving rapidly; finally, on

September 5, he wrote that he wanted to meet them in Niagara Falls on September 17. He did not say why.

Nell responded immediately: "My dearest . . . How delighted I am that you are really on your way to meet me! We have been separated so long that I can hardly believe that we are going to see each other in 10 days." Meeting at the Falls would not be possible, though. She told him of their plans: "We are going over to Lake Placid today [September 7] & will take in Saranas and Rainbow Lake before we leave on Tuesday (10th) at 11:32 A.M., arriving at Albany at 6:45 P.M. Then we will leave there Monday morning [September 18] by boat, as 'tis cheaper, for N.Y. I wish you could be in Albany in time to take that trip with us, can't you? As yet, I don't know where we are going to stop in N.Y. but if we should miss connections at all just send a line to me c/o Mrs. Cora Behrends, 40 W. 17th Str. N. Y. City. She is one of our fellow passengers on the way up & is a good substantial little German."[26]

It is obvious that she was not going to let the moment escape. She ended her letter "I can hardly wait for the 18th to come. Yours ever!"

Gonzales decided to meet them in New York. He registered at the Grand Union Hotel and wrote to Nell at Cora Behrends's. He then sent off a letter to the Art Students League of New York at their offices at 215 West 57th Street. He had heard of an art school sponsored by the League in the village of Woodstock and, in particular, of an instructor there, Birge Harrison, well known as a landscape artist and watercolorist, Gonzales's two primary interests.

Harrison, born in 1854, had studied first at the Pennsylvania Academy of Fine Arts but left with John Singer Sargent to go to Paris to study under Cabanel. His works won many medals including a silver medal in the Paris Salon in 1887 and a second medal at the Paris Exposition in 1889. Five years later, Harrison—with Winslow Homer—received a "unique medal" at the World's Columbian Exposition in Chicago. Then he won the silver medal at the St. Louis Exposition in 1904—where Boyer's works were shown in the Texas Exhibition Hall. In 1907, one of Harrison's paintings had received the gold medal at the Philadelphia Exposition.

Nell and her sister met him at the Grand Union Hotel. Gonzales told them of his plans to study at the Woodstock School with Harrison, although he had not yet been accepted. He also advised them of his desire to give up completely the cotton business and devote the remainder of his life to his art. He had enough money from his inheritance and investments to make the venture possible until the sales of his paintings made him independent.

Then, quite in keeping with his new quixotic nature, he asked Nell to marry him. Louise gave her approval, and Nell did not hesitate to accept. Arrangements were hastily made and they were married in the Episcopal Church of the Transfiguration, better known as "The Little Church Around the Corner," at 9:30 A.M. on September 21, with the Reverend George Clarke Houghton officiating. Her sister Louise and Josephine Gresham served as witnesses.[27]

Following the ceremony, they took a carriage down to the city hall, to the Department of Health, to register the marriage, then returned to the hotel. There Boyer found a letter posted that morning from the Art Students League: "Dear Sir, Your letter just received. The Woodstock School will be open until November 1st at least, and Mr. Harrison no doubt will give instruction after that to any students who care to remain." The letter concluded: "Ask for Mr. Goltz, our representative there, and he can advise you about boarding accommodations."[28]

The following day, Boyer's forty-third birthday, they boarded the Hudson Day Line Boat and leisurely sailed a hundred miles up the Hudson River to Kingston. There, they boarded the Ulster and Delaware Railroad to West Hurley.

It was only a four mile stage drive from West Hurley to Woodstock, a village comfortably nestled in the Catskills.

A Letter From Homer:
"How Happy Both of You Must Be."

Several days after arriving in Woodstock, Bo wrote to Homer at Prout's Neck saying that he was making great progress with Birge Harrison as his teacher and that he had never been happier in his life. He wrote that he owed his happiness not only to his work at Woodstock but to his recent marriage in New York, which he described in detail.

On October 4, Homer answered. But this letter different from any that Gonzales had ever received from him. There was a cold, abrupt, almost cruel tone to it that Gonzales, sensitive as he was, could not mistake or misread.

"My Dear Mr. Gonzales. It is a great pleasure to hear from you again. I certainly congratulate you on your happy life—& also on your recent marriage—How happy both of you must be." He added curtly, "I am about to hunt up some sketches to send with this for a wedding present—something that can go in the bottom of your trunk—"[29]

Absent from this letter was the usual Homerian spontaneity, wit and charm, jest, and overall ebullience and exhilaration; indeed, it was short and distant: "I am very well now. I have not worked recently having few years left to me and lots of money in which to see a thing or two—I do not know yet where I shall spend the winter—Yours sincerely, Winslow Homer."

In a smaller script, he wrote around the corner of the stationery a telling postscript: "I just found a sketch of a girl that would not go [with me] to the Little Church Around the Corner."

The terse note contained no invitation to Bo and Nell to come to Prout's Neck on their next trip to the region,

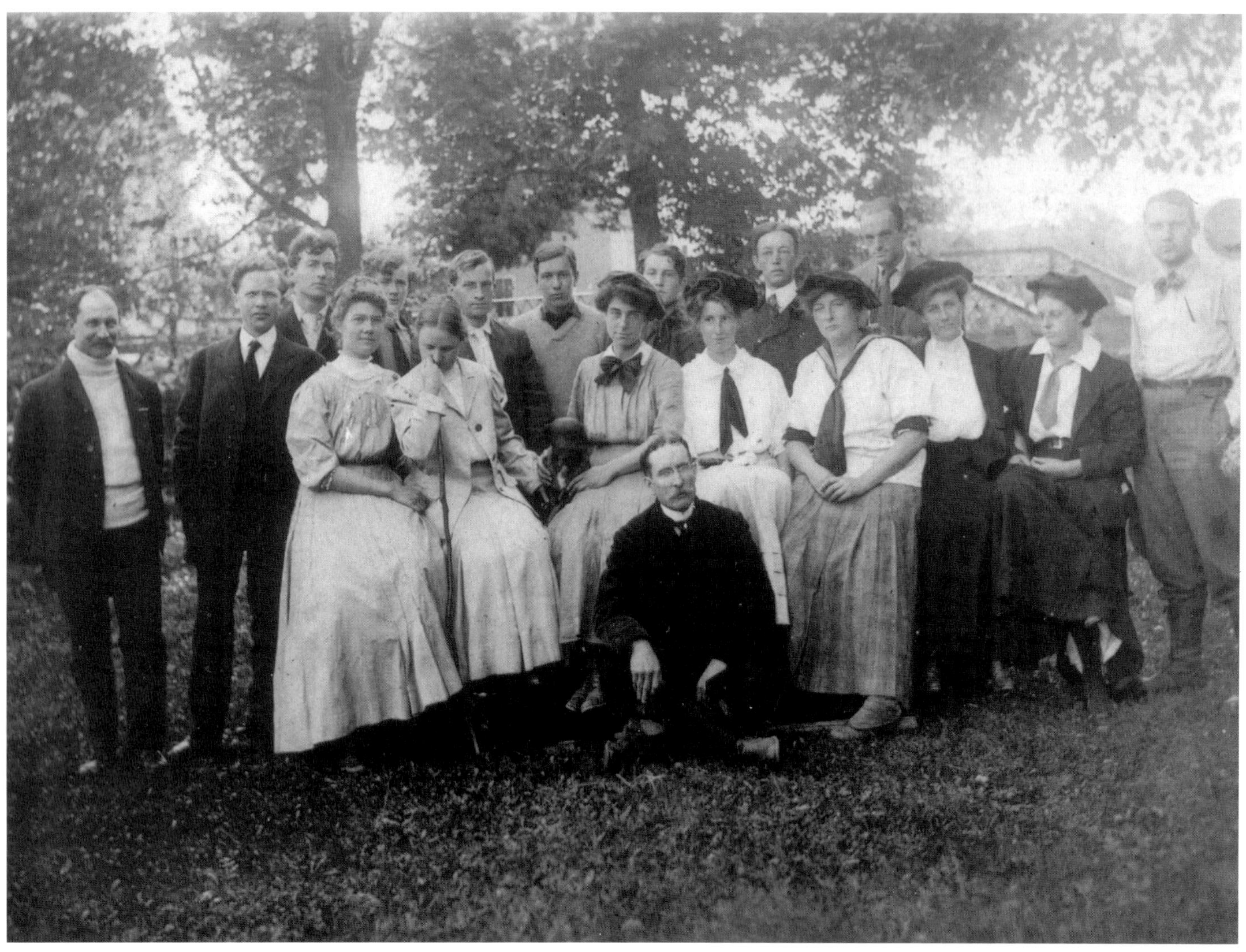

Art Students League, Woodstock, 1907

where Bo could, as in the past, paint with him in his studio or fish with him in the cold waters off the rocky coast of Maine just beneath that studio—something they had been doing for twenty years whenever Gonzales visited. Nor was there an invitation to meet in Florida and fish off the Keys. It was the letter of an old man, tired and aware of his declining age. Be-neath the casual, frigid tone is the hint of jealousy that his younger friend and fishing companion had found someone besides Homer to share his life and happy times. Gonzales never took Nell to Prout's Neck to visit Homer. Never once did he return to Maine not even after Homer's death. Nor did he ever write to him. With that one "letter of congratulations," all correspondence with Winslow Homer stopped. The once intense and lively friendship ceased.

The friendship may have ended with Homer's letter and the wedding gift of two water colors that he immediately sent to Bo and his bride, but the effect of knowing Homer so well, being with him on so many occasions, sharing his life and thoughts as no one else had ever done, would never disappear. The influence of Homer, the man and the artist, his artistic techniques and his works, would be indelibly apparent in almost every work that Boyer Gonzales would paint in the future. Even as Gonzales's technique changed as he grew older, the hint of Homer was still there. Gonzales, no matter how the relationship had ended, would forever be indebted to Winslow Homer, and it was a debt that Gonzales was always ready to acknowledge.

The letter from Homer, however, did little to dampen the spirits of Boyer and Nell. Gonzales's work went better than he expected. He got on famously with Harrison, the other artists, and students. And there were many days that he and Nell could escape and venture out into the Catskills. Their plans were to spend two weeks, but as Nell wrote to her brother-in-law, Bess Beadles, "We are so charmed with this place that instead of staying two weeks as we originally intended to, we are going to stay *five weeks*!"[30]

They left Woodstock for New York on October 28 and after five days arrived in Boston. They stayed with Bo's sister Daisy; this gave the two women a chance to meet. Two weeks later, Bo and Nell set sail aboard the *San Jacinto* for home in Galveston.

CHAPTER SIX

A Honeymoon in Europe

Once back at home in Galveston, Bo and Nell began making plans for their honeymoon, a six-month grand tour of Europe. The plans were quite general except for their intention to visit the major art galleries and museums in England, Germany, the Netherlands, France, Switzerland, and, even more important to Bo, Italy. He wanted to settle there for a while and find an artist who could help him develop his watercolor techniques. At Woodstock Harrison had given him the names of several artists living in Florence that he might consider studying with for a few weeks.

With their packed steamer trunks, passports, and letters of credit and introduction in their pockets, they left Galveston for New York via Boston and on March 19, 1908, boarded the North German Line steamer, *Bremen.* By April 1, they were cruising off the coast of England, landing in Bremen on April 5. At the time, Nell wrote to her brother-in-law, "We have not yet decided on your exact plans, & will stay in Munich if the weather is not too cold for me, so Bo says to address our mail c/o Thomas Cook & Son in Florence, Italy and we can send for it where ever we are."[1] Their time was their own to do with what they wished.

In Amsterdam, they spent two days walking about the city, spending much of their time in the Rijksmuseum. On the morning of their third day, they took the train to the Hague with the primary intent of visiting the museum and studio of Hendrick Mesdag, the painter who had indirectly influenced much of Gonzales's impressionistic style. His first contact with Mesdag and his work had been indirectly through his teacher, Walter Lansil, when he took classes in 1900 in Boston. It was Lansil who opened the door to the great Dutch painter for Gonzales. Now, he had the opportunity to see Mesdag's work first hand.

Once in the Hague, however, they could not find their way to the Mesdag museum. Nell wrote in her diary, "We inquired the way of a nice looking gentleman on the Street—he spoke a little English, and as the route was complicated and he couldn't direct us very well, to our astonishment, he insisted on taking us there. We walked together 20 minutes, he pointing out everything of interest—Even the damaged lamp post where the Queen suffered an accident. We were quite overcome by his extreme courtesy and wondered what gentleman in our own country would take the time and trouble to go so far out of his way for two strangers!"[2]

Both Nell and Bo were quite impressed when they visited Mesdag's museum. In her diary, she wrote: "Mesdag's gallery, although small, is the most artistic of any we've seen. It is attached to his studio and residence which are most picturesque." She added that they had "the extreme pleasure of visiting Mr. Mesdag in his studio. . . ." Bo noted in a postal card to his sister-in-law, Louise, "We visited Mesdag's private collection of 8 rooms of modern Dutch and French paintings and also his studio."[3]

He would have been thrilled if he could have spoken at length with the artist who had been such a profound influence in his work. But he missed his opportunity; they were in the Hague only a few hours, leaving at 2 P.M. for Antwerp.

The following morning they departed Amsterdam for Paris, with a brief stopover in Brussels. It was soon evident that Paris had been a mistake. Nell was violently ill with headaches and a fierce cold, so they hastened that very day to Germany spending the next day in Cologne visiting the Cathedral. The first part of their trip they spent mostly on trains or boats getting from one famous city to another. They sailed down the Rhine—Bo sketching as they went, just as he had done in 1892 on his way to the spa at Schwalbach. They passed a day in Nuremberg before going on to Munich where a fierce snow storm forced them to spend Easter Sunday closed up in their hotel room before a roaring fire.

After Germany, off they went seeking warmer days on the Italian lakes, stopping off on the way in Lucerne. Captivated by the beauty of the lake and surrounding mountains and the charm of the people, they lingered there five days longer than they expected to. Gonzales flourished in the solitude and beauty that Lucerne offered, and they spent considerable time walking in the countryside where Nell gathered wild flowers and Bo sketched. They spent time sitting beside the lake. The wild mallard ducks fascinated Nell

as they paraded about "right in the midst of a busy fashionable resort, never minding people, automobiles and the noises of traffic & coming to within a few feet of us in a most confidential manner & ask just as plain as if they spoke in words for something to eat." On leaving, as she wrote in her diary, they bid a "reluctant adieu to our 'views' and our 'host and hostess' and the other things we became attached to in Lucerne."[4]

The next four days they spent on Lake Como, arriving in Venice on May 2, where they registered at a small hotel that opened on St. Mark's plaza. They stayed ten days with Bo taking snapshots of Nell feeding the pigeons, throughly enthralled by the beauty they found in everything and everyone—everywhere.

On May 7, Boyer wrote his sister-in-law a long, expressive letter, illustrated with pencil sketches of scenes of the city. It was their sixth day in Venice and he waxed eloquent, "for six days, we have been in dreamland. A dreamland of enchantment. Surely it is the Show City of the World. Each moment is more alluring than the last, and we think after all Aladdin must have rubbed his lamp and made a wish here."[5]

"Today Nell and I are at the Public Garden, and I am writing this in a spot made historical by Napoleon. (Go where you will, you can see evidences of this great man's work). This beautiful spot was once part of Venice, but Napoleon decreed that it should be a park and down the buildings came and today here is a park that is artistic and beautiful. The breezes from the Adriatic are sweeping through the palms, which from under the foliage the most beautiful vistas of Venice swimming in a hazy atmosphere are to be seen. Ever changing on account of the constant moving of craft. The sky line, as I look up, is beautiful and I have adorned the first page of this with a thumb nail sketch as it appears to me. Other little sketches are made at random."

"Nell," he continued, had fallen "under the Venetian spell. I think at first she was a little disappointed because of the absence of color she had seen in Lansil and Turner . . . pictures. Temporarily, she forgot a painter's license. But as it gradually unfolded, she became more and more enthusiastic, and now she is planning a return in 1909 acompained by you and Bess.

"I think the spell was first cast upon her when she emerged from our hotel upon St. Mark's Square and saw, under a strong sun, the Church of San Marco. Soft grey, beautiful beyond description with its thousands of blue pigeons fluttering about the base of the flagstaffs that for centuries have displayed the banners of Victory from Cyprus, Morea [Peloponnesus], and Candia [Cretè]. And then, we went into the church. All guide books describe it but not one can describe the sensations of one who likes to seek a secluded corner and let his mind run back to the year 550—nearly 1400 years ago and if he be well up on Venetian history, let the story of the Venetians unfold itself. People the old church with its former worshippers. Note the marvellous marriage ceremonies—its solemn funeral processions—its ceremonies of state. Odd little shivers run down your spine as in a few moments you have over 1400 years.

"How we wish for you day by day. How you would dream and dream and dream. Gliding down the canal under the present silvery moon . . . Down the Grand Canal past palaces. Slowly falling to decay under the famous Rialto, on and on, and back to the Piazza of St. Marks, passing under the Bridge of Sighs.

"With all its Arabian Nights enchantment, we come from under the spell at times to enjoy anything ridiculous. We have met an educated Italian bookseller who speaks English fairly well, having spent six years in New York. His shop is most enjoyable to visit and his quaintness and learning very ageeable. In describing Venice to us the other day, he said, 'He (Venice) is slowly sinking. The scientists, he calculates so nice, that he say that maybe in one thousand more years,

down he go, But that, that is not my beeesneess—'

"How you would enjoy our long walks. Gradually we have made our way on foot nearly all over the place. We have been to the Rialto and miles beyond over intricate water ways and bridges. We have visited the [island of] Gidecca, nearly to the railway station, passing over the iron bridge. At night, when the streets are lighted (with gas lamps), it is fascinating. . . ."

Not all of their time was spent seeing the sights. During their stay in Venice, he reported, "I have painted several fine things [including the *Bridge of Sighs*] and Nell thinks that as soon as they are shown in Boston, they will sell on sight. Let us hope she is correct. The place is overrun with painters. Every nook contains one. But so far, we have noted none of ability save one Englishman who was making pencil drawings. He was fine."

Both Bo and Nell enjoyed receiving mail from home. In a letter to his sister-in-law, he wrote, "I want to thank you for your letter of 21st April which was received yesterday, and is the first news of Galveston since the receipt of your letter in Munich—Alcie has not written me a one, and I am so glad to learn that [his son] Julian is well. Daisy writes both Nell and me as often as her eyes will permit. [She was slowly going blind.] Write us often and tell Mr. Beadles, a line will be appreciated. Continue to address us at Florence, Italy c/o Thomas Cook and Son."

It was obvious that Boyer Gonzales had never been quite so content with himself or felt so compatible with anyone as he did with Nell. Their moments together in Venice were special: "Every evening, we go to the iron bridge at sunset and watch the twilight take possession of Venice, & the last red rays of the departing sun tinge the dome of the Salute— Watch night gradually steal over the Grand Canal and note the lights one by one come twinkling out—only when the strains of some exquisite music from some gondola party come stealing up the Canal do we realize that the day is done."

After ten days of living under the enchanted spell of Venice, they were off by train on May 12 for their intended destination: Florence. However, the hotel they checked into definitely did not suit them. It was in the town center and too close to the railroad terminal, so they moved into an inn, the Pension Suisse, that became their home for the next month. They went to Thomas Cook and Son often in hopes of finding mail from home.

The first days in Florence were spent visiting one famous work of art after another. May 17 found them at the Academy of Fine Arts where they spent time with Michaelangelo's *David.* Time was escaping and still Gonzales had found no one to study with although from his teachers at Woodstock, Boyer had obtained several names of artists in Florence that he could contact.

After two weeks of enjoying the city of flowers, Nell wrote in her diary: "Monday and Tuesday, 18 & 19 [were] spent in looking up the Italian artists. We met Geolotti, an interesting old man [and then, Arturo] Faldi [a fresco painter], whose pretty wife is partly English & who acted as an interpreter." They also called on Jorge Gambini, "who was busy painting a scene with a tired Monk in it . . . his lay figure [that he] was using as a model quite startled me."[6]

Finally, Nell reported, they "went to see and decided to paint with Giuliani who is a finished artist in the Italian technique in water color. Besides learning a great deal from him, Bo has found him a mighty fine young fellow."

Gonzales spent a total of three weeks painting with the Italian watercolorist. He also continued to do what he had been taught to do in the past: copy the works of the great masters. To do this, he often visited the Uffizi to study and sketch details of Andrea del Sarto's *The Madonna Enthroned* and the Cupid in Antonio Francescini's *Love Conquers All.*

On May 21, they began making plans to end their trip. Bo wrote to a contact at the American Line at 1 Cockspur Street in London asking for reservations. The reply came several days later. They were booked to sail on the SS *Merion* from Liverpool on July 8 bound for Philadelphia. They would have a two-berth inside stateroom in the first-class section. Once in Philadelphia, they would take the train to New York and then on to Boston.

They remained in Florence until June 12 when they boarded a train for Paris, passing through Pisa, with Nell noting in her diary that she saw the fabled leaning tower. Once in Paris, they took an obligatory side trip to Versailles. On June 22, Bo sent a card to Nell's sister saying: "We are in Paris enjoying its beauties, its history, and its art. We have lived in the Louvre and Luxemburg—the latter is disappointing—but the former affords more enjoyment at every visit. It is immense yet it grows on you."[7]

After hurrying about for two weeks on a "busman's holiday," they left for England spending most of their three weeks in London visiting the galleries and museums that Bo had been to on his first trip to Europe in 1892. They arrrived in Liverpool in time to sail for Philadelphia on July 8. After spending a day with his sister Daisy at her home in Boston, they once again set sail for home.

By the time they arrived in Galveston on August 17, Nell was three months pregnant.

"I Used to Write This in Some Lonesomeness But . . ."

On September 1, 1908, Gonzales found, and wrote again, in the diary that he had begun in 1883 where he had written "Barn swallows have been flying South since my arrival home Aug. 17th. Earlier than ever noted before, [I] saw a whippoorwill last week. Great numbers of Blue Wing teal, that harbinger of shooting, are reported down west by authentic people—Snow and frost at the North. Maybe we will have a cold winter."[8]

That was then; this was now. Gonzales had never been so content with his life. He continued to work, at his leisure, for Rogers, but for the most part, he spent his time sketching and painting and reminiscing. He was pleased with his life and the decisions he had made: to rid himself of the family business interests, to take his painting seriously and to marry Nell.

On December 21, he reminisced in his diary: "It seems like old times. Alcie and I, for the first time in four years, took an outing together—down at the Bridge. The weather was keen, a cold NEest wind blowing in, and the lake literally alive with ducks. 95% canvas backs. But all were loath to fly. At intervals, a stray canvas back would pass, then a bunch of black ducks. We had fine shooting & I missed sadly. We got plenty however. 24 in all. We lost a great many, & but for 'Beauty,' a wonderful fox terrier retriever, we would have lost all. How the old days come to me. Ed, Alcie and I. Now so long ago. We [and] the Spencer boys. then Alcie's marriage, and our drifting apart. Ah! Blood is thicker than water, & we yearn for our own. My first outing in over two years—& I hope to repeat it often. Not a goose did I see tho' I looked and longed for a sight of one. Standing on the Bridge, where Alcie, the Spencer boys & I stood, in 1900 & 1899. I looked to the North & saw mentally, the migrating flock of great brant lurch and climb—their mellow voices sending to us a farewell. I wonder if those boys ever think of those days. There were good happy days. & time is flying. How the lake has changed, the rushes everywhere fully ten feet high presenting to the eye a typical duck preserve. A walk along the shore disclosed the great havoc that hawks create with the wounded. Wings, feathers, and carcasses thrown everywhere. It's a pity that so many are wounded and lost. In the rushes, I noted the Black throated green warbler and members of the Chestnuter sided warblers seemingly making their homes in the rushes—the sauciest and cutest, however, is the marsh wren peeping at you from all sides & scolding you for being near his domain—Dodging in & out, and scolding you again & again. I love to watch the little fellows."

On January 1, 1909, he reflected with great pleasure: "1908, with all its happiness has just gone. 1909 was ushered in with the usual noises—shrieks—whistles—guns & fireworks." This night, however, was noticeably different for him: "I used to write this in lonesomenesss, but Nell has come into my life with a great deal of brightness. With Harry and Louise [Sinclair], we saw the departure of 1908, and drank a toast to our mutual and continued happiness."

That happiness seemed to increase tenfold when on February 11, he scribbled hurriedly: "Our baby came today, at 12:15 PM—8 lbs. & a dear little boy—I am having about every experience that comes to a man." He was christened Boyer Gonzales, Jr., at Trinity Church.

During the summer of 1908, Boyer Gonzales was one of sixty-seven artists invited to participate in an exhibit being mounted for the State Fair of Texas to be held in October of that year. It was to be "the finest collection of art work ever seen in the Southwest." Included were several of his well-known artist friends from the Art Students League of New York who had been with him at Woodstock in 1907: George Bellows, Robert Nesbit, Luis Mora, and fellow Texan from San Antonio, R. J. Onderdonk. It was the first invitation that Gonzales had received from the State Fair organizers. From then on the invitations came annually.

Also during the summer of 1908, instead of returning to Woodstock, the Gonzaleses stayed in Galveston with their new baby. Boyer continued to paint, spending less and less time working for Rogers. As usual, with the arrival of autumn, he was always on the lookout for the migrating ducks and geese. On October 16, he wrote in his diary: "En route to the office yesterday morning, I noted over the gulf, winging their way towards High Island, a great flock of Canada geese . . . probably 75 or 100. One long line, with eight or ten bunches at the rear end. The sight of them made me a boy again as usual." A week later, he noted: "This morning at O & Tremont a great flock of grey brant sailed majestically over me close enough for me to see the leader look down. It made me young again & all down town, my mind drifted and drifted to the past."

His thoughts were also on his very content present. On December 27, he wrote: "Xmas has just passed. The happiest since my childhood, when I heard imaginary sleigh bells, flew frantically to a window in hopes of seeing Santa Claus & his reindeer, pass over the chimney tops. Our baby enjoyed his first Christmas tree and he enjoyed it too, as young as he is—understood in his way everything that was going on. May we have many, many more."

His exhilarated mood carried over into the followng year: "December 31, 1909: 8:20 PM. 1909 is fast leaving us. In three short hours it will be gone, leaving behind only memories & for us a great deal of happiness, for it brought my baby boy. The finest, & dearest little fellow that ever came to a couple. I drink to 1910. May it be as happy as 1909."

Once again he was invited to participate in the exhibition in Dallas at the state fair. He had sent three works: *After Glow, Across the Neches,* and *Last Gleam.* As in the past, his paintings were acquired mainly by Dallasites who were willing to pay whatever he asked.

*"A Simple Gentleman.
A Good Friend. A Grand Painter."*

On October 1, he was shaken when he opened the *Galveston Daily News* to read an Associated Press release datelined, Portland, Maine, September 30, 1910: "Winslow Homer, the famous artist died at his home in Scarborough yesterday, aged 74 years. He had been ill for four days."

Gonzales had not seen Homer since the year before his marriage to Nell in 1907. The last Boyer had heard from him was the courteous but cold letter Homer had written on the occasion of Boyer's marriage. He cut out the obituary and pasted it in the small scrapbook that contained clippings re-

lated to his own life and work. Beside it he wrote: "How shocked I was to read of the unexpected death of my friend of 20 years, Winslow Homer. A simple gentleman. A good friend. A grand painter. "[9]

He began to make notes for an essay he wanted to title "Some Reminiscences of Winslow Homer."[10]

"During my delightful friendship with the late Winslow Homer, extending over a period of fifteen years or more, I can now look back upon many glorious days spent in his society. I say glorious, because they were glorious. Our tastes were identical. We loved the ocean, and uncharted seas held for us something that cannot be described, but that something belongs to every dreamer.

"Every year or so, I drifted from my winter home on the shores of the Gulf of Mexico to the stern rocky coast of Maine, where the great surges of the Atlantic roll in, unbroken from the far off Azores. On one of these occasions [in 1887], through the kindness of the late Arthur B. Homer, I came to Prout's Neck, Scarborough, Maine, a rocky promontory that juts out into the Atlantic, and as an index finger, points to Wood Island light, that flashes its beams into the ocean fastness. Here I met Winslow Homer, and there began a friendship that ended only when he died: the memory of which will never die.

"When I met him he had discarded the Tynemouth subjects. The *Fog Warning,* [1885] the *Herring Net,* [1885] and the *Life Line* [1884] had brought him fame.[11]

"A week after meeting him we took a long walk to his annex studio at Pine Point. This annex studio puzzled me. When we arrived I saw with amazement, a regular stockade that surrounded a rough one room shack. The stockade was built strongly enough to withstand the assault of Indians, too high to climb, and absolutely sight proof. A stout doubly locked door admitted us to the interior, where I saw with a thrill a dory, well-protected from the sun. Why the thrill? Because my intuition. I associated that dory with 'The Fog

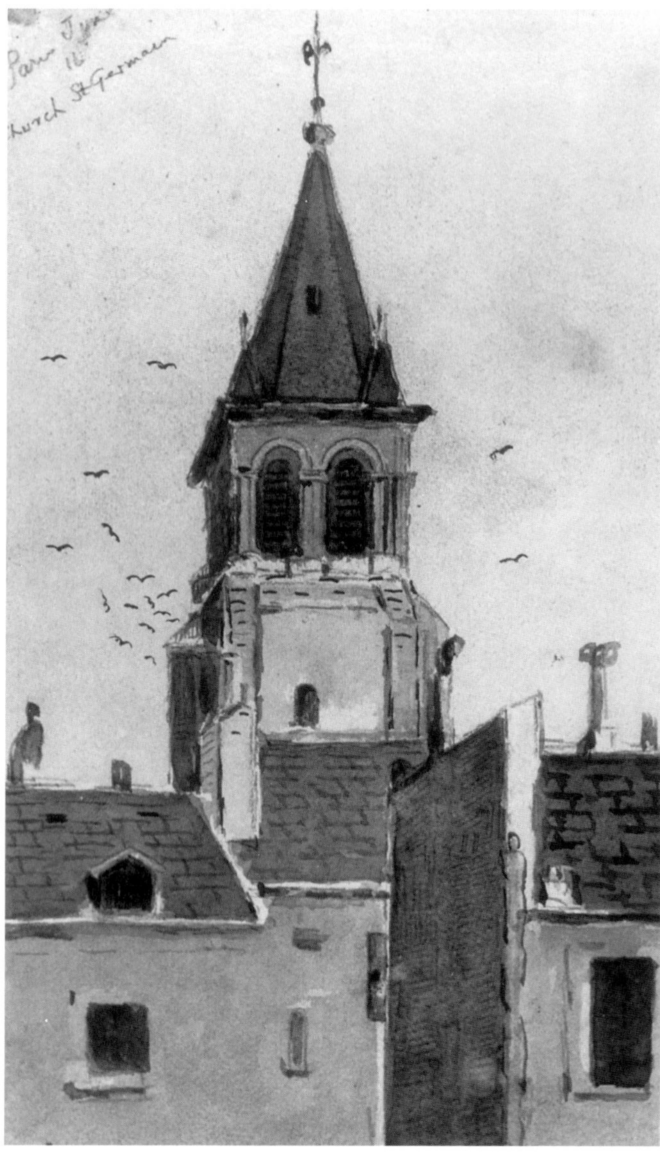

St. Germain, June 16, 1908

Warning' [1885] and my intuition was correct. I looked at Mr. Homer and at the dory. A merry twinkle came into the corners of his eyes, and then seating ourselves on the gunwale of the boat, he told me how he had painted that now famous epic of the sea.

"He detested the curious. When he painted, he wanted to be alone. Any stranger looking over his shoulder, disconcerted him so to obviate this, he built the stockade. And I can vouch for the fact that it accomplished its purpose because even an ex-ray [*sic*] could not have penetrated its solidity.

"In painting 'The Fog Warning,' by chocking up the bow of the dory, he got the exact lift. His figure was posed and the figure and the dory were completed. The sea, that wonderful piece of moving sea, was painted later. And thus came to the world one of the greatest sea pieces ever painted, a heritage to the ages.

"Mr. Homer had always a yearning to again visit Tynemouth. He seemed to have a genuine affection for the place. When we looked over his sketches of that far away English coast, there was always a dreamy look in his eyes. We planned to go there some day. The English fishwives seemed to be models exactly fitted to his temperament and work.

"He had a rooted objection to anything but a gold frame on a painting. He abhorred either a glass or a shadow box. I had been to Milwaukee and had seen in the Layton Gallery there his 'Hark, the lark' [1882]. I spoke of it when he quickly asked if it had a glass over it. It has. And he objected most strenuously. 'Why will they put a glass over an oil painting. Why when I look at a painting with a glass over it, all I can see is my bald head reflected!' he remarked with disgust.

"There was one thing that always puzzled me: his utter indifference to sales or criticism. Once he was down on the rocks fishing. His reel sang and a small struggle began and he soon landed a three pound fish. Out went the line again. At this point, a bell boy from the hotel came with a message from a noted Chicago buyer who wanted to purchase a painting. Mr. Homer was more interested in his tackle than the message. 'My compliments please to ———— and say that my paintings are for sale in both Boston and Providence.' and he continued fishing. And with more success.

"During our long friendship, I never heard him mention any of his paintings except in a general way. But I think there was something in 'The Fox Hunt' that he liked. That appealed to him. It is the only one of his paintings that he suggested my going to see in a gallery. 'It's so true to nature,' he kept repeating.

"Mr. Homer's love for the sea mounted to a passion. And as he advanced in years, humanity was left out more and more until it was the sea, only the sea. But this love was never felt when it was tranquil. The quiet trickling of the ocean over the rocks, as a gentle ground swell receded, made no impression on him, although full of gentle beauty. But when the wind came in squalls from the East and the sea picked up finally coming in crashing, tearing, plunging, throwing great clouds of spray as the giant rocks stopped it—then his sleeping temperament awoke and he looked and looked and studied.

"He loved to be in it, face it, take it! Once a sudden wind storm came tearing across the bay from Old Orchard. The clouds were ugly and gave promise of a wind of hurricane fury. Summer boarders scudded indoors. And soon we were the only humans visible. A lull. And the fury of a tornado struck. The clouds were green and coppery and sullen. The wind's fury was great. Dory after dory was tossed on the beach. Windows crashed in! Blinds and shingles went through the air. All this time, Mr. Homer's face was aglow with great excitement and eager pleasure. And he looked and studied. Neither of us spoke. The blow was a Summer squall and of short duration. And after it had passed on towards Portland, he turned to me and simply remarked, 'Wasn't it great!'

"Is it any wonder that with such a temperament we have the 'Nor Easter,' 'On a Lee Shore,' 'Morning after a Storm at Sea' and other marines that no other man can approach today. I think now what a gift to posterity his paintings are and how thankful we should be that we have them.

"He frequently reverted to our anticipated trip to Tynemouth. It was always on his mind. And he made many little plans. One of the last letters I received from him concludes: 'We will yet take that trip.' But alas! We never did."

Those reminiscences were written with the sole idea of celebrating someone whose life was over. Ironically, they were reminiscences written by someone whose life—in the artistic sense—was just beginning.

Boyer Gonzales, Artist

From 1910 until his death in 1934, Boyer Gonzales's critical reputation increased with each year. By 1911, his works were on exhibit at Vose's Gallery in Boston as well as at the Jones Little Gallery in Woodstock. It became routine at this time for the Gonzales family to divide their time between Woodstock during summer and fall and Galveston during winter and spring, where Nell's sister still lived and where they both had many friends as well as the family home. Later, as his national reputation as an artist grew, San Antonio replaced Galveston, as he could be in the company of other well-known Texas artists who lived there.

While they were in Galveston during the winter of 1910, the organizers of the Third Annual Cotton Carnival of Galveston asked Gonzales if he would assume the responsibility of mounting an art exhibition as part of the celebration to take place during July and August, 1911. With a little help from his former teachers and artist friends at Woodstock and the Art Students League of New York, he put together a show that drew international attention. Included were works by some of America's most highly respected and best known painters. The event was reviewed in the publication the *International Studio*: "Sergeant Kendall, exhibited his 'Reflection,' [which] showed his usual intimate interpretation of childhood, sharing honors with W. J. Whittemore's 'Portrait of a Girl in Red and White,' which would seem to

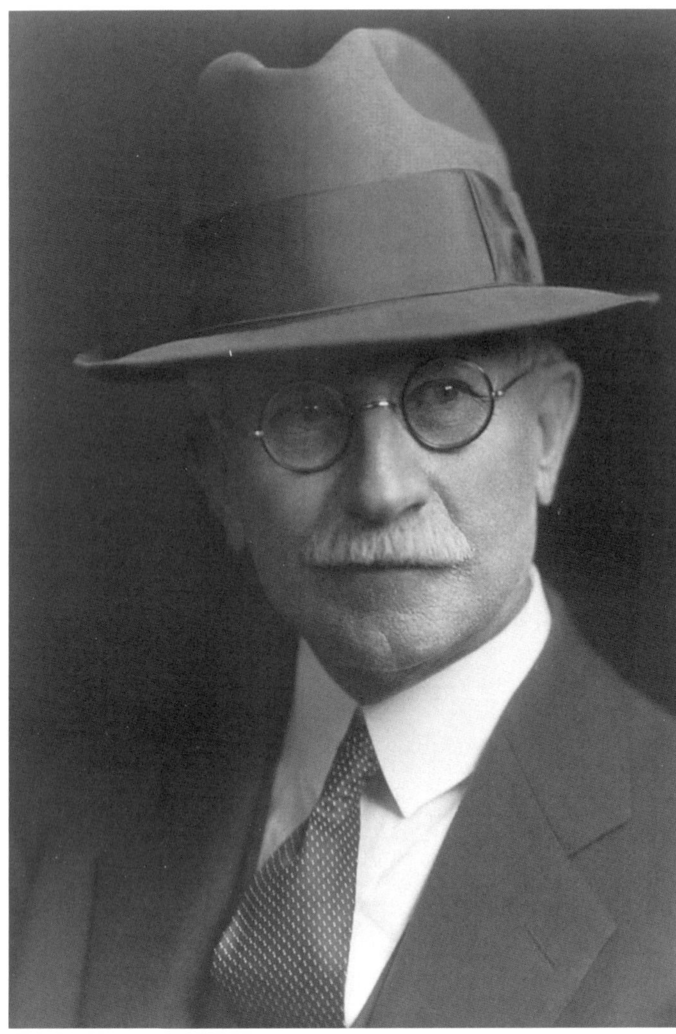

Boyer Gonzales

Gonzales—'Sunrise Off Galveston Bar, A.D. 1521.' In this the painter seems to have caught a glimpse of unknown coasts that must have been strong in the hearts of Count Bernardo de Galvez and his early exploring compatriots, who sailed these seas and made strange ports in the dawn of Amerian history. Here the old Spanish galleon, its picturesque shape agleam with delicate tints of sunrise, is standing off the distant shore of the Gulf of Mexico."[12] That was Boyer Gonzales's first review in an international publication. Many more would follow.

In September, 1911 while still in Woodstock, Gonzales took a side trip to Quebec. He had an idea for a painting of great historical importance, similar to those of Mesdag and Lansil, and, indeed, similar to his oil, *Sunrise Off Galveston Bar, A.D. 1521.* In order to do the painting, he needed more information regarding the French nobleman, René Robert Cavelier, Sieur de la Salle, who had sailed his galleon, *Belle,* into Matagorda Bay in February, 1685, and established a mission on the coast, thereby giving France its legitimate claim to the territory of Texas. He found that information in Quebec.[13]

By 1912, Gonzales had given up any pretense of working in the cotton business and devoted all his efforts to painting. In May of that year, he was invited to send works to participate in the Third Annual Exhibition of Texas Artists, sponsored by the Fort Worth Museum of Art. Among the fourteen works that he submitted were watercolor landscapes of New England as well as scenes of Italy, Holland, and England that he had painted from the sketches he had made during his honeymoon. These included *Fading Light Venice, Dutch Trawler Making Port,* and *Summer Evening, Vermont.* They had all been exhibited before in galleries in Boston and New York and received high praise from the critics. Gonzales commented, "If newspapers and critics' praise were money, I would be a millionaire."[14]

That same year he began work on his historical piece regarding La Salle and the French settlement on the Gulf

have been one of the most popular canvases in the collection. Colin Campbell Cooper's 'Portrait of a Lady' struck the forceful note which one associates with his work, and Birge Harrison showed his characteristic treatment of atmospheric values in 'The Heights of Levis' and 'Sunrise from Quebec.'"

Then the critic noted, "That it should not be assumed that all honors were carried off by northern exhibitors, mention is due of a local canvas of no small interest by Boyer

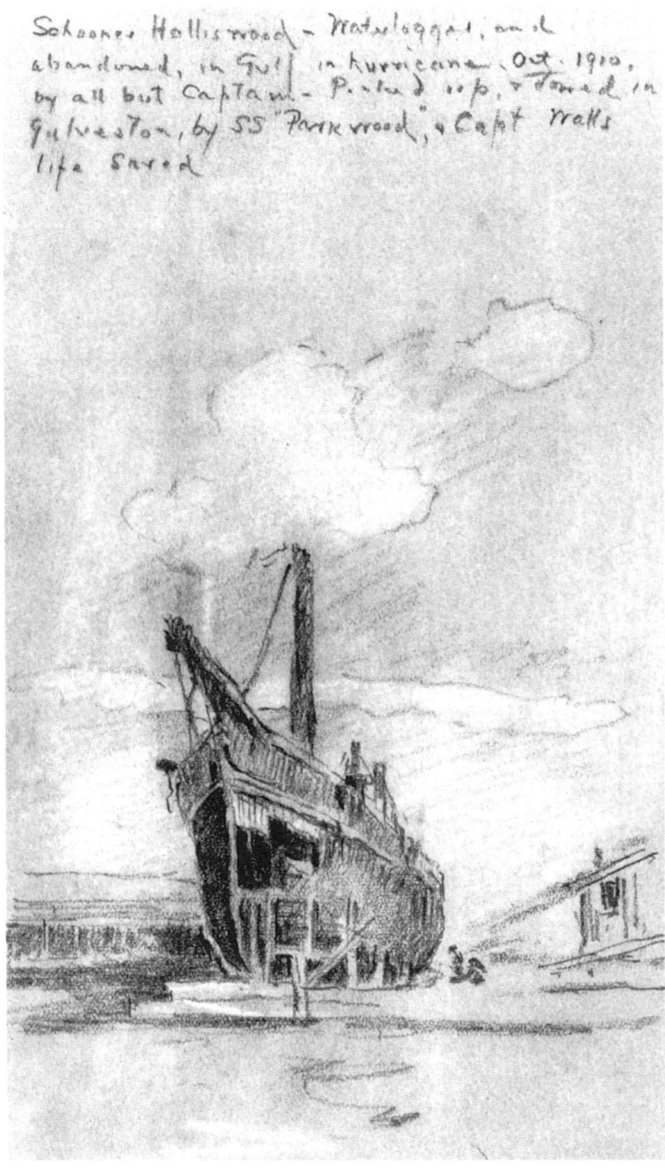

Schooner, October, 1910

Coast of Texas. Early the following year, he completed it, titling it *The Dawn of Texas*. The large oil shows the galleon, *Belle,* presented to La Salle by King Louis XIV, at anchor in Matagorda Bay at sunrise on a morning in 1685. Flying aloft is the royal blue and gold silk flag, ensign of the King of France. That painting, later purchased by the Galveston Art League and now part of the permanent collection of the Rosenberg Library in Galveston, was to become one of Gonzales's most highly regarded works of art.

In November of 1915, he agreed to show twenty-seven of his works at Purdy's Gallery at Twenty-second and Market in his home town. Seven months later, in May of 1916, the Chicago Art Institute invited him to send works for its Twenty-Eighth Water Color Annual. In the fall of that year, an exhibit at the New York Water Color Club included his work titled *Snapper Fisherman,* which was singled out as "exceptional" by the art critic for the *New York Herald.*[15] In 1917, he had one-man shows in Beaumont, San Antonio, and at the fifth annual exhibit sponsored by the Dallas Woman's Forum, where he was represented by two works: *Gilded Sails* and *The Fisherman.* Of the latter, one critic noted that it was "indeed a masterpiece of thought and time. No need here of dreamy gazing—the picture is there and painted with such depth and feeling that it takes no imagination on the part of the spectator to see the actual scene before him."[16]

Sadly, neither his younger brother nor his sister lived long enough to see Gonzales realize his dream of being a successful, full-time artist. Alcie had died in 1914, and on December 6, 1918, word reached Galveston that his sister, Daisy, had died. Gonzales wrote in his 1883 diary, "Daisy the last died."

A month later, on January 10, 1919, Gonzales was invited to become a member of the highly regarded New York Water Color Club, which had a limited membership of seventy-seven.[17] During that same summer, while he and Nell were disposing of the effects of his sister in Boston, they began building a home in Woodstock. In an attached studio, he painted with added vigor, producing some of his more impressive works, most of which sold immediately. His reputation grew rapidly and soon he was being asked to show in exhibitions throughout the country.

Critical praise came with each show. On March 5, 1920, he received an invitation to join the professionally prestigious Salmagundi Club in New York, and later that year, he was accepted as a member of the exclusive and very fashionable National Arts Club on Gramercy Park in New York City.[18] Being a member of the NAC meant that they would never again have to stay in a hotel or rent an apartment when they went to New York; the Club on Gramercy Park became their home-away-from-home.

In March, 1921, he had paintings in shows sponsored by the Salmagundi Club in New York as well as in an all-southern show in Charleston, South Carolina. In April, he received his first gold medal: the Arthur A. Everts Award for best landscape at the Tenth Annual Dallas Women's Forum.

In March, 1922, his work, *Above the Rapids,* was declared "deserving special mention" at the Twenty-First Annual Art Association of New Orleans show, held at the Delgado Museum. In June, he participated in the combined watercolor exhibition sponsored by the New York Water Color Club and the American Water Color Society. In October, he was invited to have a one-man show of twenty-three works at the Arts Club of Washington.

That December he received a personal letter from a family friend, Congressman Clay Stone Briggs of Galveston, which began "My dear Bo." It seems that Congressman Briggs had taken time from his work in Congress to go "around to the Arts Club for a view of your pictures on exhibition there and certainly enjoyed the opportunity of seeing them." He noted, "The scenes on Galveston with the dock front and elevators in the background and ships in the harbor, were certainly suggestive and intimate pictures of home. I also like particularly the bayou and marsh scenes. The painting styled, I think, 'On the Way to the West Indies', is another impressive picture." He observed that Gonzales's "work appears to be growing bolder and stronger, and has certainly assumed a more pretentious character when contrasted with your simpler and earlier work with which I am more familiar." Congressman Briggs then wished him all the best: "I sincerely hope that the art world accords you the distinction which I feel sure your work deserves, and that you will experience the pleasure not only of accomplishing the most successful results, but also having it fully appreciated."[19]

Indeed it was. The November 1 issue of the *Christian Science Monitor* featured his painting *The Wings of Morning,* which he had done while the Gonzales family was on vacation in Laguna Beach, California. The critic wrote that the work "depicts the on rush of the Pacific during a heavy northwest wind over the outer reefs at sunrise. It is a painting of great action and brilliant color."[20]

The collection of paintings from the one-man show in Washington, D.C. was so successful that they were exhibited at the Salmagundi Club before going on to Detroit and Philadelphia and ending up as one of the highlights at the State Fair of Texas in Dallas in October. The front page of the *Dallas Morning News* on October 17, 1923 proclaimed: "Texan Art Wins Acclaim at Exhibit / Landscapes and Marines of Boyer Gonzales show spirit of Sea." The newspaper's art critic noted: "The former Galvestonian is a protégé of that great New England artist, Winslow Homer. . . . While Mr. Gonzales has learned to love the sea and the small types of coastwise vessels, as much as Homer did, he quite escapes any imitation of that great artist. All of his work is strikingly individual."[21]

During the first two weeks of November, 1923, he had another one-man show at the Ainslie Galleries on Fifth Avenue in New York. The critic for the *New York Post* noted that his watercolors "have a pleasing freedom of movement and good color. The simplicity of the 'End of the Lane, Rockport' with the big outlines of the house and its bit of walled-in seclusion, has the reserve of statement that makes one feel power behind it. The wide sweep of white cloud strewn sky over a blue sea in 'Fine Weather' has sparkle and a swift vigor of movement. In quite another key is 'Nutting Time,' with a richness of foliage and a feel of autumn through it all." Another critic called him "an individualist in water color. He eschews brilliance and aims at lightness, clarity and thinness. His landscapes are highly personal, extreme in their simplicity, although not impoverished as to detail. Lightness of touch also runs through the marines but is not so dominant as in the landscapes."[22]

In November, 1924, he had paintings accepted in the 29th Annual Water Color Exhibit sponsored by the Washington Water Color Club, of which he was a member. The exhibit was presented at the Corcoran Gallery of Art. Shows in New York, Chicago, and Los Angeles, as well as in San Antonio and Dallas, came with regularity. Boyer Gonzales was now sought after, and his works sold in the most highly respected galleries throughout the United States.

In the April 10, 1925 issue of the French magazine, *Revue du Vrai et du Beau,* Gonzales's *The Dawn of Texas* was featured with the critic commenting that it was "a work of magnificent conception and unusual interest from the historical point of view." Of his total work, it was noted, "We owe to Boyer Gonzales a collection of marines worthy of much appreciaton, which, having been displayed many times in principal American exhibits, have always had the best word of the critics, as well as won the admiration of the layman." It added that Gonzales "possesses a very individual art. His profound technical knowledge, joined to the deep understanding of his truly artistic soul, has made him the creator of perfect works of real interest."[23]

On April 29, 1925, Gonzales was honored once again when the Dallas Woman's Forum awarded his oil painting *West of the Brazos* his second Arthur A. Everts gold medal for the best landscape at their fourteenth annual exhibit of Texas artists.

Two years later, in March, 1927, the Museum of Fine Arts of Houston presented an exhibition of twenty-four water colors, with Birge Harrison writing the catalogue: "I have known Boyer Gonzales for a number of years. He was a pupil of mine in the summer school of the Art Students League of New York, which was situated at Woodstock, New York. His marines, fishing vessels, coast scenes, and the old fashioned square rigged sailing ships are full of charm, and have a delicate and lovely color, which only those who know and love the sea can give. Also his paintings of winter landscapes in the north are beautiful and deserving of the highest praise and I certainly hope that his exhibition of water colors at the Museum of Fine Arts of Houston, Texas, may have the success which its high artistic quality should bring it."[24]

In November of the following year, the career of Boyer Gonzales reached new critical heights when his one-man show in New York opened at the highly regarded Brown Robertson Gallery. The critic of the *New York Tribune* noted: "Boyer Gonzales, a protégé and friend of Winslow Homer, who is exhibiting a series of water colors at the Brown Robertson gallery, also is attracted by the sea as well as other subjects which were typical of the great American water colorist. But his manner is his own. His impressions of the Indies are radiant with light and atmosphere, though there is nothing subtle or impressionistic in his method. He paints directly in washes of thin color giving stress to form and detail. The New England coastal environment induces him to use stronger color and he warms up these impressions with more enthusiasm. The bleak impression of winter, 'The Two Crows,' is one of the most successful in quality and perspective." The *American Art News,* also noted that Gonzales was a "protege and friend of Winslow Homer" and found "his schooners, ships and boats are the real thing. He not only knows how they are rigged, but the erratic manner in which they act at sea." Other glowing reviews appeared in the *New York Evening Post, New York World,* and *New York American.*[25]

The invitations to exhibit continued unabated. In May,

1929, he was included in the Nineteenth Annual Exhibition of Selected Paintings by Texas Artists at the Fort Worth Museum of Art. The August 26, 1929, issue of the *Christian Science Monitor* once again featured another of Gonzales's paintings, *Voice of the Rapids,* and in October he had another invitation to show at the 46th Annual Exhibition at the State Fair of Texas in Dallas.

During this period, the Gonzaleses spent more and more time at their home in Woodstock, winters and springs in San Antonio, often taking short vacations in Taos, New Mexico, where Boyer always seemed to have found inspiration.

On one occasion in March, 1930, while they were in San Antonio, Gonzales and his wife took two artist friends on a brief trip across the border at Eagle Pass where they spent several days traveling around the state of Coahuila, painting the brilliant Mexican landscape and scenes from nearby pueblos. Unfortunately, when they tried to return to the United States at Piedras Negras, the Mexican authorities abruptly stopped them. What transpired made the newspapers. It was later reported, "Nothing would appease this servant of the law but a surrender of their work. The water colors were confiscated, the canvases were smeared over and the painters were allowed to go free."[26] No explanations to the authorities helped, nor did the fact that his father had been born in Mexico. Neither did it matter that Gonzales had a profound affection for Mexico nor that he had been traveling and painting in Mexico for thirty-five years.

Strangely, the confiscation and destruction of the finished paintings do not seem to have daunted him. He was still able to bring back dozens of sketches, which he immediately turned into paintings. Later that year, he had another show at the Jones Little Gallery in Woodstock, which included several paintings of Mexican scenes, including one of his best. He thought so much of it that he never sold it: *A Street in Mexico—Watching the Buzzards.*

Another honor came when late in 1933, several of his

marines were presented at the First Annual Exhibition of Water Colors, sponsored by the California Palace of Legion of Honor in San Francisco.

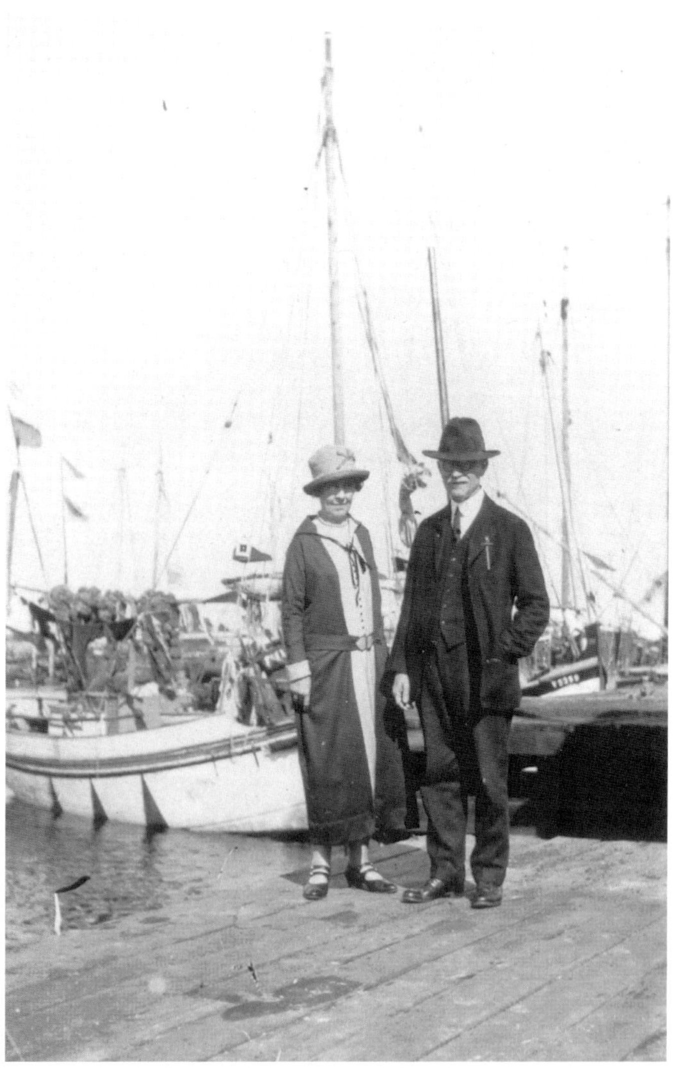

Boyer and Nell Gonzales

Throughout their lives, the family of three—Bo, Nell, and Boyer, Jr.,—always remained very close. They were never out of touch or ever very far apart. Boyer, Jr., attended the Mercersburg Academy in Pennsylvania and was graduated from the University of Virginia with a Bachelor of Science in architecture. After his graduation he returned to Woodstock and, as his father had done, began to study painting with various artists from the Art Students League of New York, including Henry Lee McFee and Yasuo Kuniyoshi. In 1932, the family took a trip by train to Mexico City. In addition to just being tourists and visiting the gardens at Xochimilco, Gonzales took time to paint a few scenes typical of the Mexican countryside, as he had when he first visited Mexico in 1895. One of his most successful paintings was his rendition of the volcano, Popocatepetl, which he titled *Mighty Mountain.* This was a painting which neither he nor his son could bring themselves to sell.

As the years passed, the Gonzaleses spent less and less time in Galveston. In fact, Gonzales became known as being "formerly of Galveston, Texas." But as his son Boyer, Jr., later pointed out, his father never lost complete touch with the island or the big house on Avenue O, which he refused to sell "because it was the tie with his family and his anchor to windward, as it were."[27]

Occasionally, the Gonzales family did find time to pay a visit and spend a few days with family and friends, as they did in February, 1934. Since Thanksgiving, they had been in San Antonio where final preparations were being made for an exhibition of his latest paintings that was to open in March at the Witte Memorial Museum. It would stay at the Witte until late April, then travel first to Austin and later to Beaumont. The show first opened in January of that year at the Museum of Fine Arts in Houston, where one critic hailed Gonzales's most recent work as one "of appealing beauty and sentiment," noting that it "reveals Gonzales as a vigorous man with a great love for the open spaces. He paints a fiercely beautiful, calmly all-powerful sea and his brush is kind to the ships that sail her, depicting them in all their rugged, heroic strength." The critic, like others in the past, was especially impressed with the "surging unrest of mighty water, its angry spray and delicate foam [which] are superbly caught in the artist's swift medium. Water and sunlight are probably the most difficult qualities a painter has to transcribe, and Mr. Gonzales has approached mastery in his bold use of color where the former is concerned."[28]

After visiting the show in Houston, Bo and Nell arrived by train in Galveston on Sunday, February 9, and went directly to the Broadway home of Nell's sister, Louise. The extravagant annual Mardi Gras festivities were in full swing, and they were there to help celebrate. Boyer spent Monday with members of the Galveston Art League who had come to ask Gonzales if he would agree to have his latest exhibition shown in Galveston after it closed in Beaumont. As usual, he felt honored and graciously consented. The Art League was special to Gonzales; it had been his idea to organize it, modeling it on the one he belonged to in Woodstock. A group of local Galveston artists formed the league in 1914 and elected Nell the first president. Gonzales not only agreed to have the show, he promised that they would return to Galveston to inaugurate it.

But unexpectedly two days later, on Ash Wednesday, Boyer Gonzales suffered a stroke and was taken immediately to the hospital. Later in the day, he died and his body was removed to J. Levy and Son Funeral Home. Listed as his only survivors were his wife, Nell, and his son, Boyer, Jr. The following morning, with the Reverend Edmund Gibson of Trinity Church officiating, he was buried in the Episcopal cemetery on Broadway.

Boyer Gonzales, the critically acclaimed, award-winning artist, had come home to Galveston.

Part 2

BOYER GONZALES'S ART

The Art of Boyer Gonzales:

Conversations with Lise Darst

Throughout the writing of this biography, I have had the pleasure and good fortune to have worked closely with Lise Darst, the museum curator at the Rosenberg Library. Lise, an award winning watercolorist herself, took time out during the summer of 1995 to discuss with me Boyer Gonzales and his work. Surrounded by paintings included in this book, we talked.

Edward Simmen: Let's begin by saying something about how you became acquainted with the Boyer Gonzales collection held by the Rosenberg Library. Approximately how many paintings are there?

Lise Darst: There are 551 paintings and drawings in the collection. This includes watercolors, oils, and several sketchbooks that contain pencil, pen and ink, and thumbnail watercolor sketches to be used later for larger paintings. But there have always been paintings hanging in the library by Boyer Gonzales. Most well-known is his *Dawn of Texas,* a large oil painting of the La Salle galleon anchored in Matagorda Bay. Everybody who grew up on the Island and used the library knew that big Gonzales painting, which hangs on the wall of the main stairway. It became part of the library's permanent collection when it was donated in 1982 by the Galveston Art League, whose first president, by the way, was Gonzales's wife. We also have several watercolors that have been donated by people over the years to the library's permanent painting collection, but nothing like this collection that came when the son decided that the library should be a repository for the majority of his father's work.

ES: Boyer Gonzales, Jr.

LD: Yes. He was an artist of reputation in his own right. He had retired in 1978 as the drector of the School of Art at the University of Washington in Seattle. Earlier he had been a member of the faculty, and, later, chairman of the art department at the University of Texas in Austin prior to moving to the northwest, where they lived for over twenty-five years. His father's paintings were to be his gift to the Rosenberg Library.

ES: When did all of this take place?

LD: The initial contact with the library was made in 1980.

ES: When Boyer, Jr., was about seventy years old.

LD: He was a very charming man and, as I said, a prominent artist. One of the reasons he gave the paintings was that he always felt that his father was sentimentally attached to Galveston. The first collection of sixty-seven paintings arrived in 1980. The following year, we had an exhibition of the father and son's work. The paintings of Boyer Gonzales, Sr., were taken from the recent acquisition. Boyer, Jr., and his wife, Betty, came for the opening of the exhibition and Boyer, Jr., gave a rather poignant lecture about his father and his life as an artist. Being the curator, it was my job to catalogue and photograph each of the paintings. Gonzales, Jr., had tried to date each of the pictures from memory and by the subject matter as well as by the technique Gonzales was using at the time. The library received donations again in 1982, 1988, and finally in 1990.

ES: These, of course, were in the family's possession.

LD: Yes, and there are the sketch books and some oils, but the majority of the paintings in the collection are watercolors.

ES: Gonzales, Jr., died in 1987 and the remainder of the paintings and documents and other family papers came to the library. . . .

LD: After the death of Betty Gonzales in 1989. The library also received an endowment to care for the collection.

ES: But as a Galvestonian and a watercolorist, you had known of Boyer Gonzales before this.

LD: Boyer Gonzales, Sr., had always been someone that I had heard of, though I never knew him. I was barely alive when he died, but as it happened, he was a good friend of my grandmother and grandfather Robertson. In fact, in June, 1905, they received as a wedding gift a framed watercolor from Boyer, Sr. It's a small sailing ship entitled *Red Sails* and it always hung in my grandmother's house. It was a part of my growing up and it now hangs in my living room. So I was most excited to meet Boyer, Jr., and to know that his father's paintings were coming back to Galveston.

ES: But you had some other memories of the Gonzaleses.

LD: Oh, yes. There is a story in my family about the courtship of the Gonzaleses. Evidently the young couples on the island in the early 1900s decided that they would "match" Nell Hertford and Boyer, who was already in his mid-thirties. Nell had been an attendant in my grandparents' wedding. Boyer, at the time, was living alone in that large house on Avenue O. He needed a "push." So after my grandparents were married, they would have small dinner parties and invite them both. The match was successful and my grandparents congratulated themselves on getting the two together. That is the story. Boyer married Nell and, I guess, lived happily ever after. My mother also knew the Gonzales family from their annual visits to Galveston to visit Nell's older sister, who lived just around the corner from us on Broadway.

ES: Then you have more than a casual relationship to the collection.

LD: Yes.

ES: Let's talk about the early works that are here. We should, I suppose, begin by saying something about the sketch books in the collection. First of all, we had better explain that there are no existing paintings that we know of prior to 1888. I assume they were all destroyed when the Gonzales house burned in the Galveston fire of 1885.

LD: Paintings, no. But we have the sketch books. The first of those begin with drawings done in 1883 and show him as a very meticulous recorder of what he sees. It is obvious from the sketches that he liked to draw. In the 1880s, a person who wanted to be an artist was not necessarily out to rebel against society. Of course, Boyer Gonzales was luckier than most. He never needed to rely on the sale of his paintings to make a living. The family was quite "well off," and he had an income from working in the family businesses. Being an artist was evidently just something that he wanted to do. Still we have to say that in the early years, painting was a hobby for him, perhaps an escape from the business world. Later, of course, painting became his work, his way of life.

ES: What precisely do you think of his early sketches?

LD: The earlier sketches are ink and wash. At this time, he had no formal training. But he shows definite talent. His sketches are accurately drawn and display, for example, an understanding of water. Even at this early stage, he is able to capture the feeling and movement of water. And he would paint water throughout his career. Later, he would do landscapes of the hill country of Texas and the mountains and countryside in Mexico and the area around Woodstock, for example, but he always returned to the sea where he was eminently successful in capturing, whether it was in Galveston or Florida or California or Maine. But the sketch books. In a sense, Boyer Gonzales's sketch book is his diary. He took that sketch book wherever he went. And as some people write a diary, he has kept a diary through his drawings.

ES: These are mostly sketches of places he visited and people he observed in the travels he took as a young man to the East to visit his sister, who lived with her husband in Boston.

LD: Yes. He would leave Galveston by sailing ship, stop off in Key West, Florida, and continue on to Massachusetts, then up the coast to Prout's Neck in Maine where he would be with Winslow Homer. Ships would become one of his favorite subjects. Not people. He doesn't display a facility for drawing people. His renditions of people are very labored.

ES: His son was well aware of that. When he came to Galveston to inaugurate the father-son show, he admitted, "My father was not interested in figure painting per se; he was much more interested in the landscape . . . he was satisfied to look for beauty in the world around him and particularly beauty in nature."

LD: True. When it came to capturing the coasts of Maine and Texas, that is something different. He is so very careful to draw the same subject over and over to free his hand until the drawing becomes an automatic reflex. This can be seen in the trees he would draw in Maine, for example. There may be a three-by-five thumbnail sketch of a particular tree and then there will be a larger one, maybe a five-by-seven, of the same tree and then it comes out as a regular size watercolor. It happens over and over again. Take the mountain that he could see out of the window of his studio in Woodstock. It is the subject of numerous paintings at different seasons. In the fall. In the winter when it is snowing. In the spring.

ES: Before we go any further, we should say something about yourself as an artist.

LD: (Laughter) An artist in the Galveston tradition. I am a watercolorist. I have done watercolors of the old houses of Galveston and I must admit that I have achieved some notice for my painting. And this is primarily why I can relate to Gonzales's watercolors and perhaps bring some better understanding of his art. Watercolor is my medium and I have taught watercolor to other people.

ES: Back to Boyer. Do you see any more or less systematic development in his work?

LD: Yes, there are clues in the early sketches in the 1890s. His understanding of nature is there. The water. The trees. Rocks. Birds. He has an eye for nature. The early watercolors, like the sketches, are painstakingly and accurately drawn. He is developing a pattern which will last throughout his life. From the beginning, he made thumbnail sketches and then developed these into paintings. In this early period, the colors are light washes, not very bold. But there is something different about them. What stands out is the water and the sky. That's his forte. Then in his Mexican paintings he begins to change.

ES: Those were done on a business trip he made for his father in 1895 just following the death of his mother.

LD: Something happens. Suddenly there is color. Vibrant color. He just couldn't avoid the color in Mexico. It's everywhere.

ES: Are they unusual in any way?

LD: Certainly. That he traveled to Mexico before 1906, in the first place, is unusual in itself. As far as I know, he was one of the first Americans to go to Mexico and paint. Even if he had gone there on business, once there, the country, its scenery and the color would capture him. These watercolors are again the real diary of his trip. It must also be noted that again he is drawing from nature, making copious notes with his brush.

ES: Would you say that the Mexican works, then, represent a move in the development of his art?

LD: Yes, but the development is going to be gradual. He will go through several distinct periods in his work, taking from the styles of others, accepting and rejecting until he affects a style which is distinctively his. But here in the Mexican paintings, compared with the early sketches, he is beginning to feel more at home with his media, his tools, and his subject matter. The paintings do not look labored. The execution seems to come much easier. By this time, he had been with Winslow Homer on numerous occasions and much of what he saw Homer doing must have encouraged and influenced him. He was obviously a very careful watcher of Homer.

ES: He certainly did admire and respect him. He later wrote a short essay about Homer and his visits to Maine.

LD: What an opportunity! I mean, after all, how many young painters get to spend time with someone of Homer's incredible talent.

ES: You are quite right. In his letters to Gonzales, Homer often compliments him.

LD: Well, in the Mexican works, he seems to have control of his media though still in an academic way. And we will see that control develop more and more as he comes into his own style.

ES: Do you see much of Homer in his works?

LD: Not in these early works. But definitely in his later paintings. Very much. We have several small sketches that are exactly copies of some of Homer's works. I doubt that Homer thought his young friend was doing it. He knew that Gonzales had talent. If he did know, however, I'm sure he would have been complimented. You can certainly tell that even though Gonzales at this time in his career had no formal training to speak of, it is easy to see he has a talent. He can draw although he is timid about his color. But in the Mexican scenes, we can see that he has learned how to use his washes, how to control the color with the brush. He is now becoming very conversant with his tools and knows how to make them work for him. And he stays within his landscapes and seascapes, which in the end will be what he was recognized and praised for.

ES: That seems to be what he was attracted to.

LD: Of course, he grew up in Galveston with the water and the sky and the clouds. The birds and the boats and the ships. He is very capable of recording the rigging on the ships. Very accurate. He was interested in the little working boats, like the oyster boats.

ES: And his father had the offices of their company on the Strand where he worked from the time he was a child and he had a constant view of the harbor and Galveston Bay with the ships tied up to the wharf or anchored in the Bay.

LD: Yes. And he does the same thing when he travels to the East Coast, doing the working boats, the tugs in the Boston harbor and the sketches he did on their trip to Seattle. He was fascinated with the paddle boats on Puget Sound. Then the mackerel boats and the lobster boats in Maine. It just depended on where he was. And water. He just has no trouble doing water at all. This is very interesting because water is not easy to do.

ES: But during this period, the 1890s, he rarely sold anything. There is a reference in one of the letters that his father wrote him during his Mexico trip in 1895 telling him almost offhandedly that one of their friends had bought a painting for fifty dollars. But I found no other. Not even in his diaries. I am sure that he would have recorded any sale. But no. Selling comes somewhat later.

LD: Actually, I think he gave a lot of pictures away. A small watercolor became his standard wedding present. There are many people in Galveston who have small Boyer Gonzales paintings like mine. People whose families have lived here since before the turn of the century.

ES: And as you said, the Gonzales family was "well off" and he never really had to make a living from painting. When his father died in 1896, he took control of the business. Actually, he didn't devote the major part of his time to his art until he had sold most of the family businesses during the first five years of the twentieth century.

LD: And he married Nell Hertford in 1907. But by this time he was beginning to receive some recognition. In 1904, he was invited to display one of his paintings in the Texas Pavilion at the St. Louis World's Fair. Around the turn of the century, the paintings begin to take on a style, a style which is individual to him and at the same time he is building a reputation. And there is something else that is very important. I think it is very difficult for an artist who has lived in one town all of his life to build a reputation. The town may accept him as an amateur artist, but it doesn't encourage him to go on. It is as if the town never takes him seriously.

In effect, the town tolerates a local artist but rarely recognizes or understands him.

ES: It really wasn't until he got away . . .

LD: Yes, but once he left Galveston and he had Nell to encourage him, his work began to sell. He sold in New York, Washington and San Francisco and Chicago. He was especially popular in Florida, which he often visited. And in Dallas and San Antonio. And Houston as well as here in Galveston. Anywhere his paintings were exhibited, they sold.

ES: His records show that beginning in 1915, he began having one-man exhibitions throughout the country with greater regularity and with stunning success. For example, from that date onward, he was always invited to participate in the very prestigious annual watercolor shows, such as those sponsored by the Chicago Art Institute or the New York Water Color Club.

LD: And the pictures won prizes and awards. It would be interesting to know how many Galvestonians bought his pictures in those days. Or did they just wait for Gonzales to give them one as a gift? Do you see what I mean? I am sure that people in Galveston had difficulty understanding why he sold his father's businesses and went off to study painting after he was forty years old.

ES: Ten years after his father's death, there was nothing left for Gonzales to administer. He had sold all of the family businesses and holdings.

LD: Granted, he left Galveston, but he was sentimentally attached to it. After all, they came back to the Island at least once a year and maintained the family home here. But he certainly went on to make his own life in Woodstock in the summer and fall and San Antonio in the winter. He simply threw off the yoke of the cotton business and the family. Nell, I think, had a great deal to do with that. She was his support, his encouragement.

ES: After he became recognized, and his name was mentioned in publicity, it was always "Boyer Gonzales, formerly of Galveston" or "Boyer Gonzales, a former Galvestonian."

LD: I doubt very seriously that he would have been accepted into organizations and clubs like the Salmagundi Club or the New York Water Color Society if people did not have a respect for his work. After all, membership in the New York Watercolor Society is limited. But again the respect for Gonzales came from outside of Galveston. He had to shed the stigma of being Boyer Gonzales, local artist.

ES: All of that really began after Boyer and Nell were married, when he spent five weeks at Woodstock with Birge Harrison and others from the Art Students League. More study took place the following year when they went on a belated honeymoon, taking the grand tour to Europe with the primary intention of settling in Florence for an extended period as Boyer wanted to find a watercolorist to study with.

LD: Yes, the trip took them to Venice and we have several paintings from that visit. The ones included in your book fall into what can be called the classic English watercolor tradition. [*Grand Canal* and *Doge's Palace*] Very nice rendering of the architecture of the city. The detail is done with the brush as opposed to the pen. I am sure there were preliminary sketches of each one because the subject matter in these is quite difficult to capture.

ES: He obviously thought that he had progressed considerably. He makes the comment in a letter that Nell thought that they would sell in Boston.

LD: Yes, I would think that they were very salable because they are of subjects that people are familiar with. Not just people who had visited Venice. These are well-known landmarks. The Bridge of Sighs. The Lido. The working boats. The canals. The gondolas. All of these are there in his paintings. The technique he uses here can be found in his earlier paintings, two in particular: *In the Rockies* and *Caulking, Galveston,* both painted in 1902. This technique is what I referred to earlier as the "classic watercolor style." Then, the series of 1908 European paintings contain excellent examples of what Gonzales was capable of achieving at this point in his artistic development. Technically, these particular paintings are accomplished watercolors. The architectural details are reduced to a minimum and the colors are clear and clean.

ES: After the European trip they returned to Galveston and began the routine which would permit them to spend the winters in Galveston or San Antonio and rest of the time in Woodstock, where they built a home with a studio for Boyer in 1919.

LD: And he began to make painting his life. And it is obvious that around 1914, he has begun to develop his own style. He is beginning to cast off the more-or-less classic traditional English style that is so evident in the early works and to adapt his technique to a more colorful pallete. The *Wrecked Sloop Down the Island, Galveston* [1915] shows this and also shows that he is strongly influenced by Homer. This is repeated in another painting, dated 1916, *Campeche Fisherman.* Now he has really hit his stride.

ES: His son singled out 1916 as being the year that his father "really broke into the big leagues of the art world." That was when one of Gonzales's watercolors was selected to be in the watercolor show mounted by the Art Institute of Chicago. What made it more important, the painting was among those selected to go on an extended tour throughout the country.

LD: He now has a style that is recognizable as Gonzales. We can see this in *The Danish Barque* [1918]. With a minimum of effort, he is able to capture and record his subject. There is less detail. In other words, he knows what to leave out to make a more interesting composition. Oddly enough, he is never going to be able to break completely with the influence of his mentor, Homer, until, perhaps, the last years of his life. This is especially true of the seascapes and landscapes.

ES: But he doesn't try to hide the fact that Homer had such a strong influence on his work. When critics reviewed his shows, they always noted that he had been a friend and protégé of Homer. By the 1920s, Gonzales was probably pleased to be identified with a painter of such international fame. Let's back up for a moment. Do you know anything about Winslow Homer ever being in Galveston? In conducting the research, I have come across stories that he was here.

LD: If he did come here, it was to visit his brother [Arthur] and his family. That would have been in the early 1880s, I suppose. I don't think there are any paintings of Homer's of Galveston scenes. And there are no sketches of Galveston in any work that I've seen. I can't imagine Homer being in Galveston and not recording something of the ships in the harbor. Or the beach. If he had been here, certainly he would have taken time to do something.

ES: And I haven't run across anything in the Gonzales documents to indicate that Gonzales ever met him when he was here if as you say, Homer was ever here. And he doesn't mention it in the essay that he wrote about Homer after Homer had died. He surely would have made the connection.[1]

LD: About Homer. Let me tell you a story. In the early 1980s, the Brooklyn Museum mounted an exhibition of the watercolors of John Singer Sargent and Winslow Homer, which I happened to see. As I walked into the room, I was speechless. The influence of Homer on Gonzales almost jumped off the wall at me. Since I had been working with the Gonzales collection here at the Rosenberg, they were familiar to me. I had known that Homer's influence on Gonzales was strong but not as powerful as what faced me that afternoon in the Brooklyn Museum.

ES: Since you know something about both artists and have read the Homer letters to Gonzales, could you say something about their friendship or their working relationship?

LD: I would begin by saying that the two men had one important "love" in common. They both shared a great love of nature. When Boyer, Jr., was here, we talked about the two artists. I honestly believe that Homer was almost complete unto himself. A real loner. I have never read that he had any protégés. He, like Degas, was a misogynist, known for his solitary way of living. He seemed only to tolerate everyone, even at times his family.

ES: But then there is Gonzales. Homer took him into his studio and even shared with Gonzales his innermost thoughts about his most famous paintings. He seems to have honestly enjoyed those visits.

LD: Well, he first took Gonzales into his studio at the request of his brother. And he liked him. As I said, the two of them shared this great love for nature, especially the sea. He accepted Gonzales and encouraged him to "do his own thing." And Gonzales's personality was quite different from Homer's. From what I can ascertain from his son and from what I heard my grandmother say, Boyer Gonzales was a gentle, warm, and caring man. She called him a "wool gatherer." A dreamer. He needed his family and friends as a support system. Certainly his son adored him. He was definitely not the loner that Homer was. Their paintings display a tremendous difference in the way they captured nature. Homer's oil paintings are simply powerful. There is a lot of emotion in the sea, in the faces of his subjects. Gonzales work is not that of a powerful emotion. It is more a gentle understanding of nature. And Gonzales didn't use figures in his paintings or do portraits. That's what keeps him from ever becoming a major painter. On several occasions, he did try his hand at history painting. For example, the La Salle ship anchored in Matagorda Bay that is in the Rosenberg. But obviously Gonzales absorbed a lot of Homer during the vacations he spent in Maine.

ES: I have a specific question for you. Are Gonzales's works characteristic of what American artists were doing at this time?

LD: Yes and no. His work is more characteristic of American Impressionism. The subject matter of American Impressionists remained defined, and their palletes, more subdued than the French. American painters who were considered American Impressionists are, for example, William Merritt Chase, Sargent, and Homer. All three were accomplished watercolorists. At the 1893 Columbian Exposition in Chicago, the American Impressionists were highly praised by the critics.

ES: In the same vein, how does Gonzales's work compare with the work being done by other Texas artists at this time?

LD: That particular point is really interesting. As a result of reading Cecilia Steinfeldt's book *Art for History's Sake: The Texas Collection of the Witte Museum*, I found several interesting correlations between the painters living and working in San Antonio between 1900 and 1930. And how their lives and careers meshed with that of Gonzales, who is, by the way, one of the artists included in Steinfeldt's book. The Witte has several paintings, one of a landscape, the hill country outside San Antonio, and another of the Alamo in the rain. It turns out that San Antonio was the center for many Texas painters when Gonzales first started painting at Woodstock. By spending his winters in San Antonio, he joined this group of artists. These were active painters and teachers. Fellow artists. All of them scenic painters. The ages of the men vary. Some are younger, some older than Gonzales. The Spaniard José Arpa y Perea [1862–1952] and Robert Onderdonk [1852–1915] were both prolific painters as well as teachers and both were responsible for the early organization of art groups in San Antonio. The landscape painters such as Julian Onderdonk [Robert's son, 1882–1922] had the same profound respect for nature as Gonzales. Many summered in Woodstock. Dawson Dawson-Watson [1864–1939] was a friend of Birge Harrison, Boyer's teacher, and a member of the Woodstock Art Colony. Arpa y Perea and Charles Frank Reaugh [1860–1945], the prominent West Texas landscape painter who lived in Dallas, were both included in the 1893 Columbian Exhibition in Chicago.

ES: Which Boyer Gonzales attended.

LD: Yes. Well, all of those I mentioned and others as well including, of course, Gonzales, were participating and winning awards in the major Texas exhibitions at this time. He would have found in San Antonio a congenial atmosphere, a fellowship of friends and associates conducive to his intellect and his creativity. You might say that San Antonio was not at all unlike Woodstock where he spent the summer and fall.

ES: Back to Boyer's style. When do you see the style change? When does he explode out of that classic style?

LD: By 1915. What you see is an artist who has now simplified his approach to composition and color. He has perfected his sense of color while still retaining the luminosity that is so important in a watercolor. Then, several years before his death in 1934, another vivid change occurs. This is evident in *A Street in Mexico: Watching the Buzzards* [1930] and *Making Camp* [1932]. He is compacting his compositions and simplifying his subjects by using just a few bold brush strokes. He now applies almost pure color.

ES: It is quite bold, isn't it.

LD: Much bolder. He has, in a sense, freed his hand. He is now very secure and spontaneous in the way he works. Again, I refer to the Mexican scene, *Watching the Buzzards* [1930]. The trees are reduced to a wash of color, as opposed to his earlier trees which have detailed depiction of branches and leaves. All of that enhances the simplicity of the composition. He is becoming a master of letting the white paper work for him. This gives the painting that luminous quality. He has worked for years to achieve this spontaneity. He has gained control of this difficult medium.

ES: What about the later works?

LD: The subject matter is much like his earlier ones. As I have said, Gonzales used the same subjects throughout his life. Here we have examples in *Three Crows* [1933], *Deep Lake, Maine* [1933], and *The Old Chestnut Tree* [Woodstock, 1933]. However, they all show how bold he has become at using color. Especially the use of blue. Look at the blue mountain. He no longer tries to imitate nature's true colors. In this painting, *The Old Chestnut Tree,* he has succeeded in doing something which doesn't always work. He has used almost pure color in the distant ground. There is no middle ground. In this way, his painting has become more of a design than an accurate rendering of a mountain landscape. But the tree remains a tree. Look at *Backwater* [1932]. It's another work from the later period that is very skillfully done. His landscapes remain indicative of his intense feeling for nature. In the late 1920s and early 1930s, he has reached a point when he really gets his own style. There is still Homer there, but Homer was such a powerful figure in the art of the time that he could not help but influence everyone in the early part of the twentieth century. Another is *Beached Boats in Florida* [1929]. Once again he is getting almost abstract with his composition. He has reduced everything to a form and left out a lot of details so that everything still has a natural shape. His skies are getting less detailed. Just a few slashes of color or wash. I think it is very interesting that this one has details, but the details are done with a brush rather than with a pen or pencil or have been penciled in very carefully before he painted. This one, *Backwater,* is 1932, and he has almost an abstract pattern done solely with the branches, with the rock and with the branches of the tree that surround the rock. There is nothing tight about these paintings. Look at the ships in these paintings. They have to be done naturalistically; otherwise, you will look at the painting and say, "That ship isn't floating, it'll sink." It has to be done correctly to make it appear to be what it is so that you know that it is a functioning object. A tree has to be planted in the ground. A boat or a ship has to say to the person who is looking at it, "I can float! I can go through the water." He manages to do that with just a few strokes of his brush.

ES: The sense of the movement in this one of the tree!

LD: In *A Sudden Squall* [1922] he has done something different. The tree is opaque in certain places. He has used white to mix his light green so there is an opacity there which is a little unusual. Maybe he didn't like what he had done. And in a water color you cannot go back and take it out once it is there. So he would have put some white pigment in his paint to make the light. He can put it in, but he can't take it out. Watercolorists have to be fairly accurate. When they sit down to do the painting, they have to know what they are going to do and just do it. Because when you make a mistake, you have to start over, more often than not. You can't repair it. You can't paint over it. Otherwise, you lose what a watercolor is all about. The lightness. The movement. It becomes heavy and opaque and that is not what a real traditional watercolor is. If you are going to do that, then you are going to paint in gouasche or tempera or nowadays in acrylics. *Watching the Buzzards* [1930] is a prime example of leaving the artist very much in command of how an artist wants his painting to turn out. He has left a great deal of the white paper showing. His brush knows exactly what it is doing. It is very controlled. There is nothing stilted or stiff. The colors are all bright. There is nothing dirty about the colors. That can happen in a water color. The canoe in the woods is a Homeresque subject, but it is not executed in the Homer fashion.

ES: What about his oils?

LD: Well, just that at the same time he is doing watercolors, he is also doing oils. The same thing holds true. The later ones are the thumb-box shows at the Salmagundi Club. He has become almost abstract. In his rendering of nature, he has used just color to define the mountain and the foreground. He has used just one stroke of the brush. In the other painting, the rocks. He has used a lot of color in the sea. You can see the strokes of the brush. It is really almost an abstract pattern. Yet at a distance, it is very realistic. There is a lot of movement in the water, but he is definitely not going to be an abstract painter. His son was. But it is obvious that Gonzales, Sr., understands his subjects so well that he can almost reduce them to an abstract design, which basically tells you he had a very good sense of design. He had a good sense of color and he was certainly extremely skilled at handling his brush and late in his life his paintings have become very bold, very colorful, almost abstract in their design.

ES: Some of his contemporary critics always thought of him as a naturalist.

LD: Yes, he always had a great respect for nature. Birds. Fish. Trees. Flowers. The sea. The sky. From the time he was a boy, he hunted and fished. Nature simply fascinated him.

ES: Just before he died, he was talking with his son and he said something to the effect that there was much more he needed to know about painting. He said, "If I could just have a few more years, I think that I would really know what I'm doing."

LD: That is what makes a good artist. You are always anxious to learn. You are never satisfied with what you do. Always working to perfect. Obviously, Boyer Gonzales worked constantly throughout his life. Look how much he produced. If the Rosenberg collection contains five hundred works, imagine how many other Gonzales paintings there are in private collections as well as those in museums. He had an inquiring mind, experimenting over and over again to try to see things and record them in a different way.

ES: One last question. When Gonzales died in 1934, he was nearly seventy years old. And as you have said, he was at the height of his career as an artist. He was highly regarded by the critics and patrons alike. He had lived long enough to make a comfortable living as an artist. Why did he drop out of sight?

LD: That is something that happens to most artists who achieve the type of success and respect that Boyer Gonzales did during his lifetime. Granted, he was not a Homer. Gonzales, as a painter, never received the reputation of some of his contemporaries. What can be said about Gonzales is that he was a very competent and highly respected painter who reflected an intimacy with his subjects. He was, it can be said, a man of his time. His paintings gave a great deal of pleasure to a great many people.

ES: Let Boyer Gonzales, Jr., have the last word on his father's paintings. These comments come from the address he gave at the Rosenberg Library in 1981: "I've been studying these paintings for some time now and they look better and better to me . . . [Consider] the breaking water. He did this a great deal . . . [but] in no sense did he have a patent way of showing a wave and repeating it and repeating it. Each wave was a new experience. . . . A very simple subject, but it moves. The water moves. The design moves." Gonzales, Jr. had a profound respect for his father's artistic abilities but, curiously enough, never followed his father's impressionistic style. Boyer Gonzales, Jr., was an abstract artist. He knew, however, how fine an artist his father was and he freely praised his work. He said, "Right until the end it seems to me his paintings had a fresh vibrancy, a quality that reflected his optimism. . . ." He ended his talk saying, "I came across this quote from the German author Goethe some time ago: 'It is more pleasing to do than to say, and more pleasing to feel than to do, but most pleasing of all is simply to look.' And I would encourage you all to look at my Dad's paintings. . . . So much is written about art, so much is said about art, but the painting is the thing." With the publication of this book, a new public will have the opportunity to enjoy the work of an artist who "understood so intimately the moods of the sea and the ways of the seabirds."

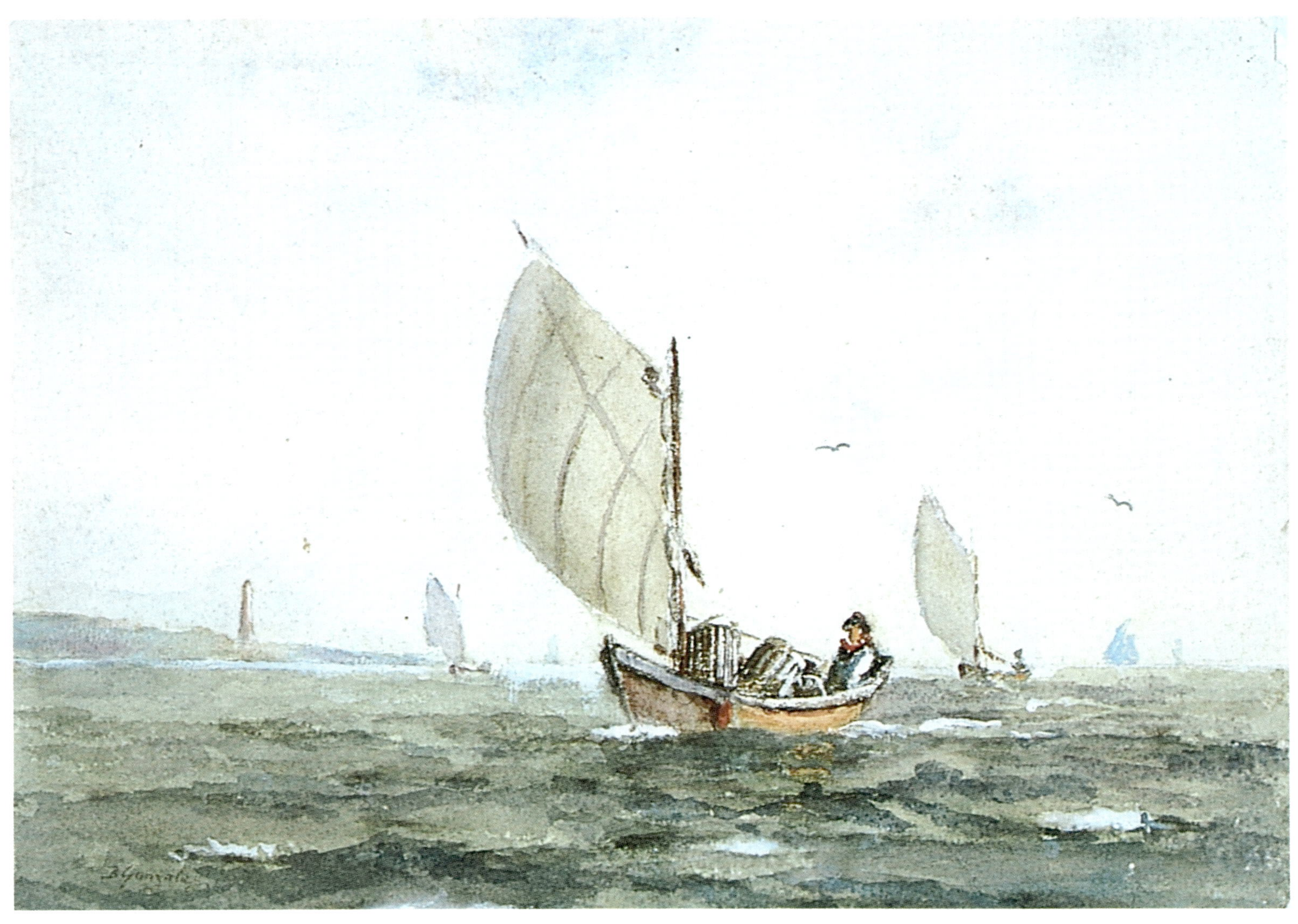

Homeward Bound, ca. 1885–90

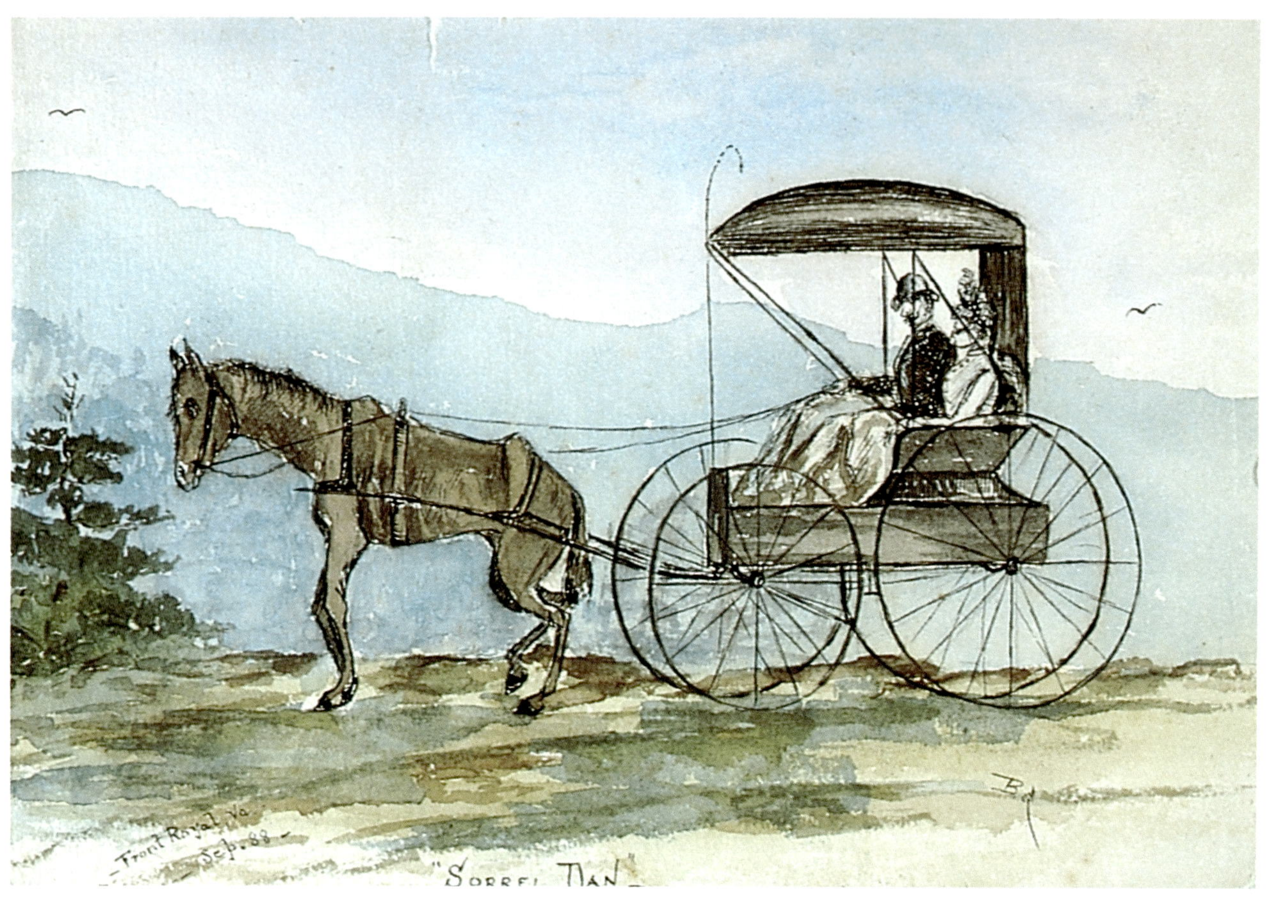

Sorrell Dan, 1888

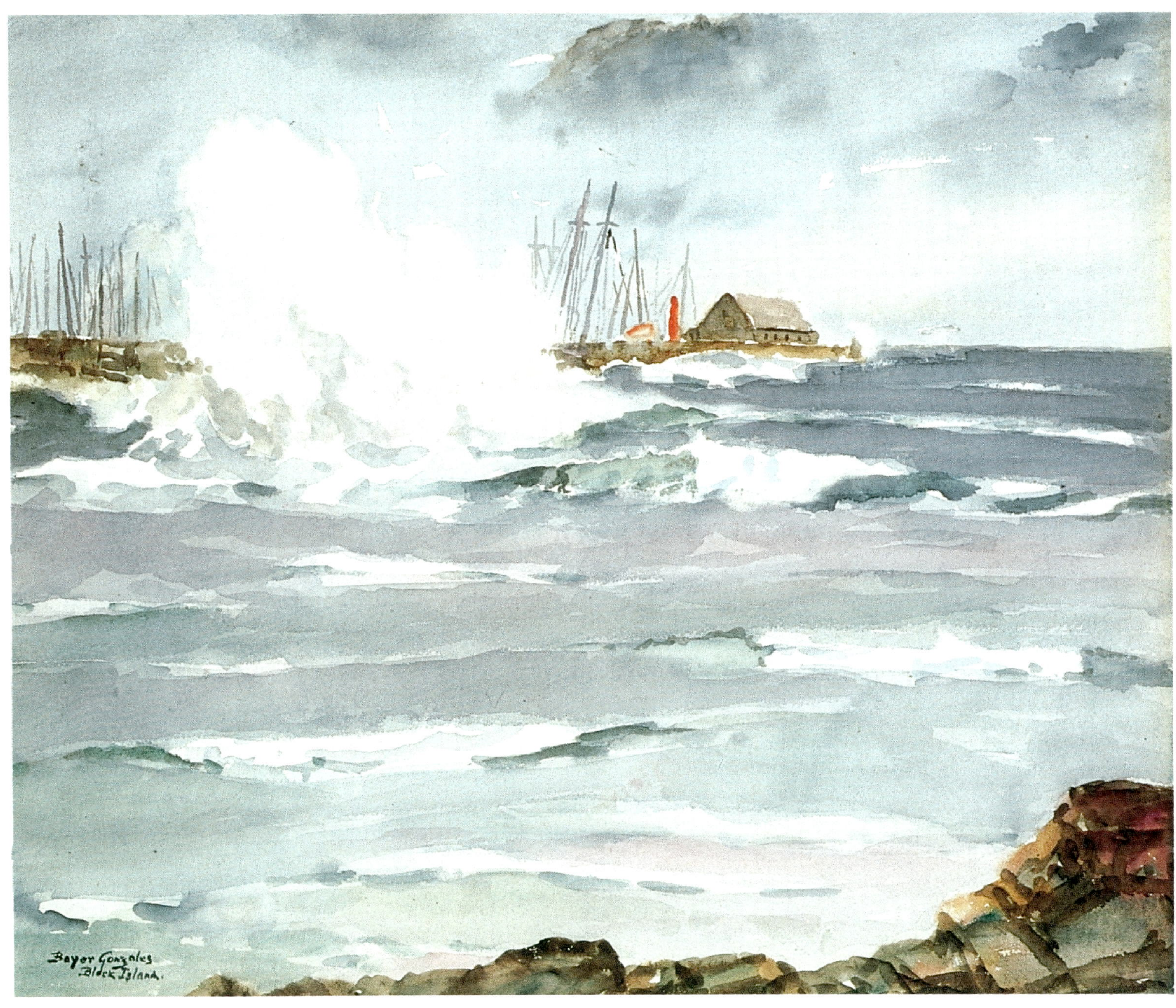

Block Island

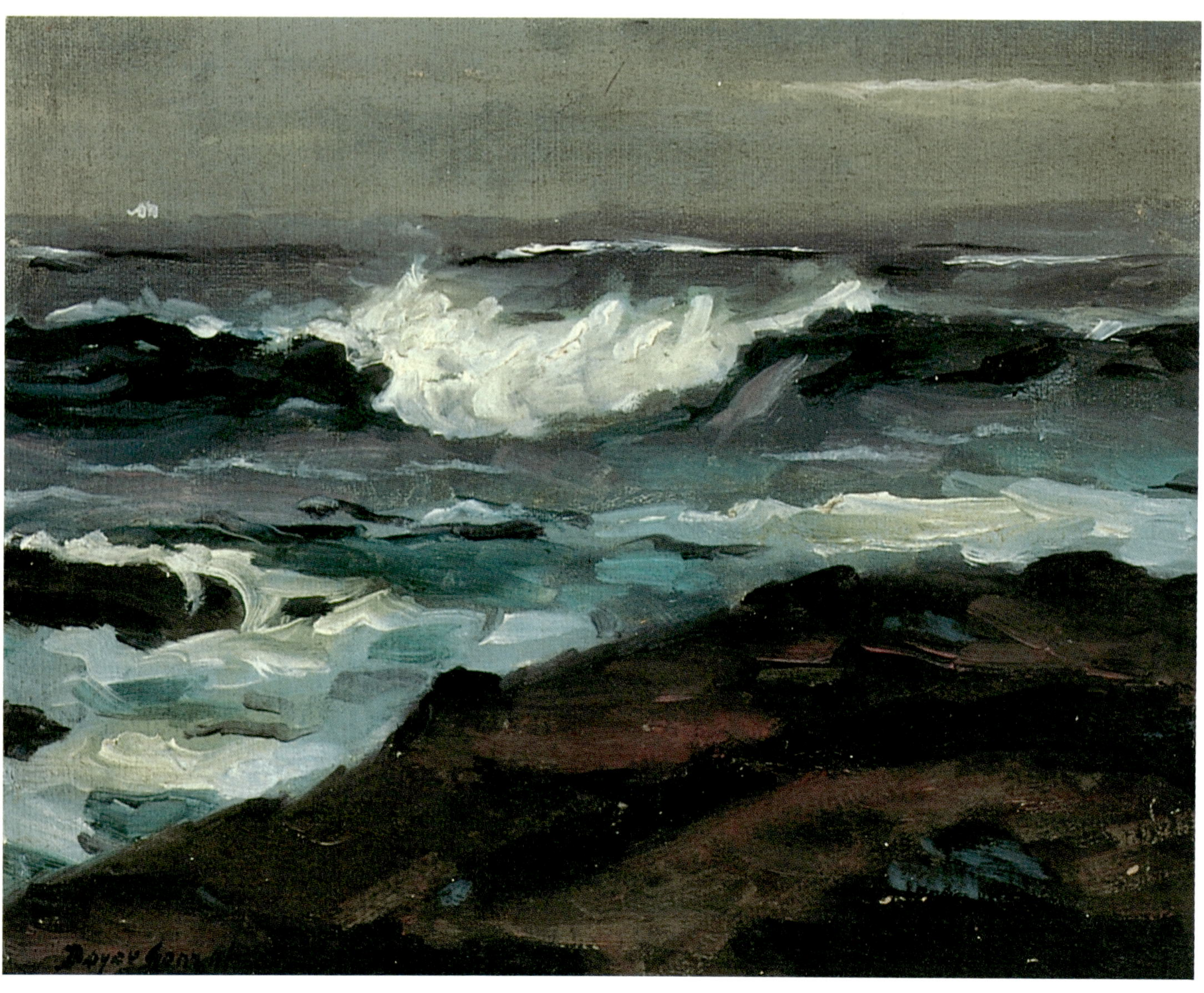

Monhegan Shores

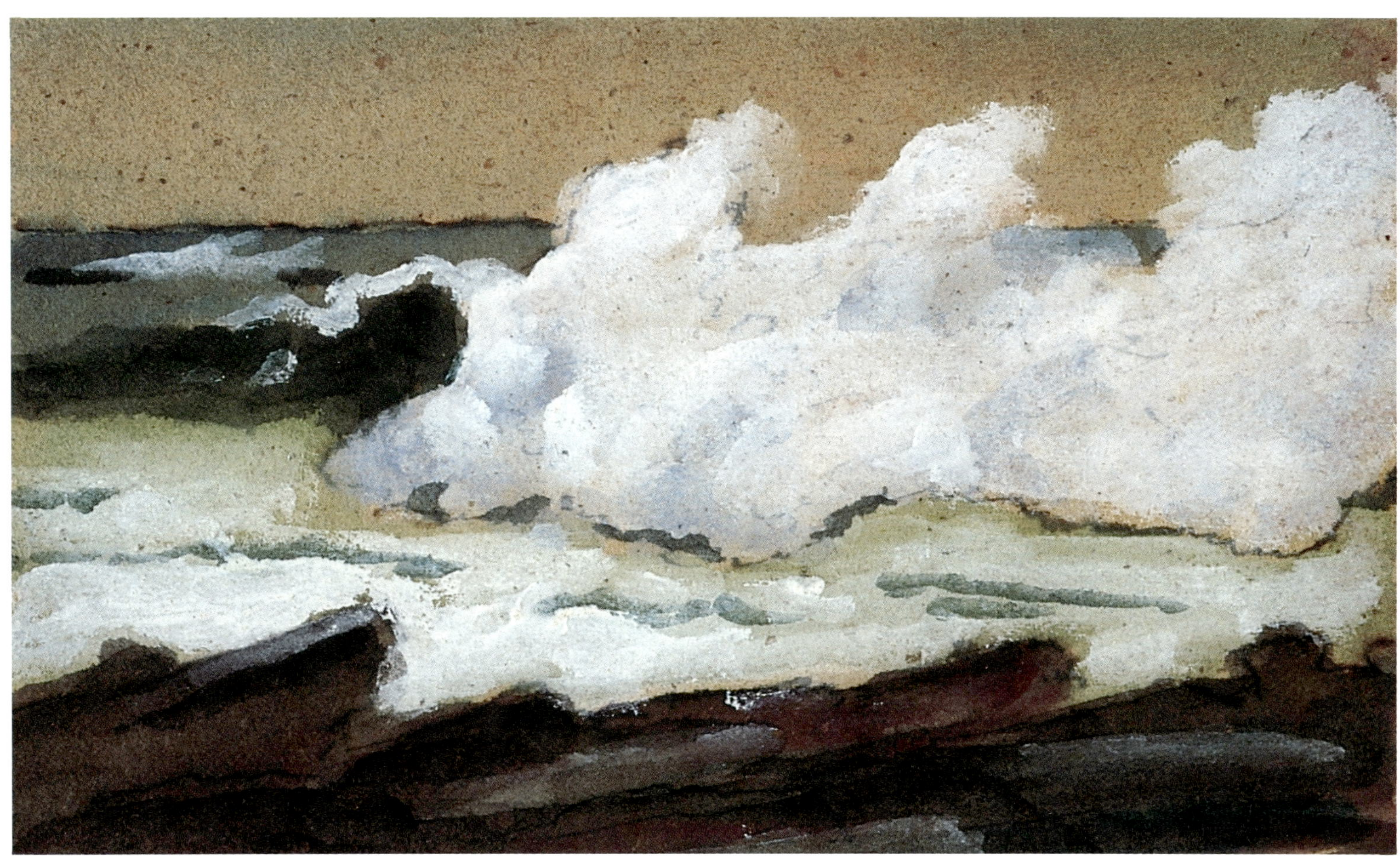

Untitled

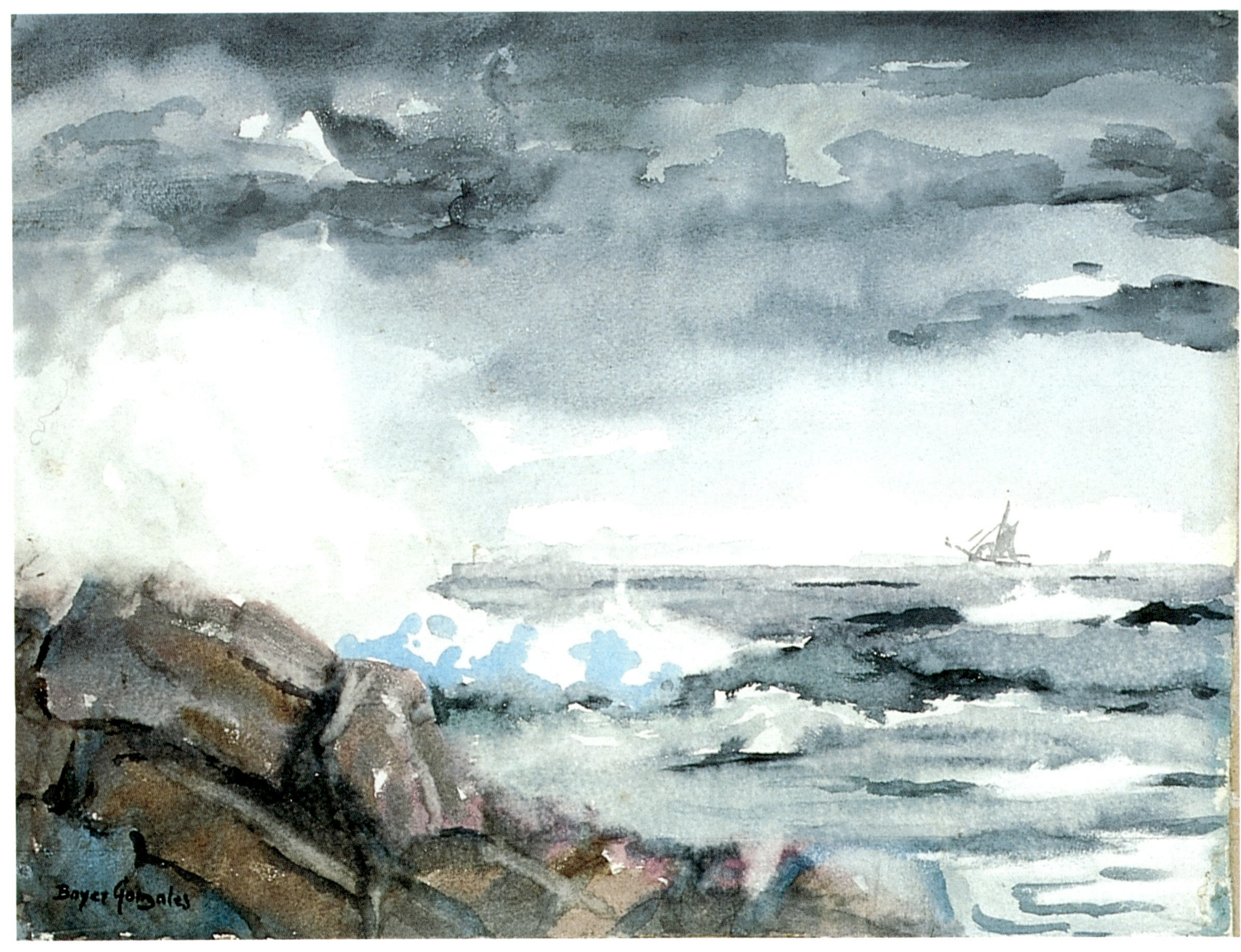

Untitled

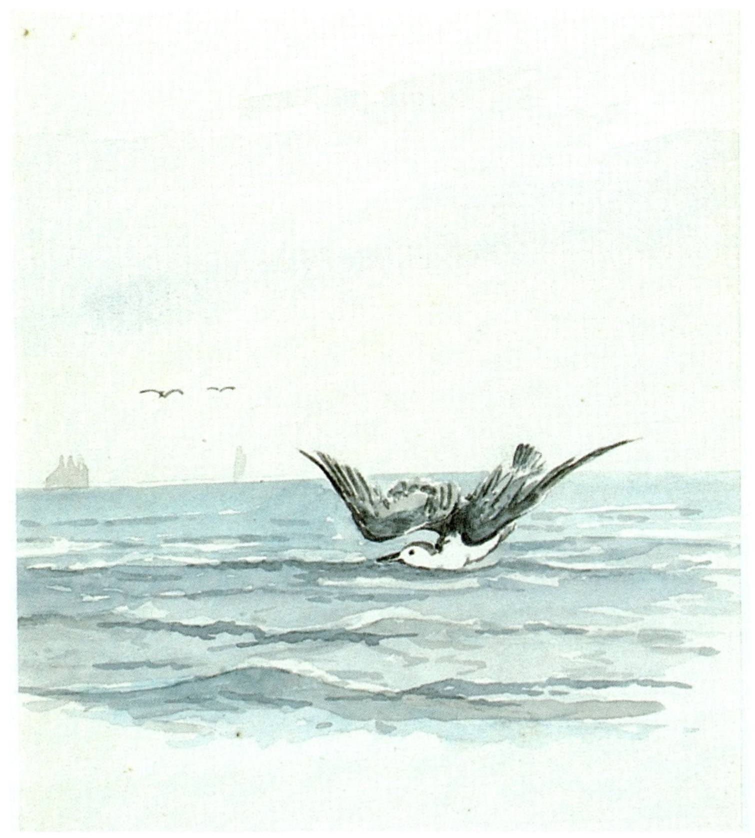

Flight, ca. 1894

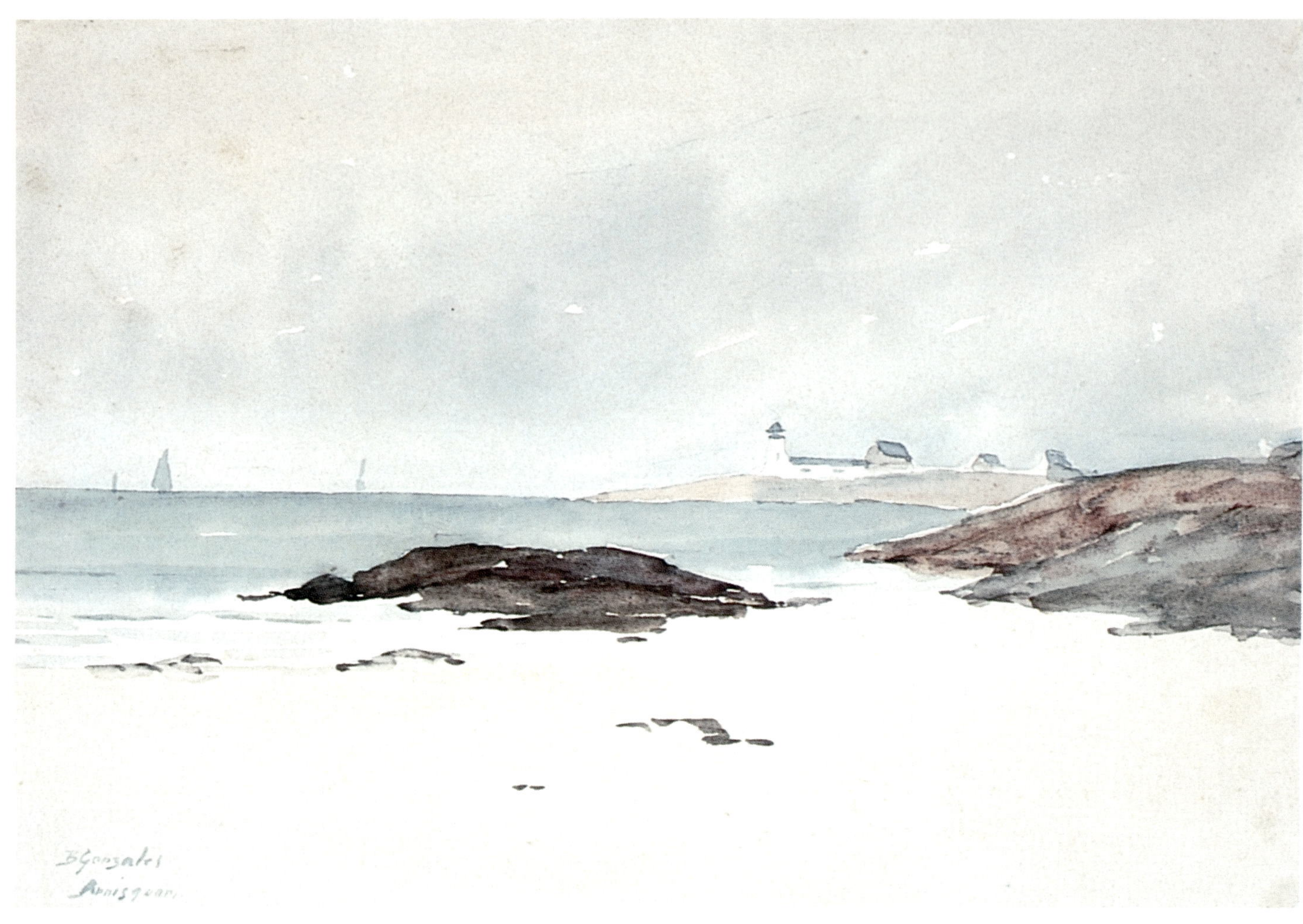

Annisquam, summer 1894

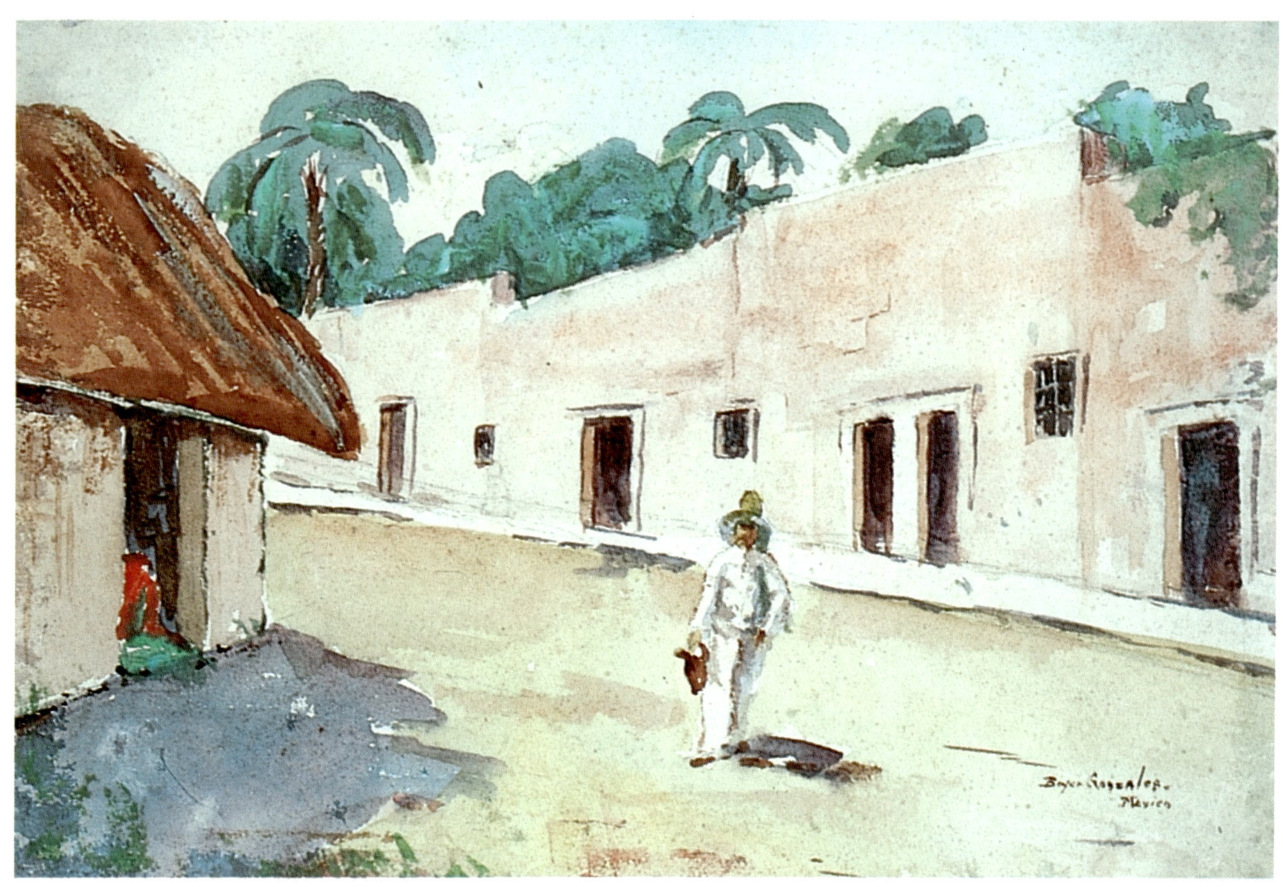

Mexican Street, 1895

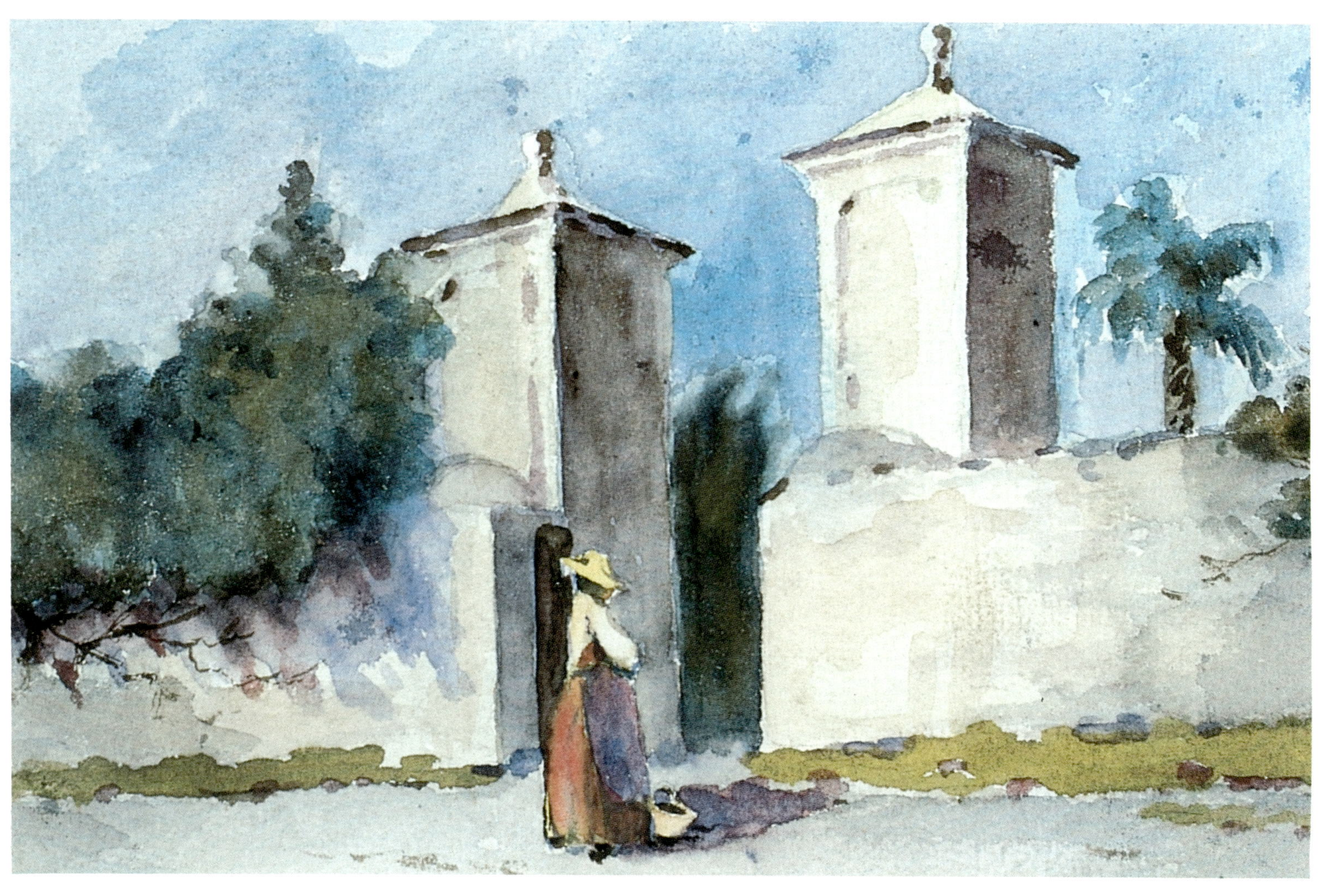

Gateway—Tizapan, 1895

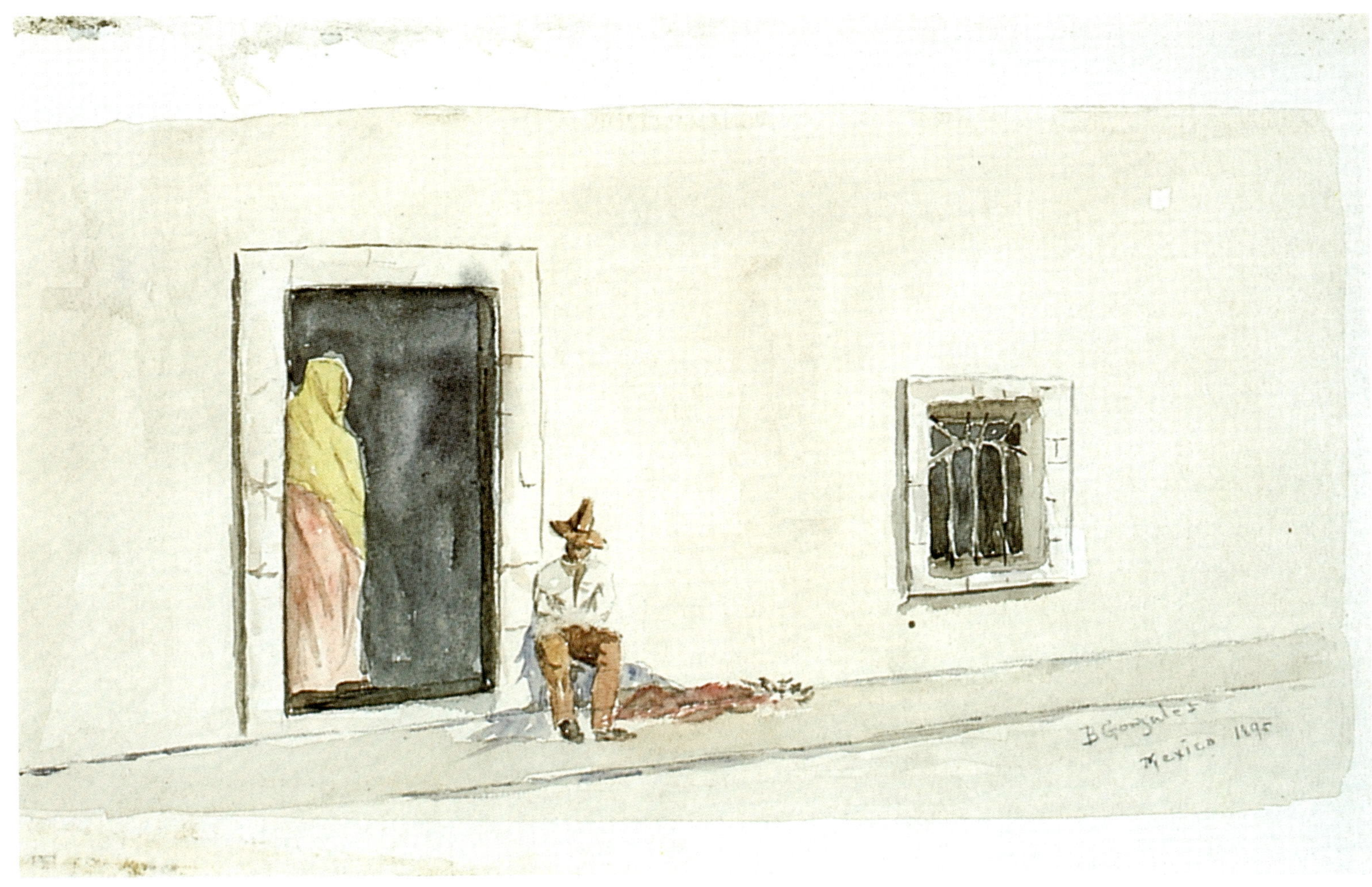

Mexico, 1895

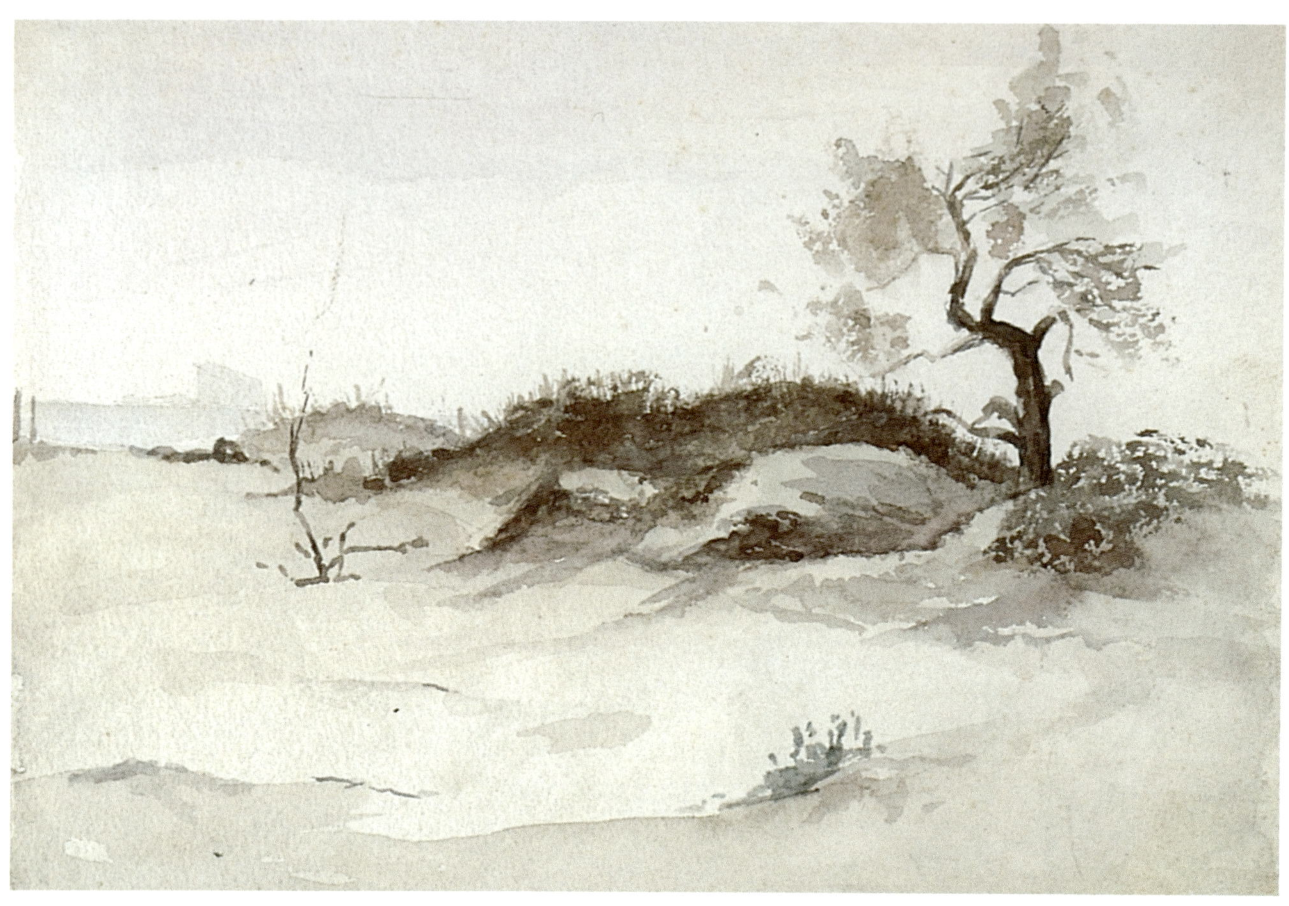

Virginia Point, ca. 1898

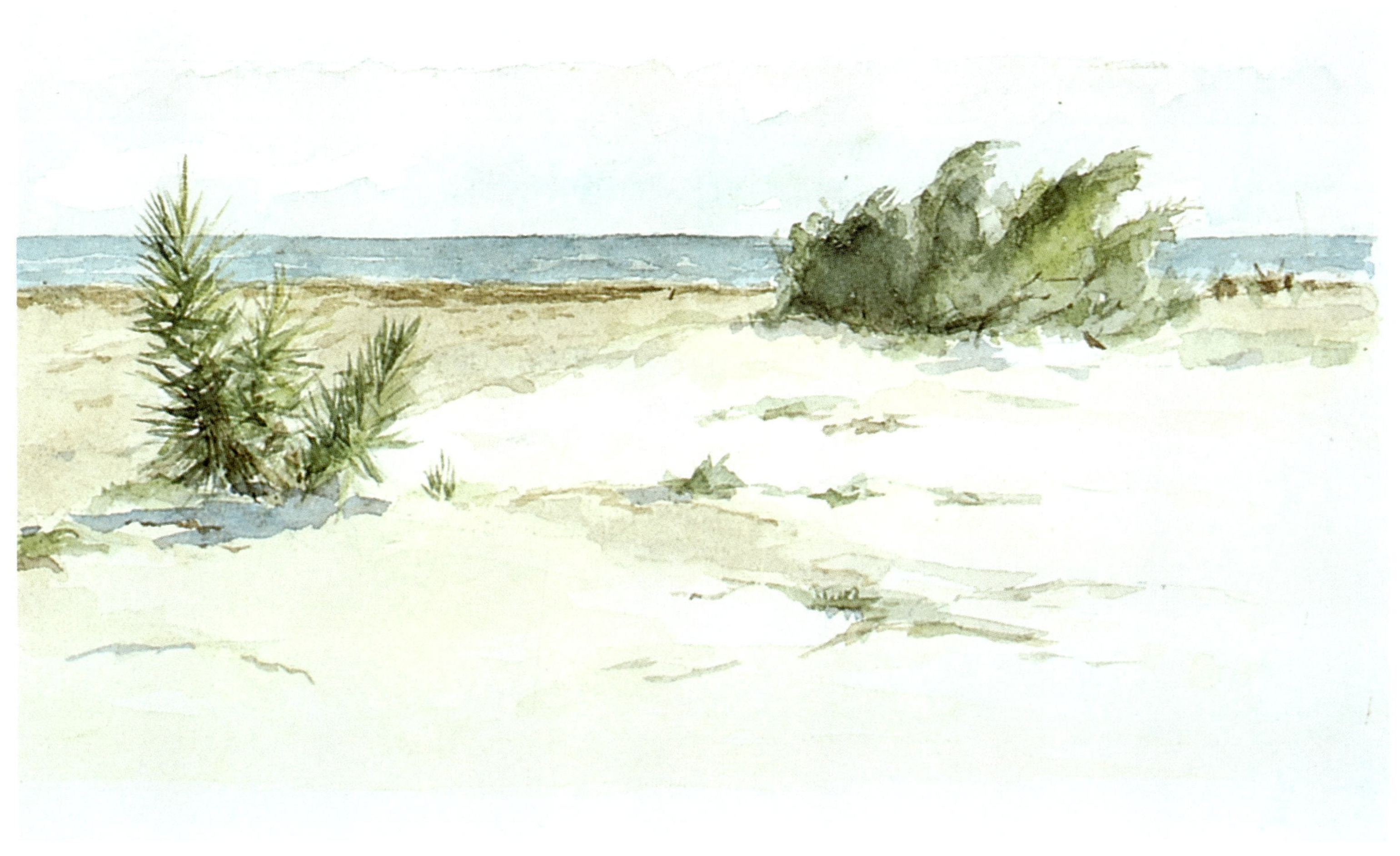

West Beach—Galveston, ca. 1898

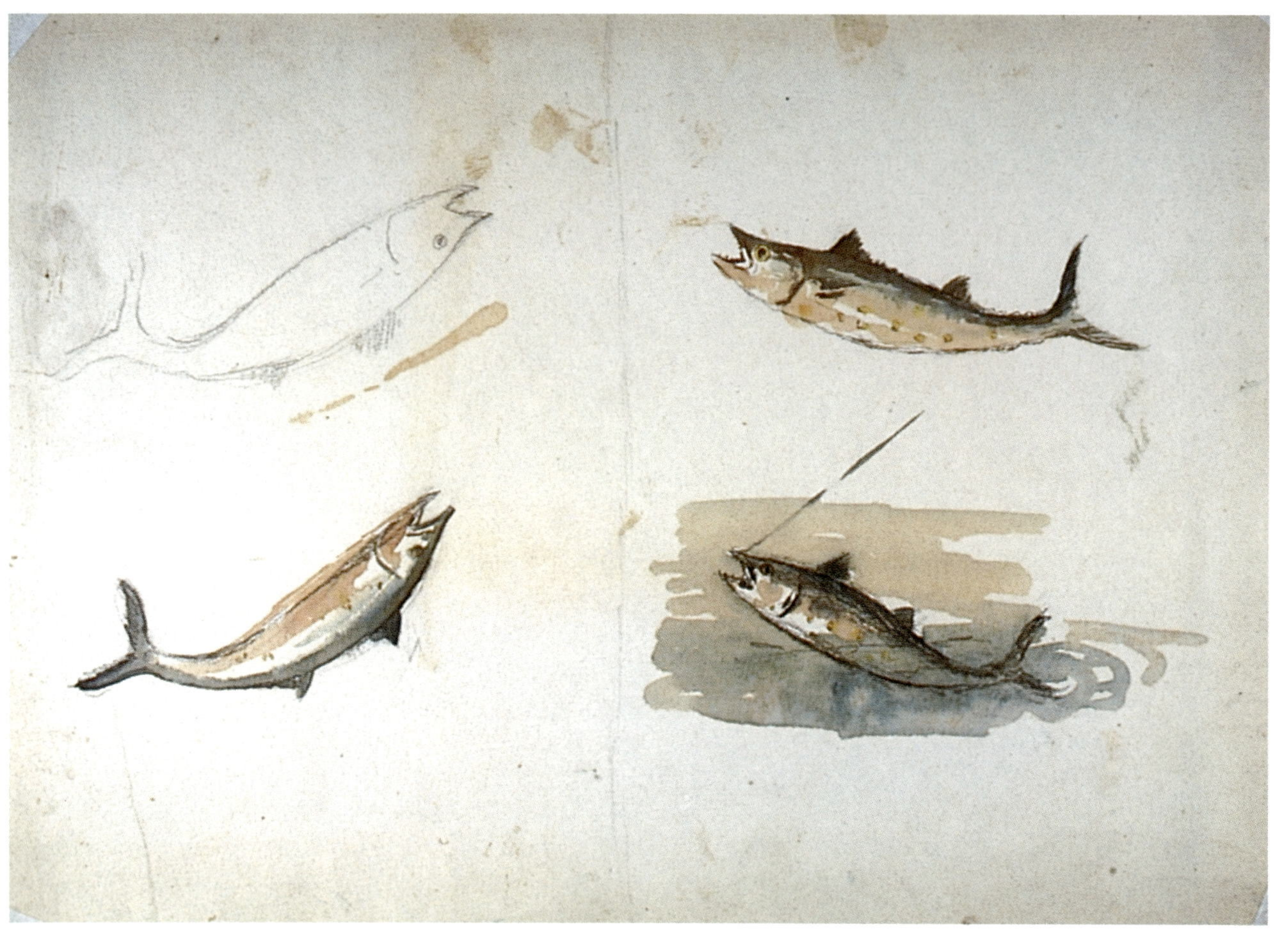

Four Spanish Mackerel Studies, ca. 1901

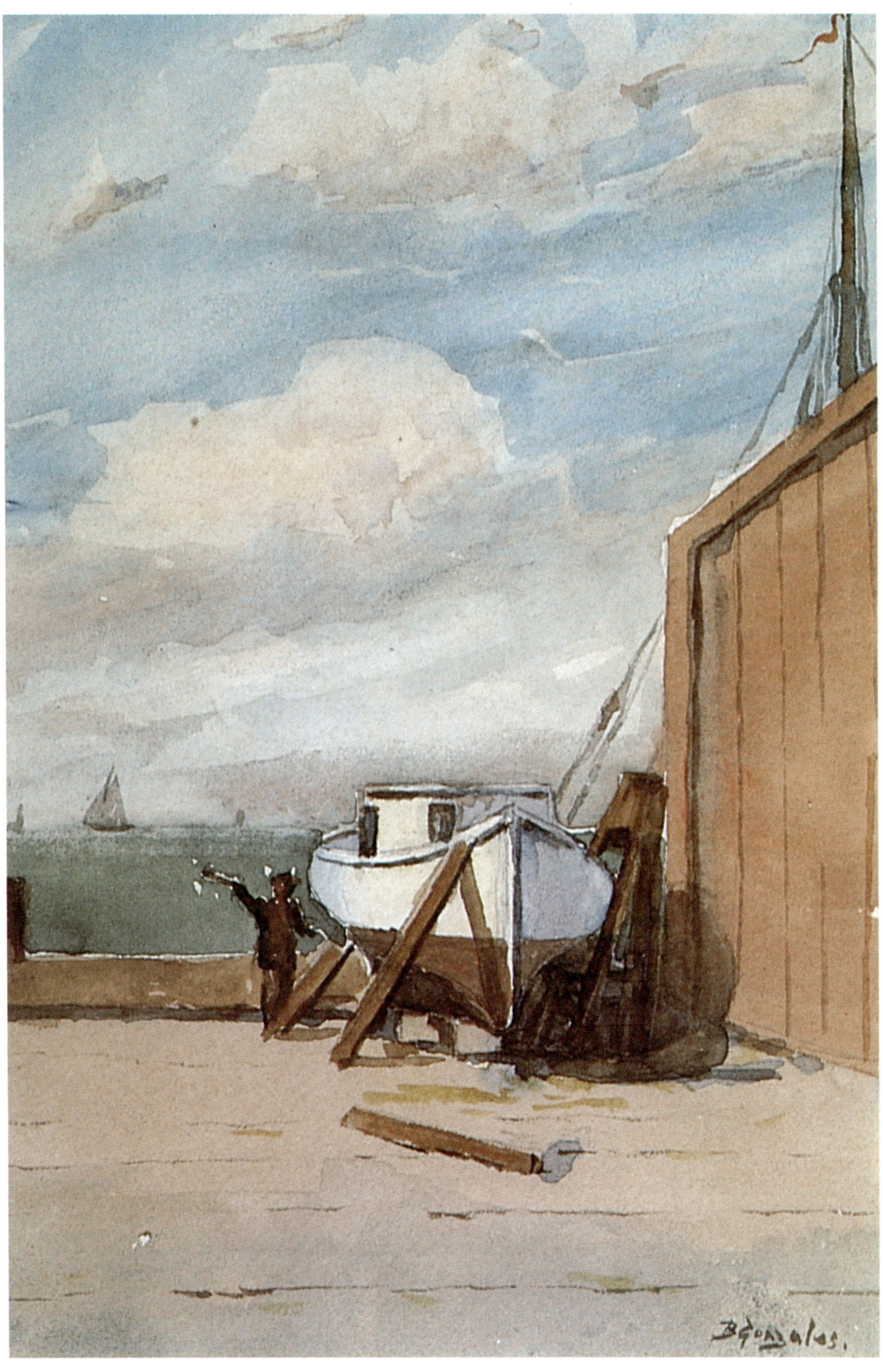

Caulking—Galveston, ca. 1902

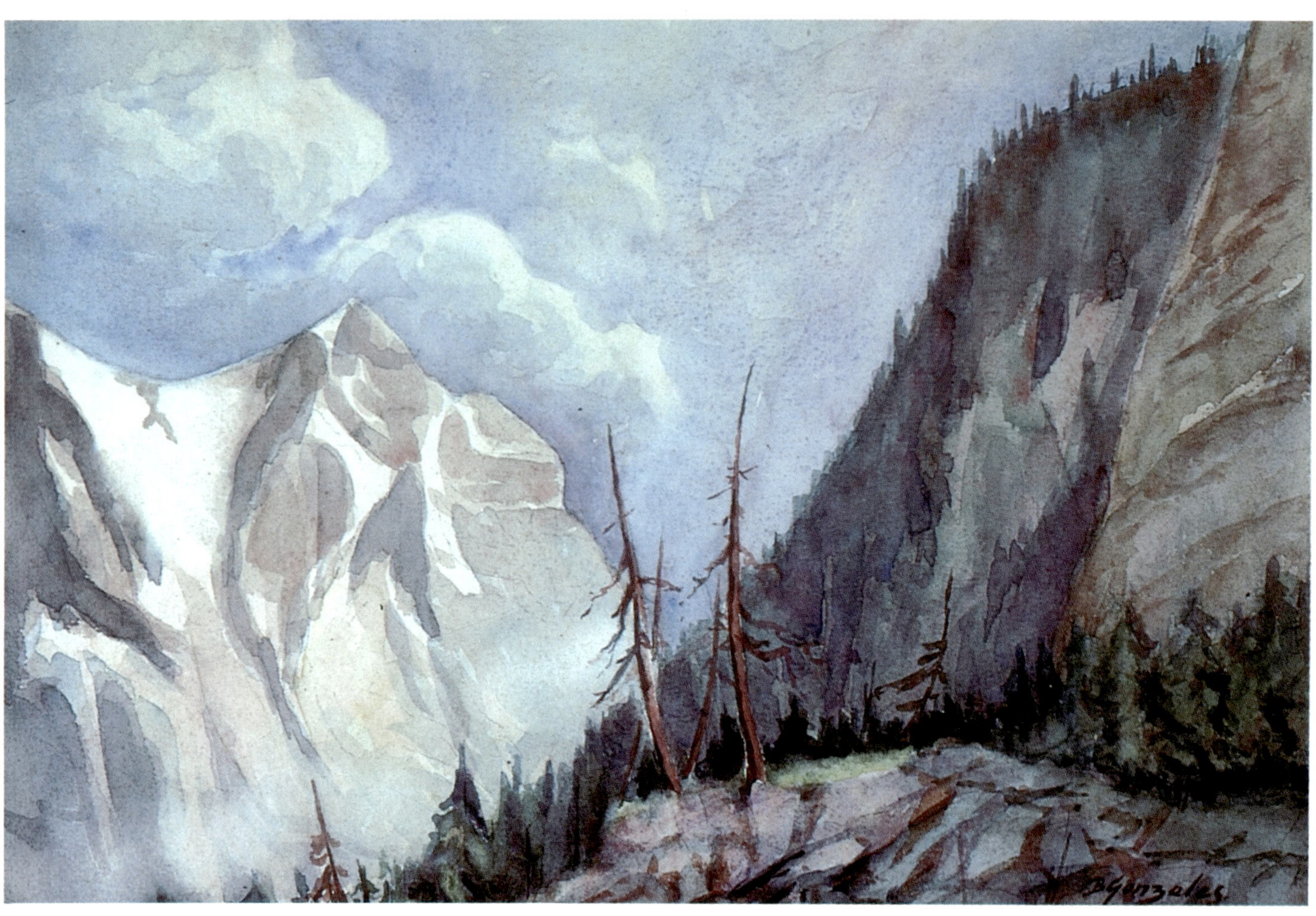

In the Rockies, ca. 1902

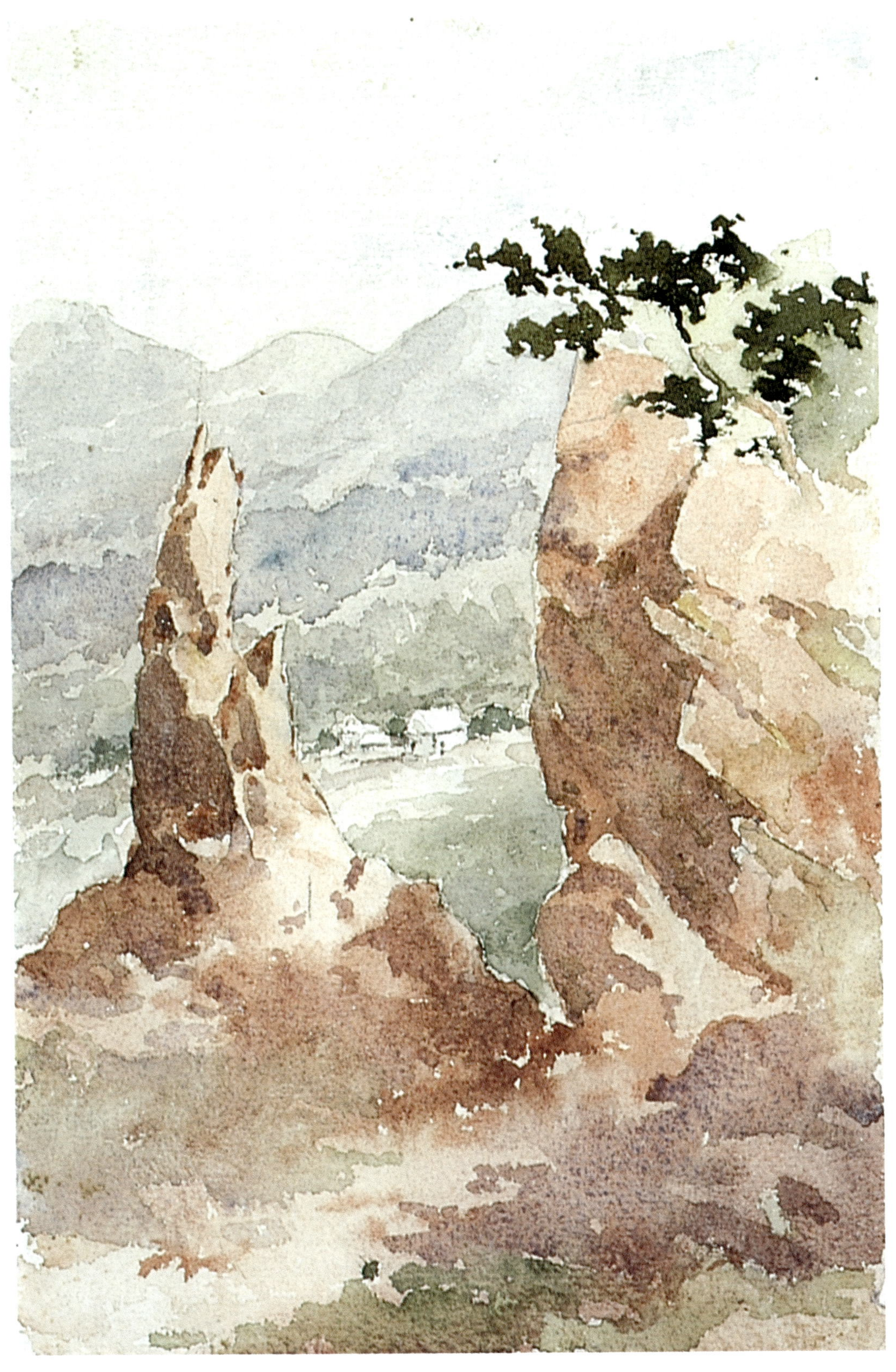

Colorado Springs, 1905?

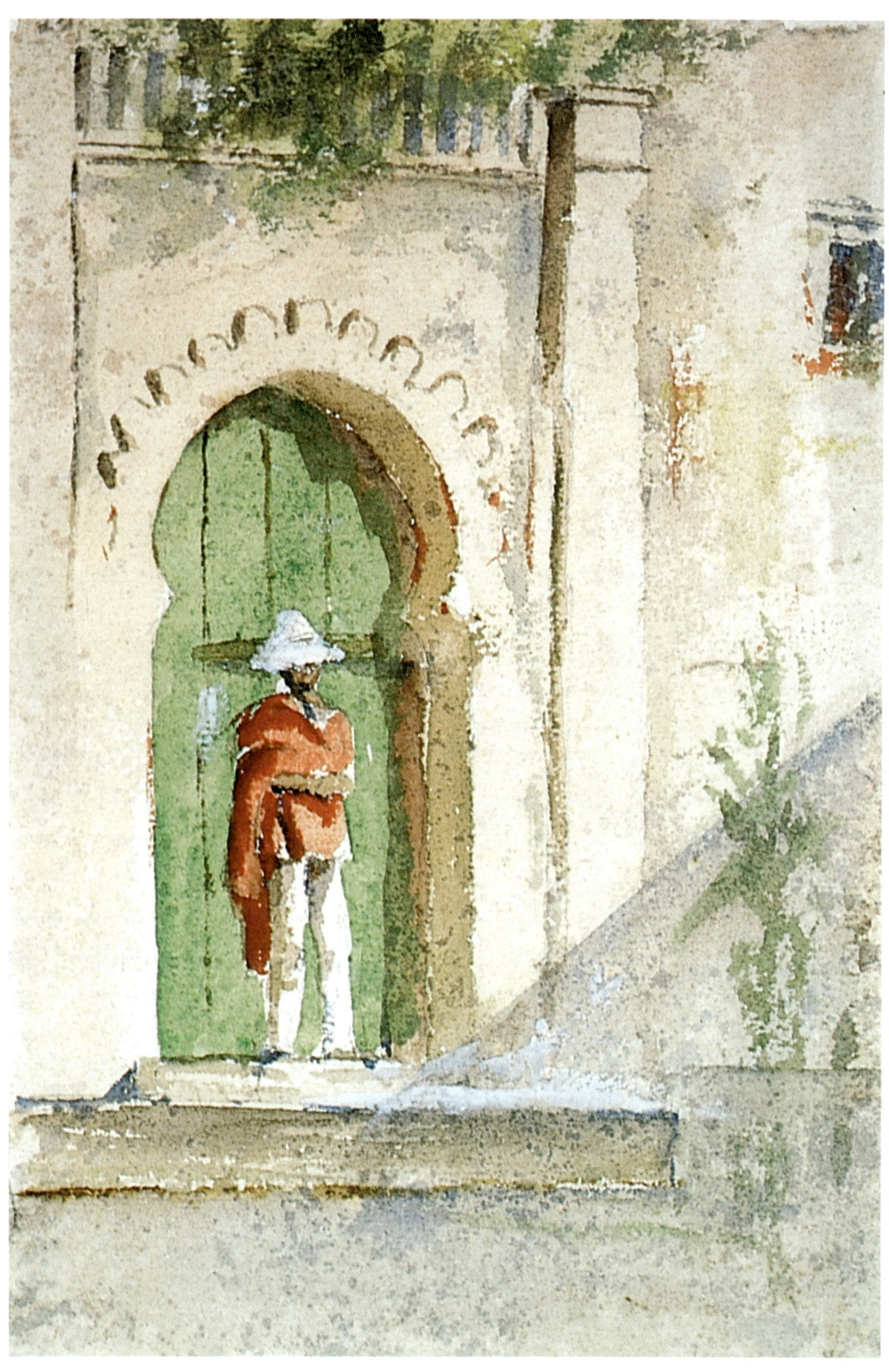

Doorway Mexico, ca. 1905

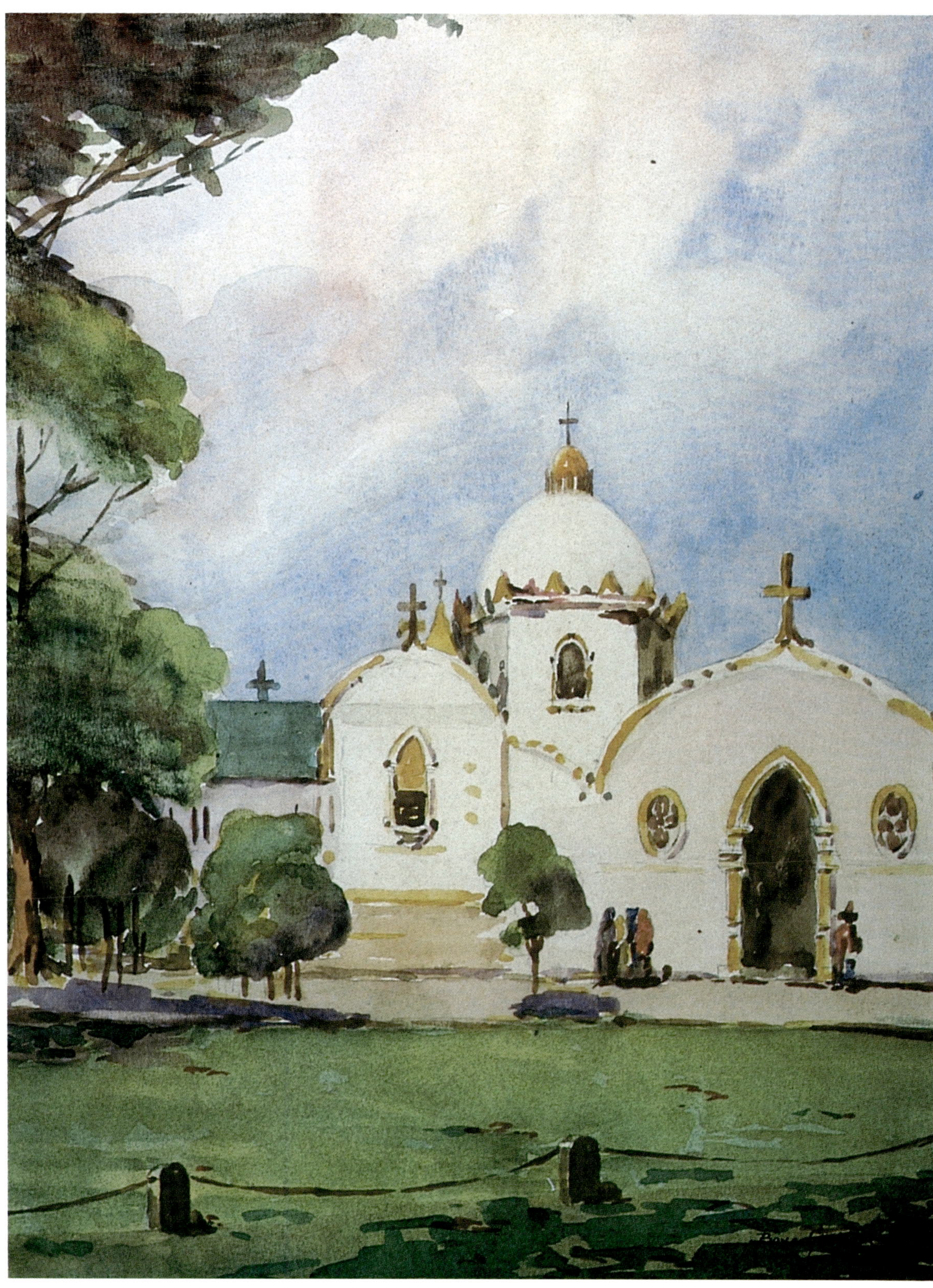

Mexian Church, ca. 1905

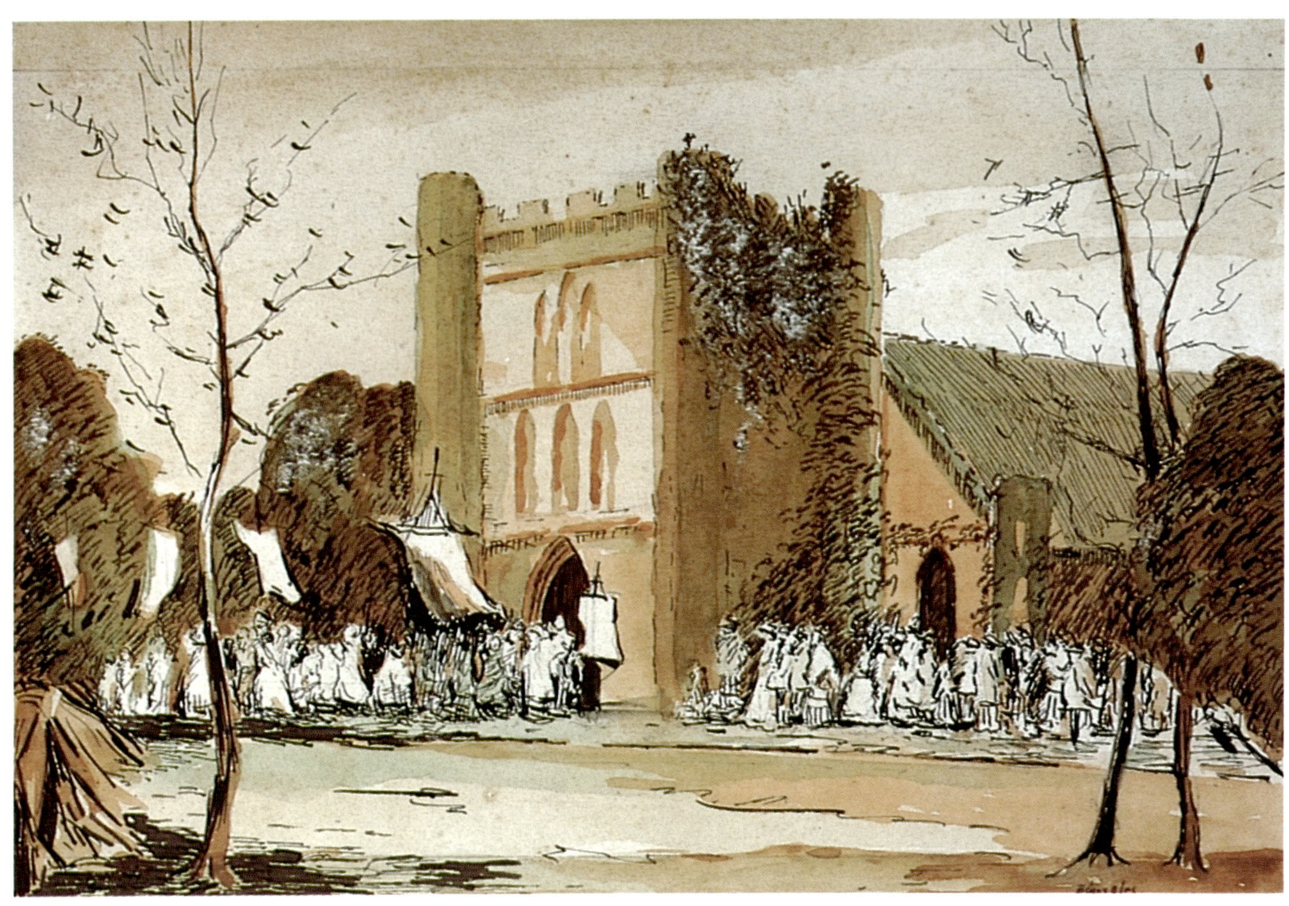

"Children's Easter, Trinity Church," 1908

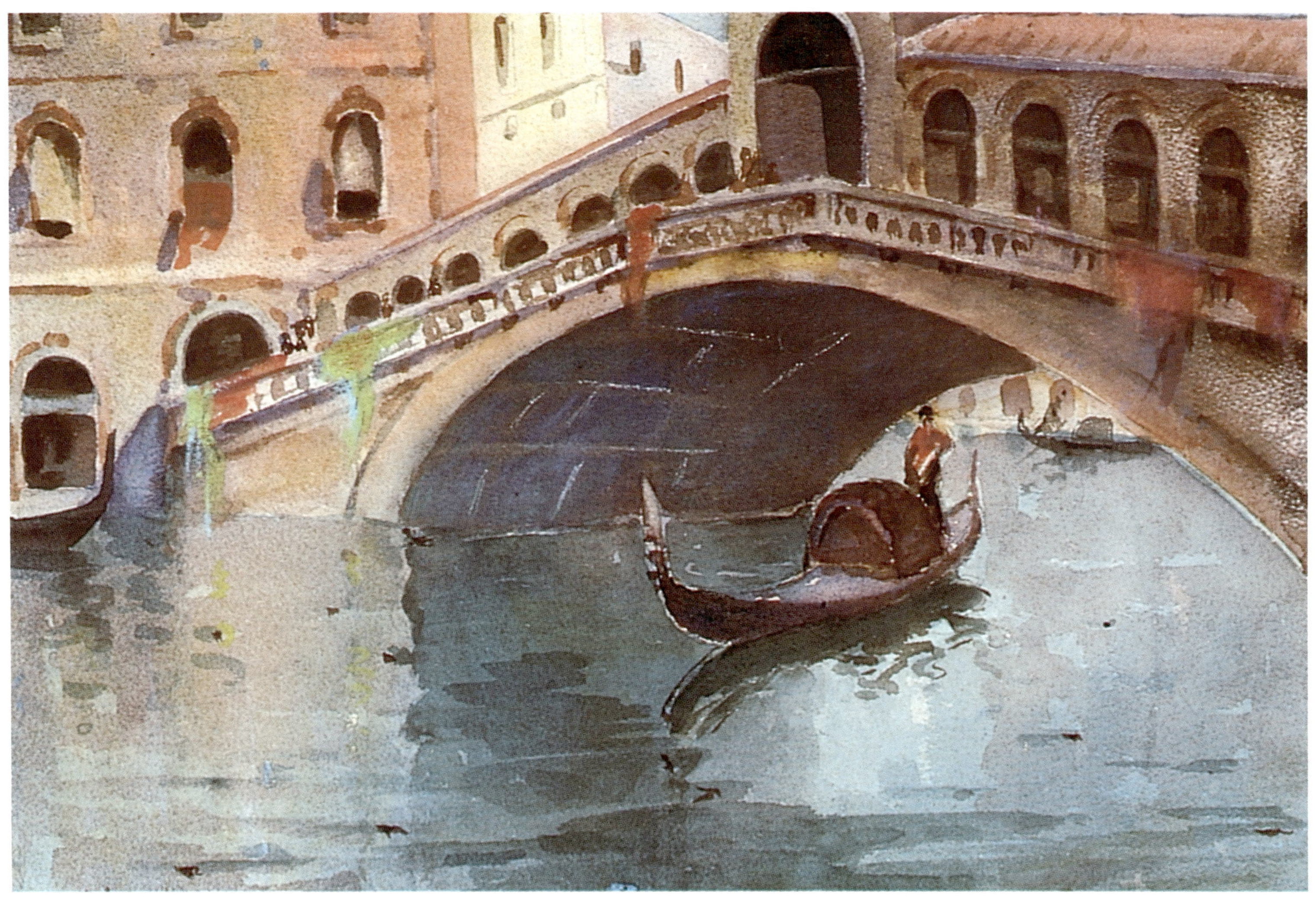

Grand Canal, 1908

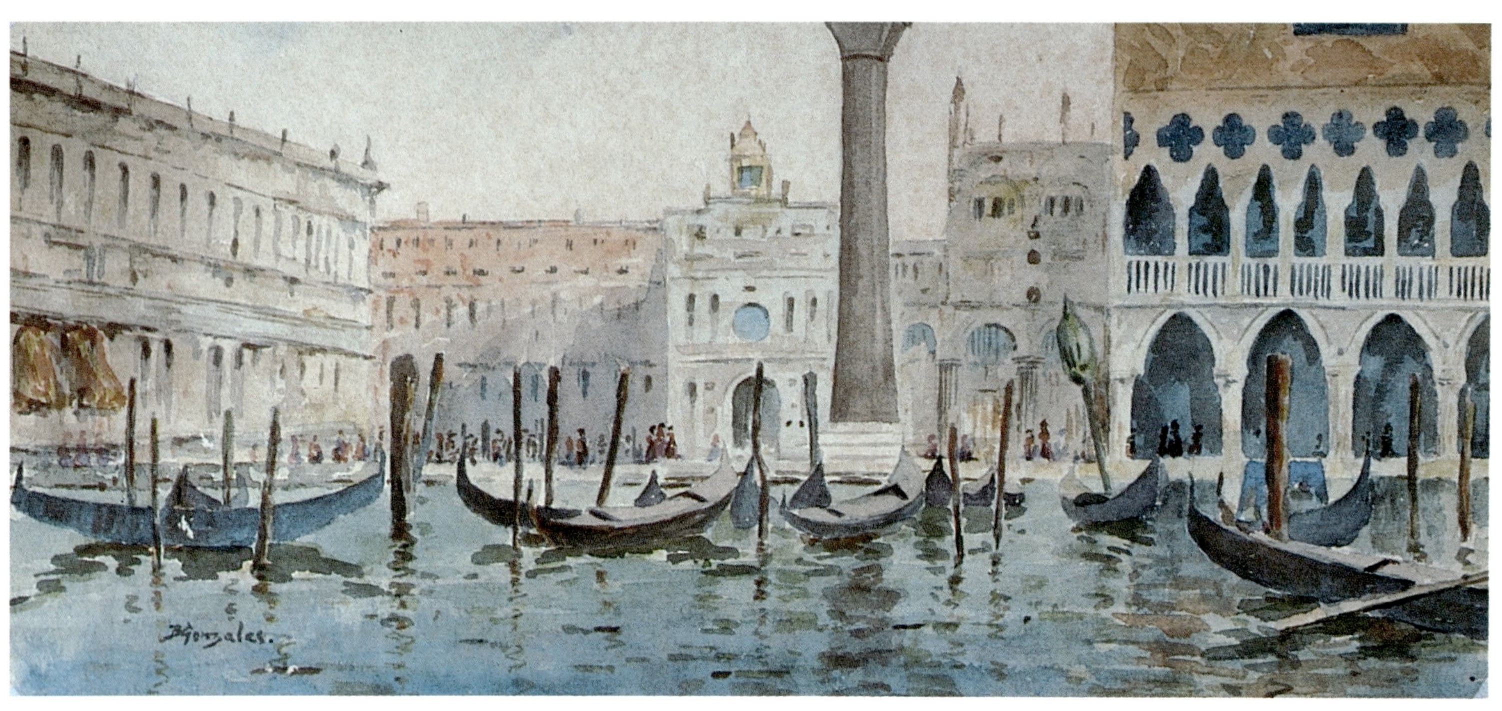

Doge's Palace, 1908

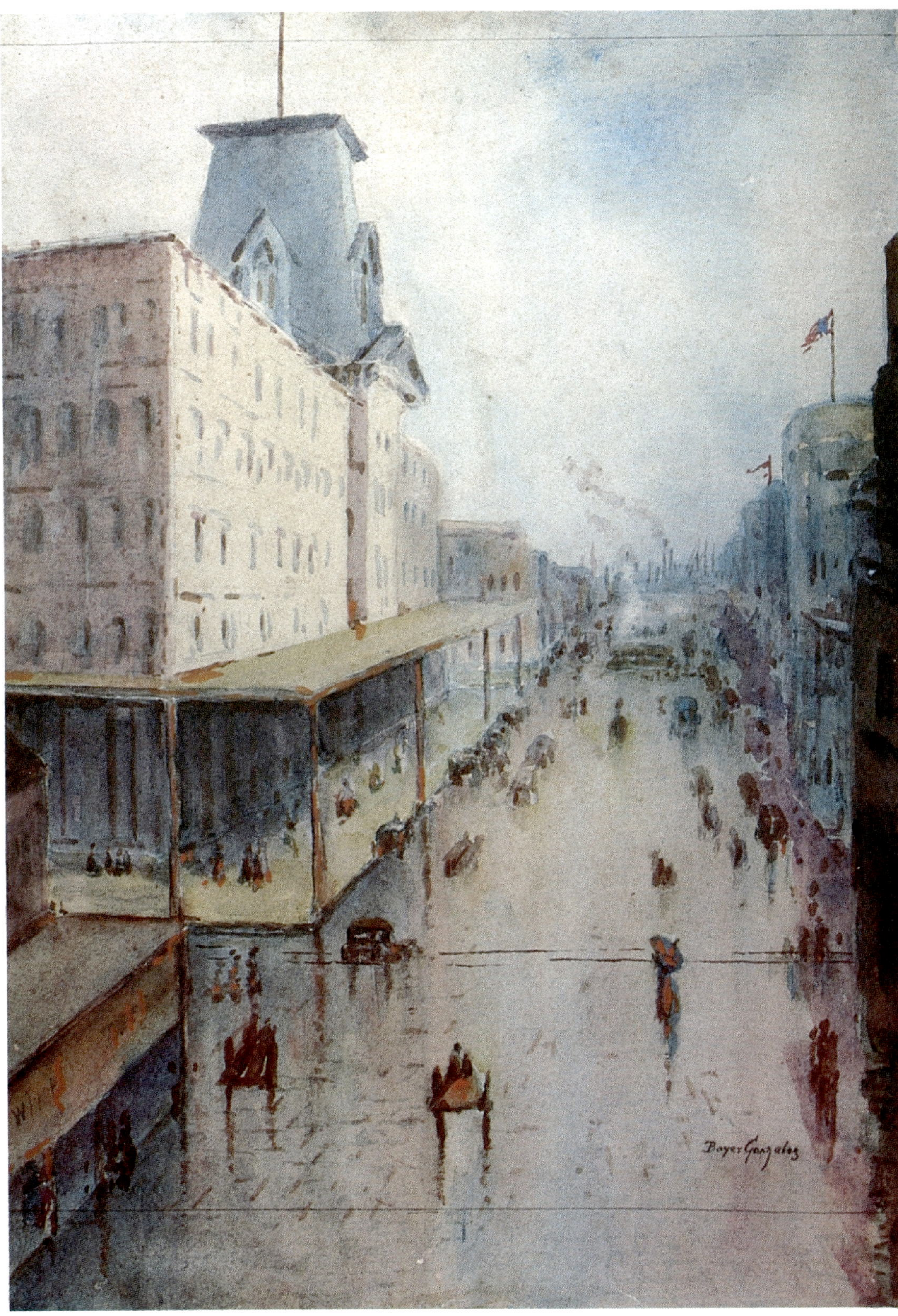

Street in Galveston, ca. 1910

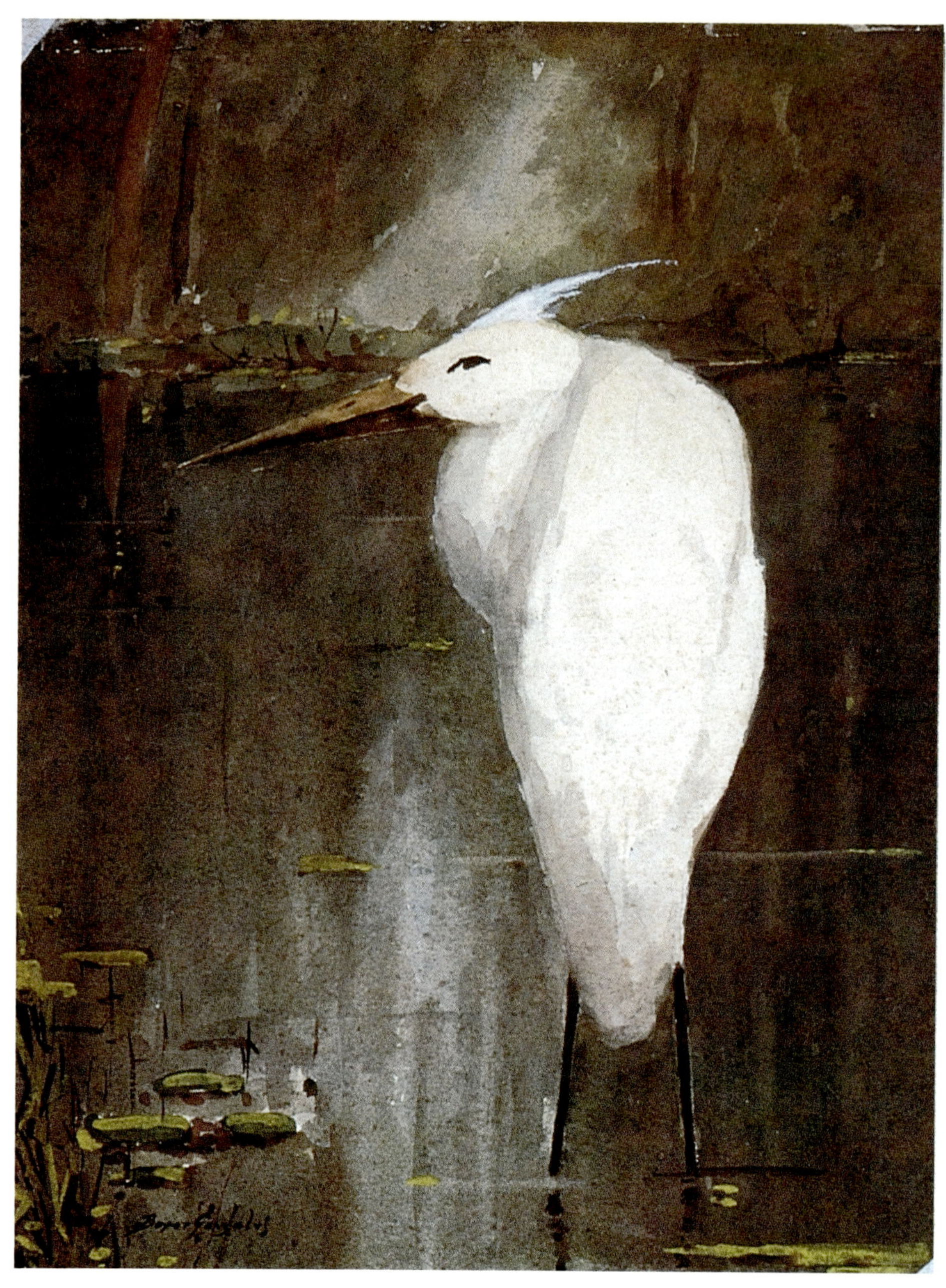

Egret in Swamp, 1912

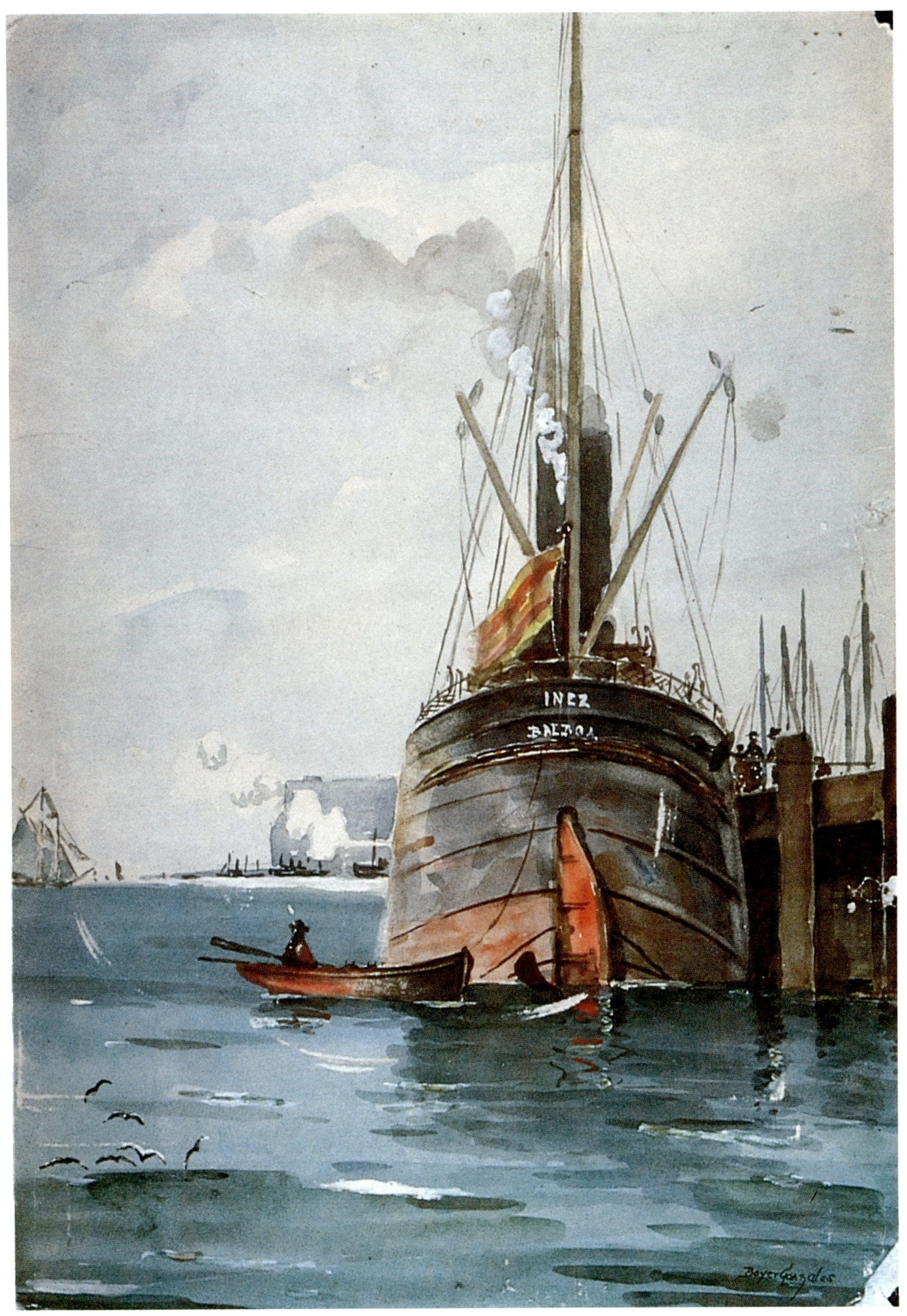

"Inez" Spanish Freighter,
Galveston, ca. 1914

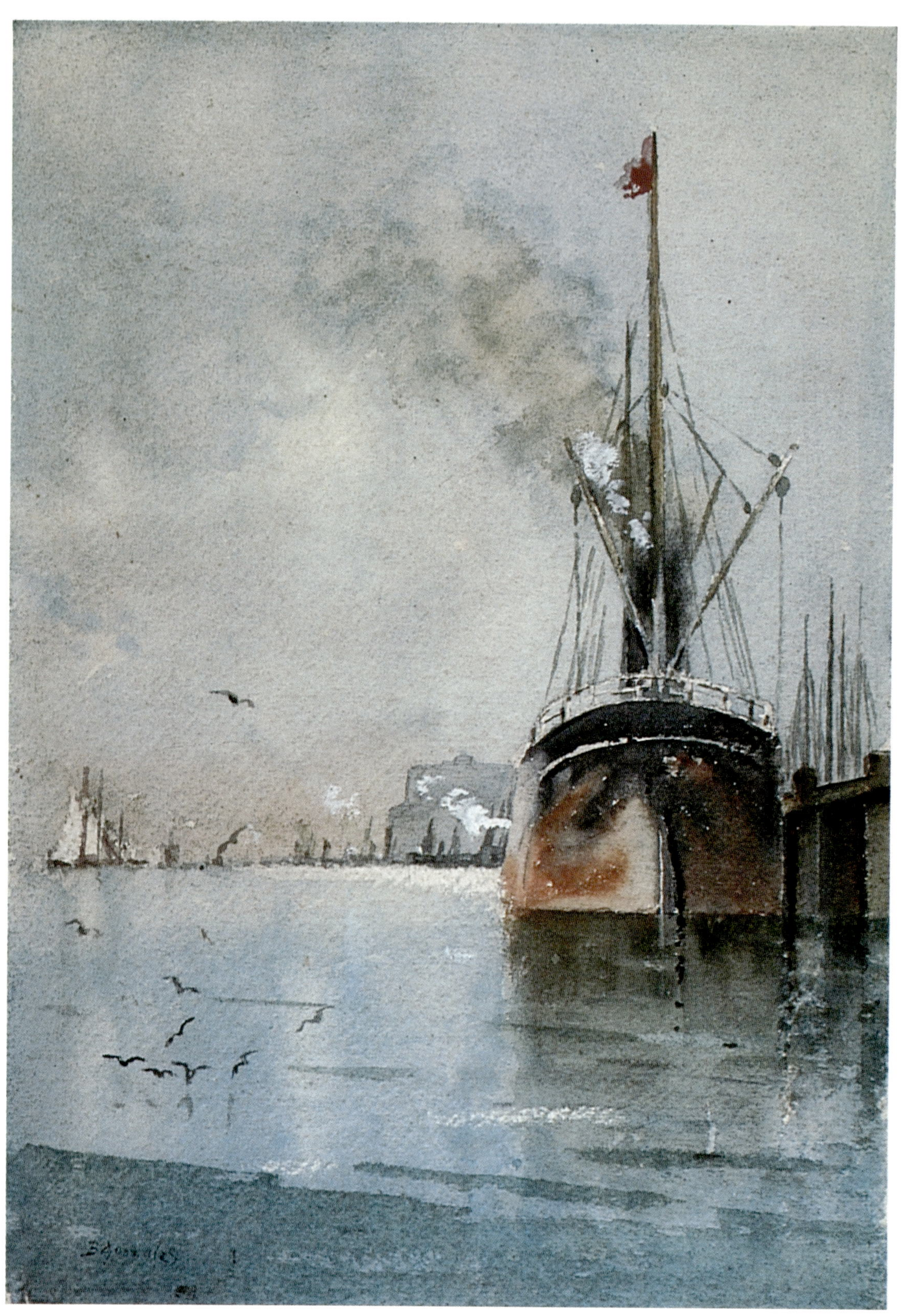

Galveston Harbor—
Steamer at Dock, ca. 1914

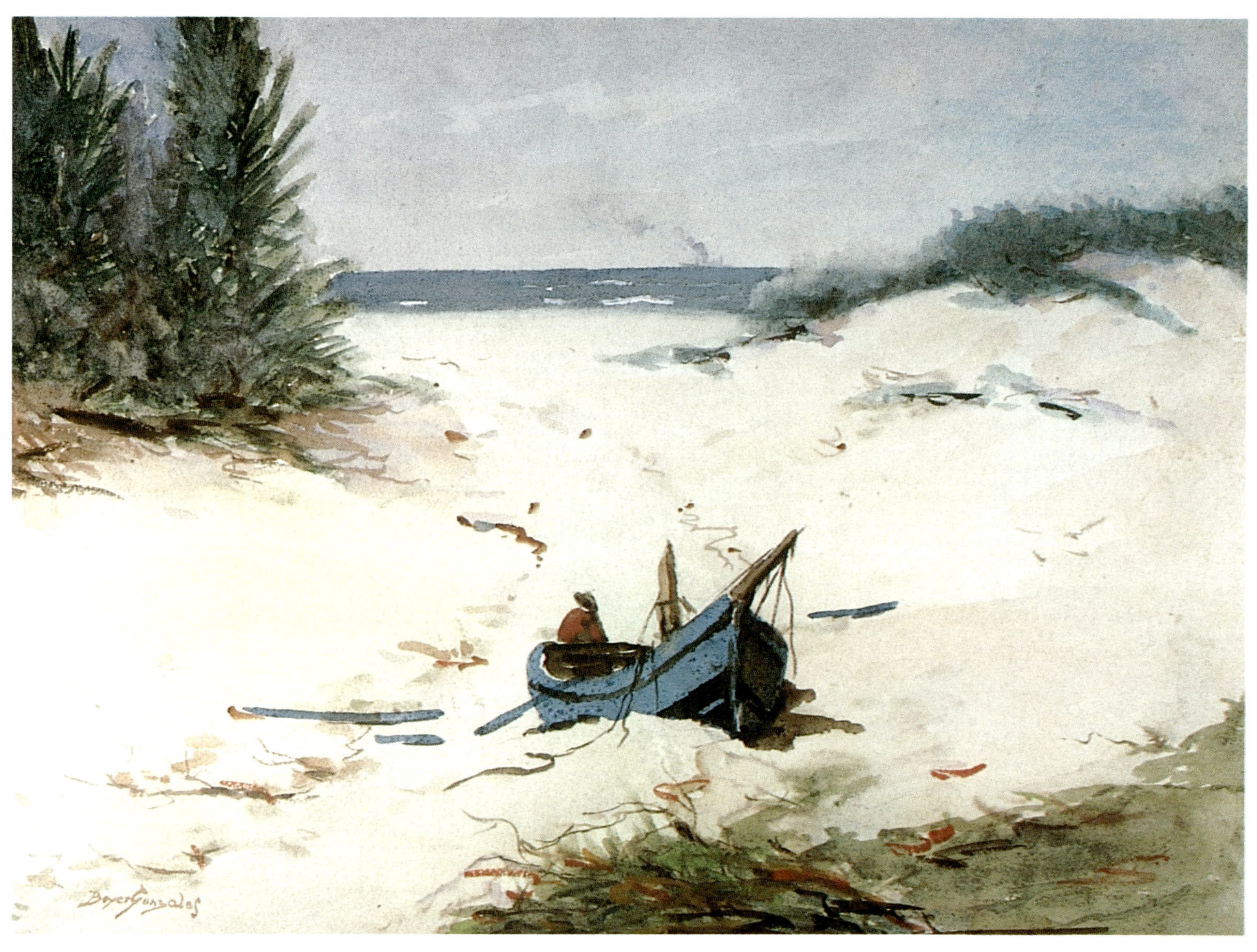

Wrecked Sloop—Down the Island—Galveston, ca. 1915

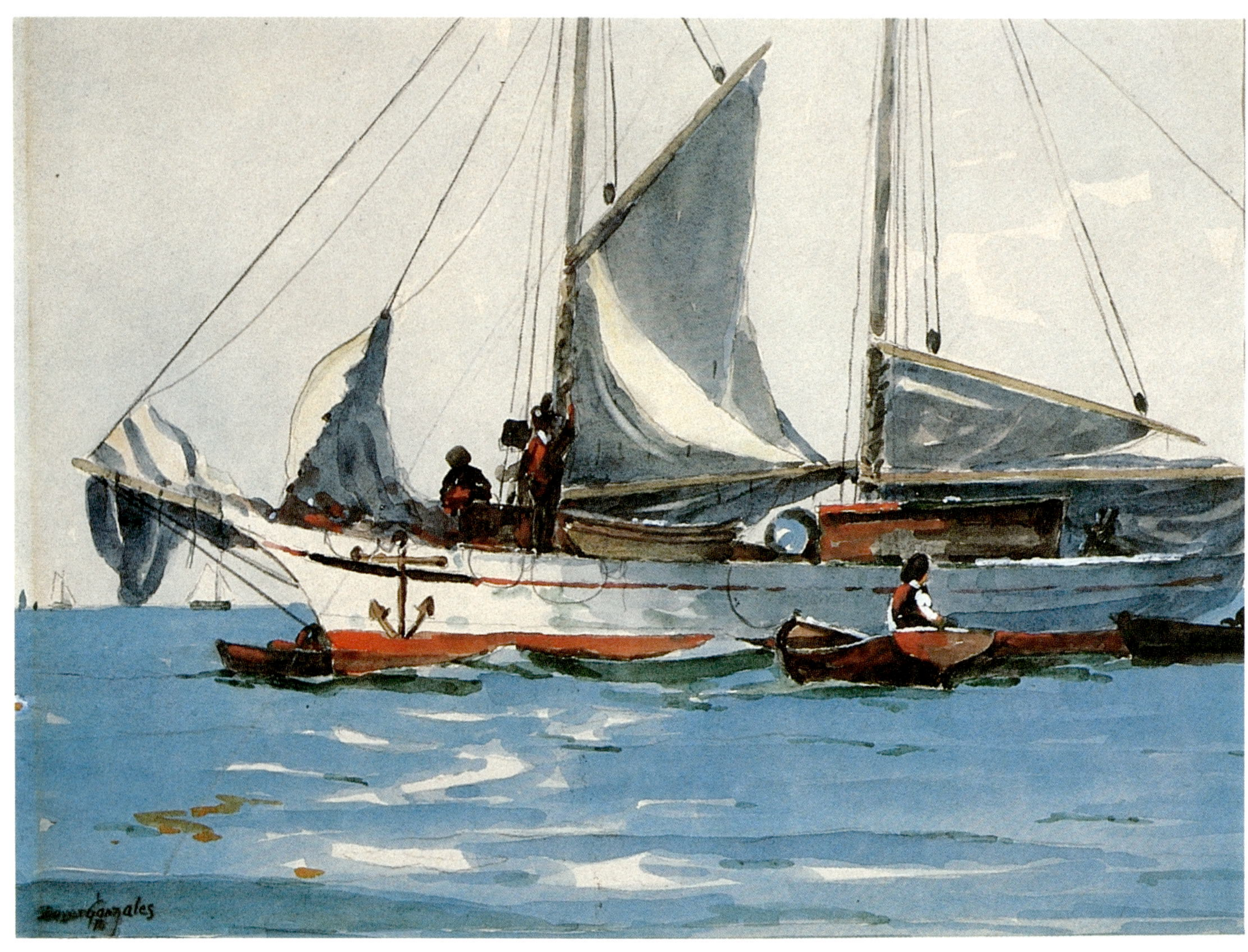

Campeche Fisherman Taking on Provisions, ca. 1916

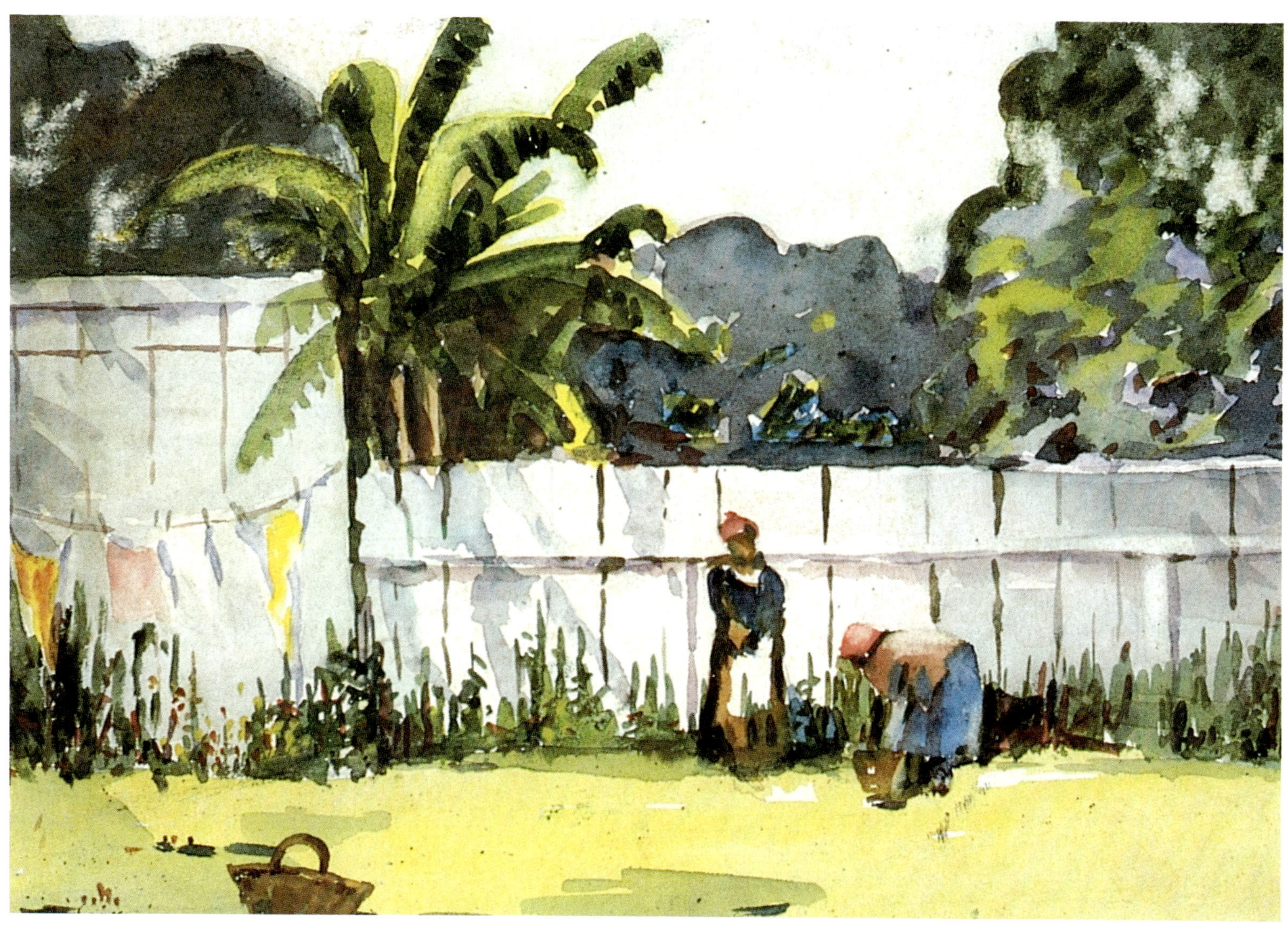

Galveston Spring, ca. 1916

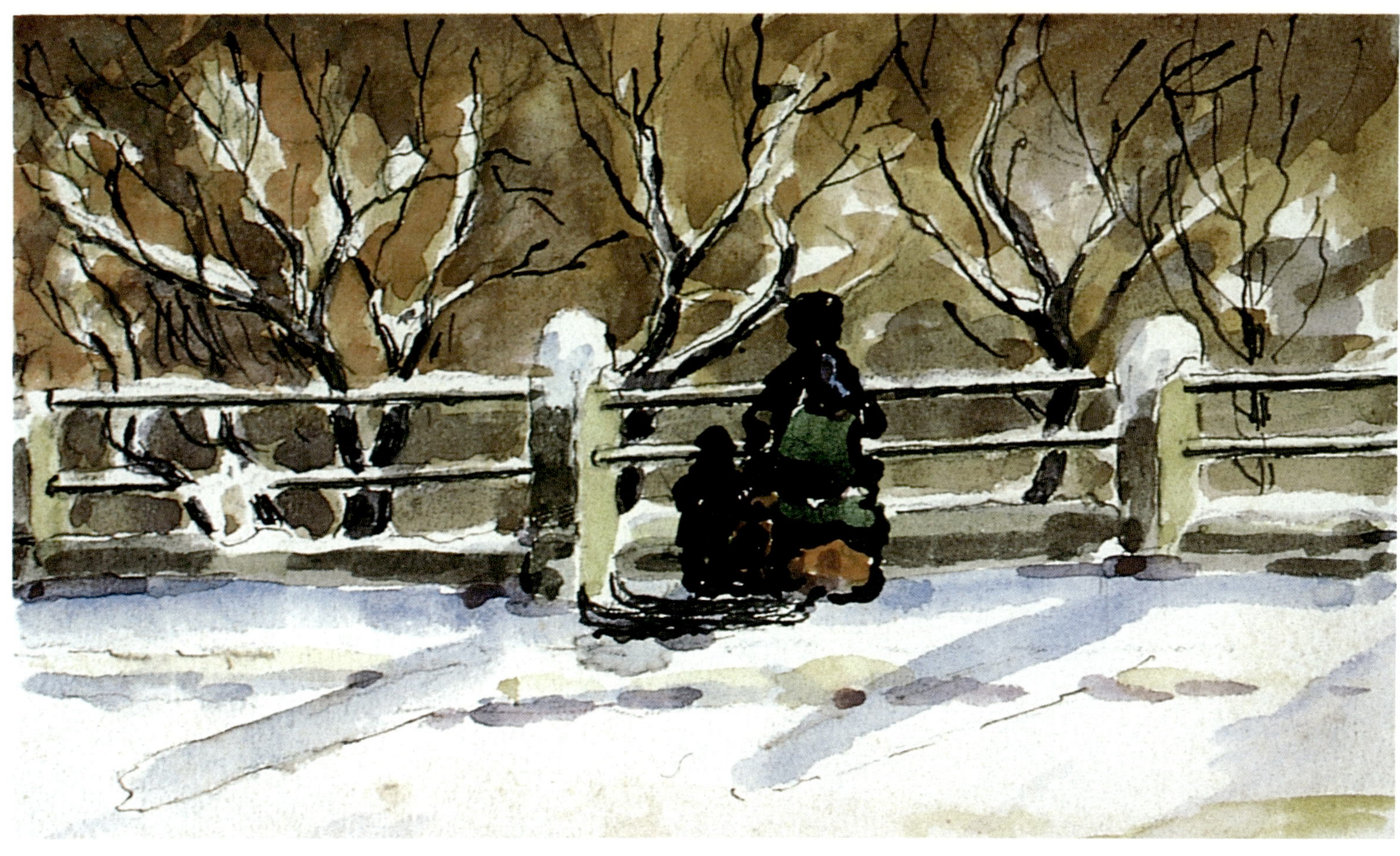

Untitled

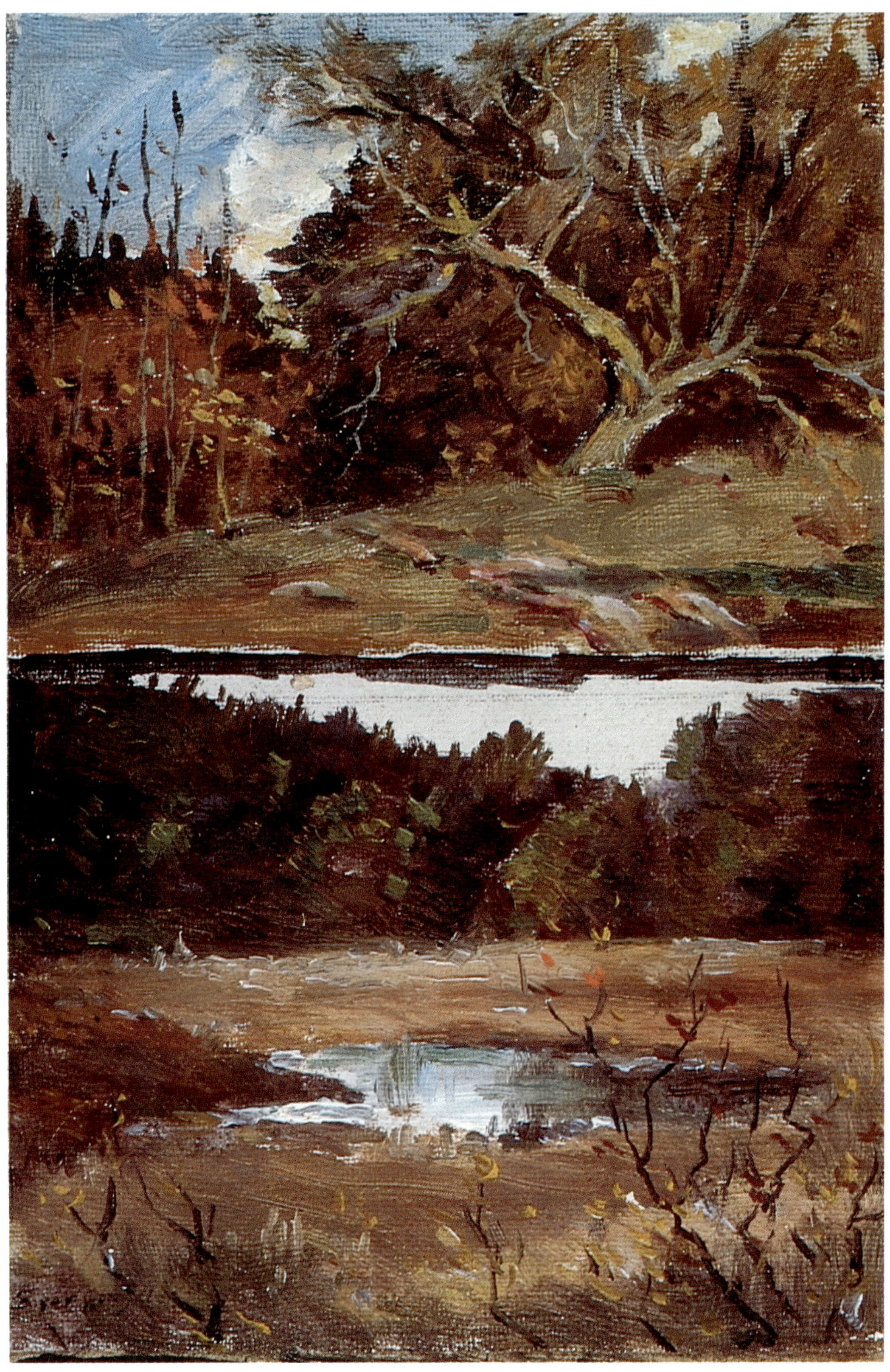

In deep woods, South Orleans,
Mass., November 7, 1918

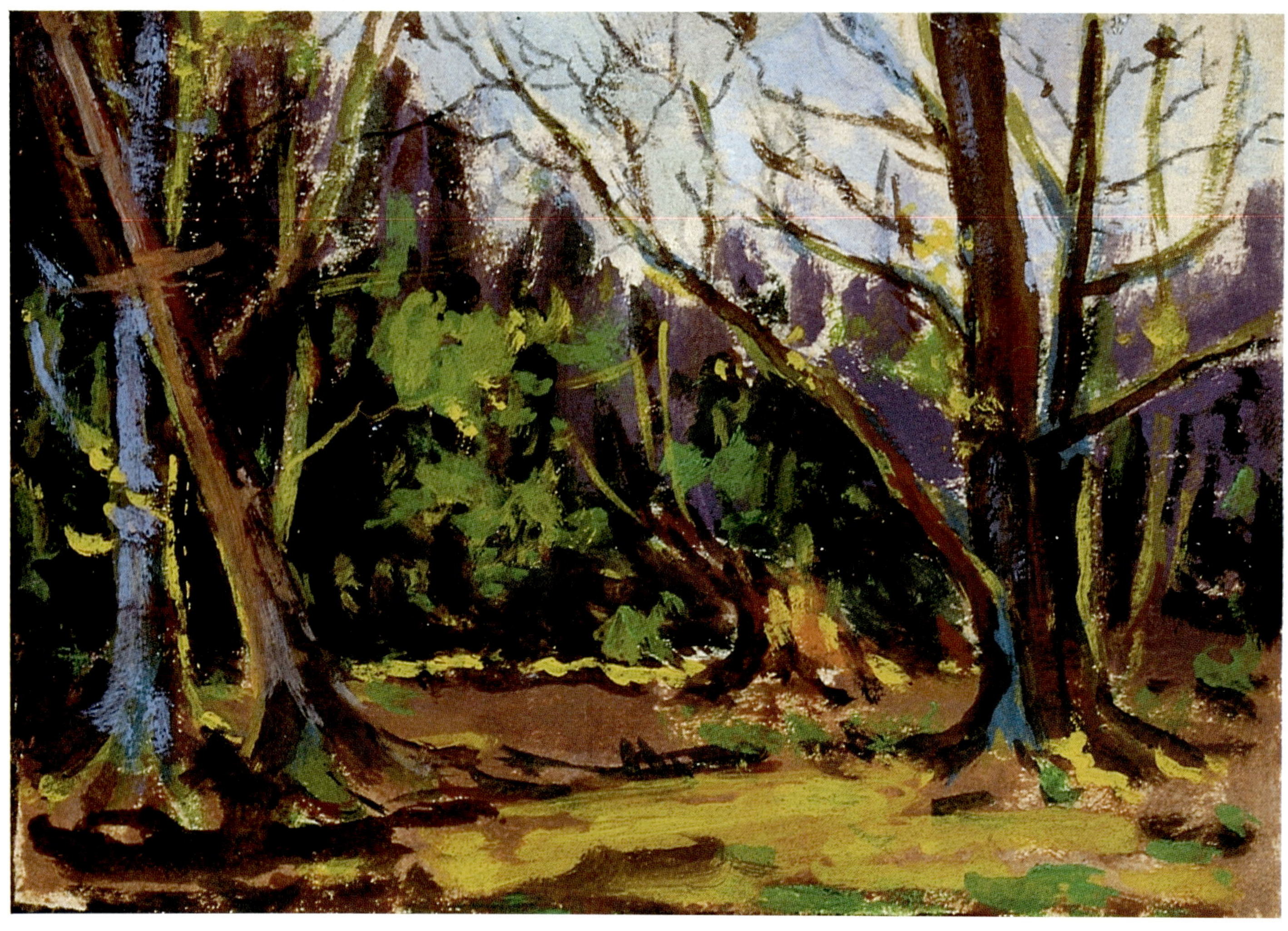

Untitled

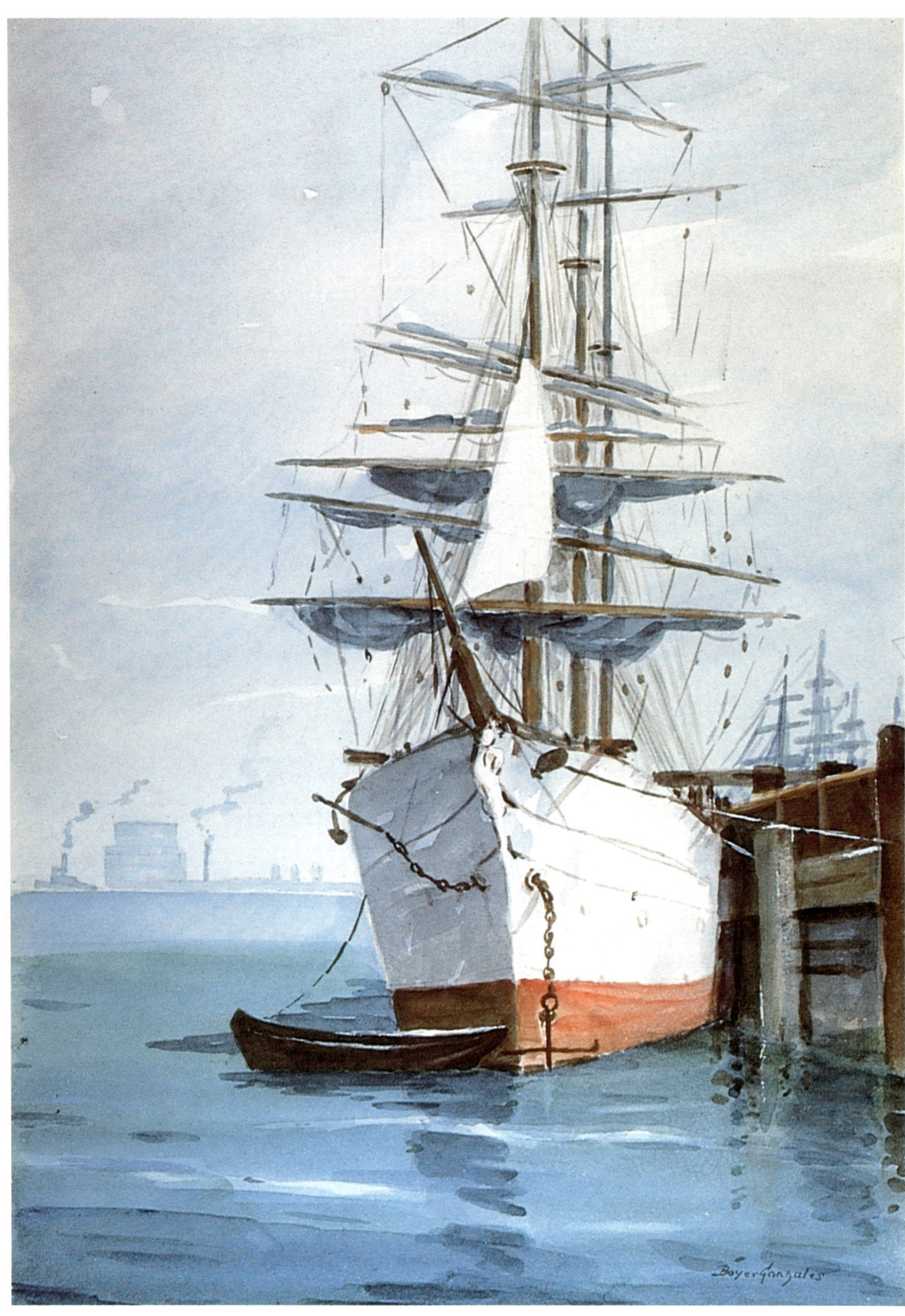

Danish Barque—
Galveston, ca. 1918

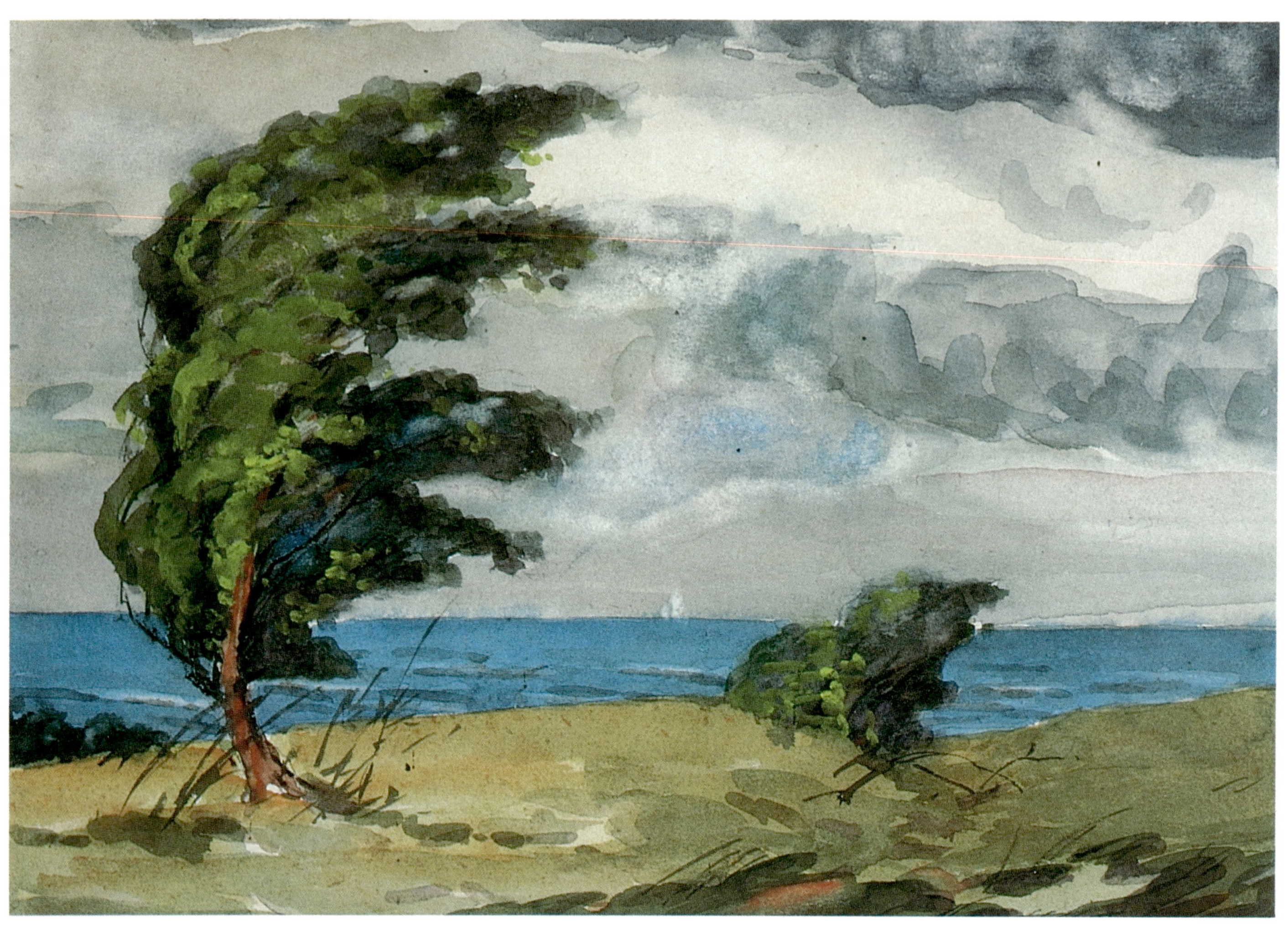

A Sudden Squall, ca. 1922

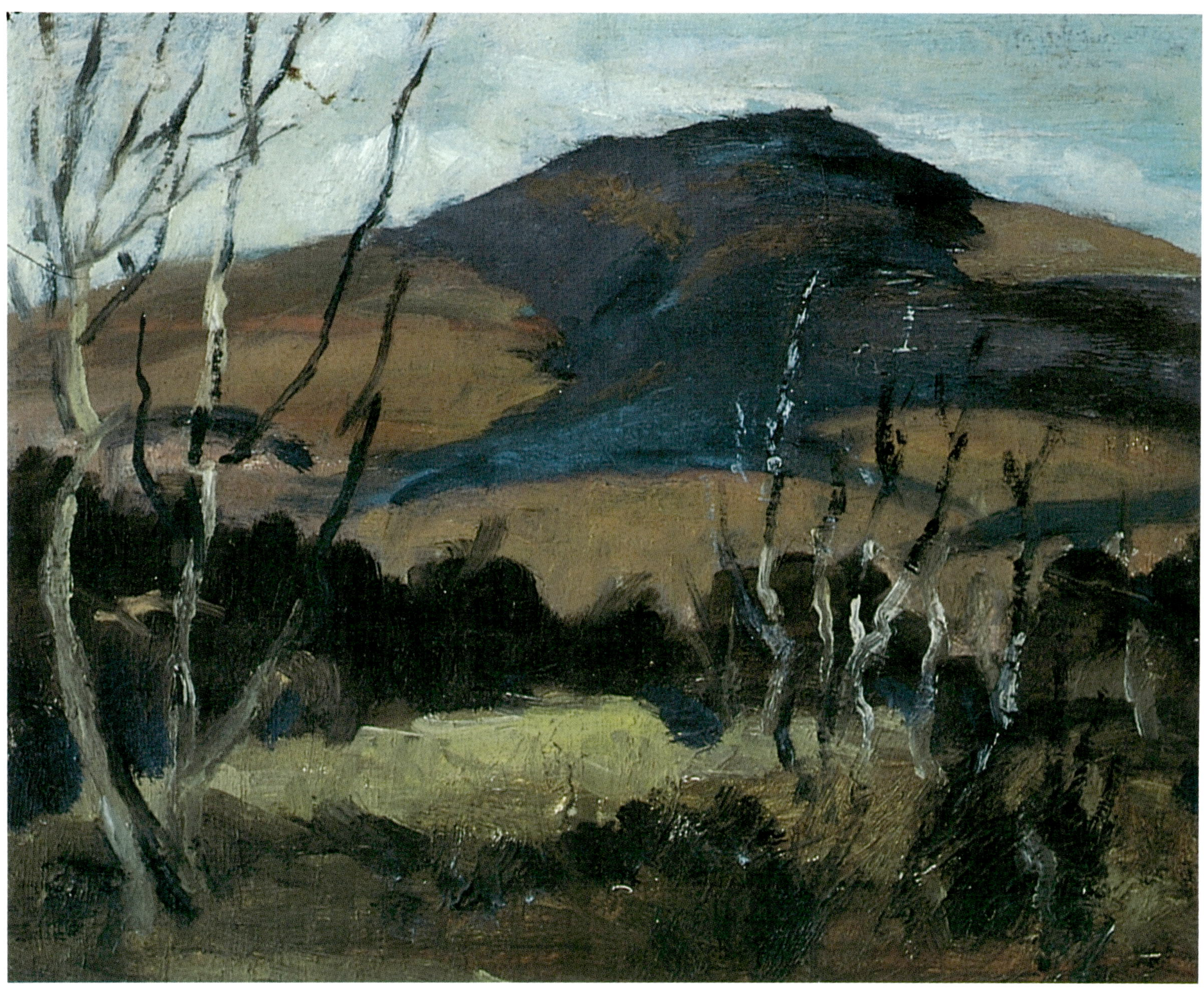

Autumn Sunlight

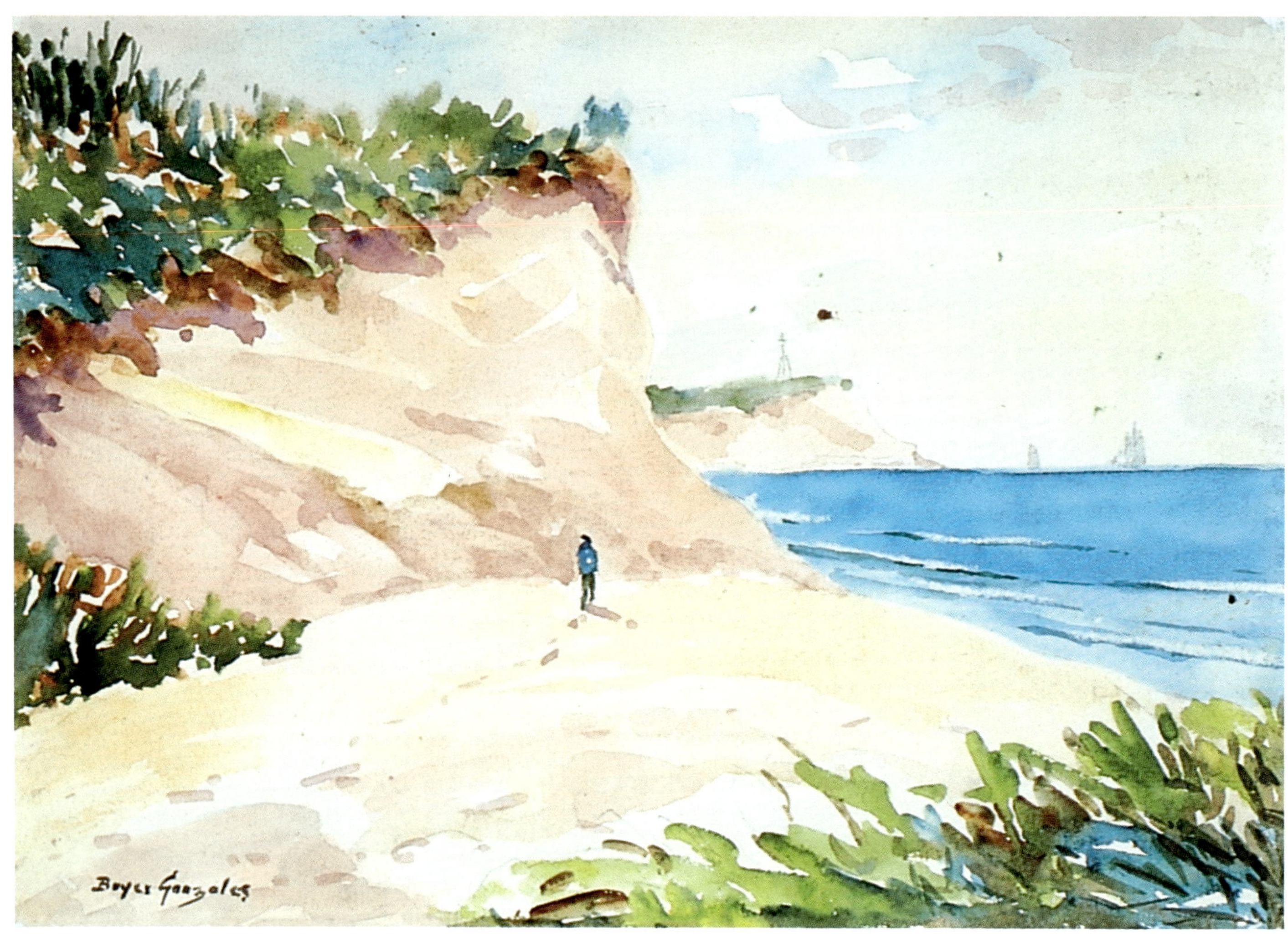

Dunes, ca. 1928

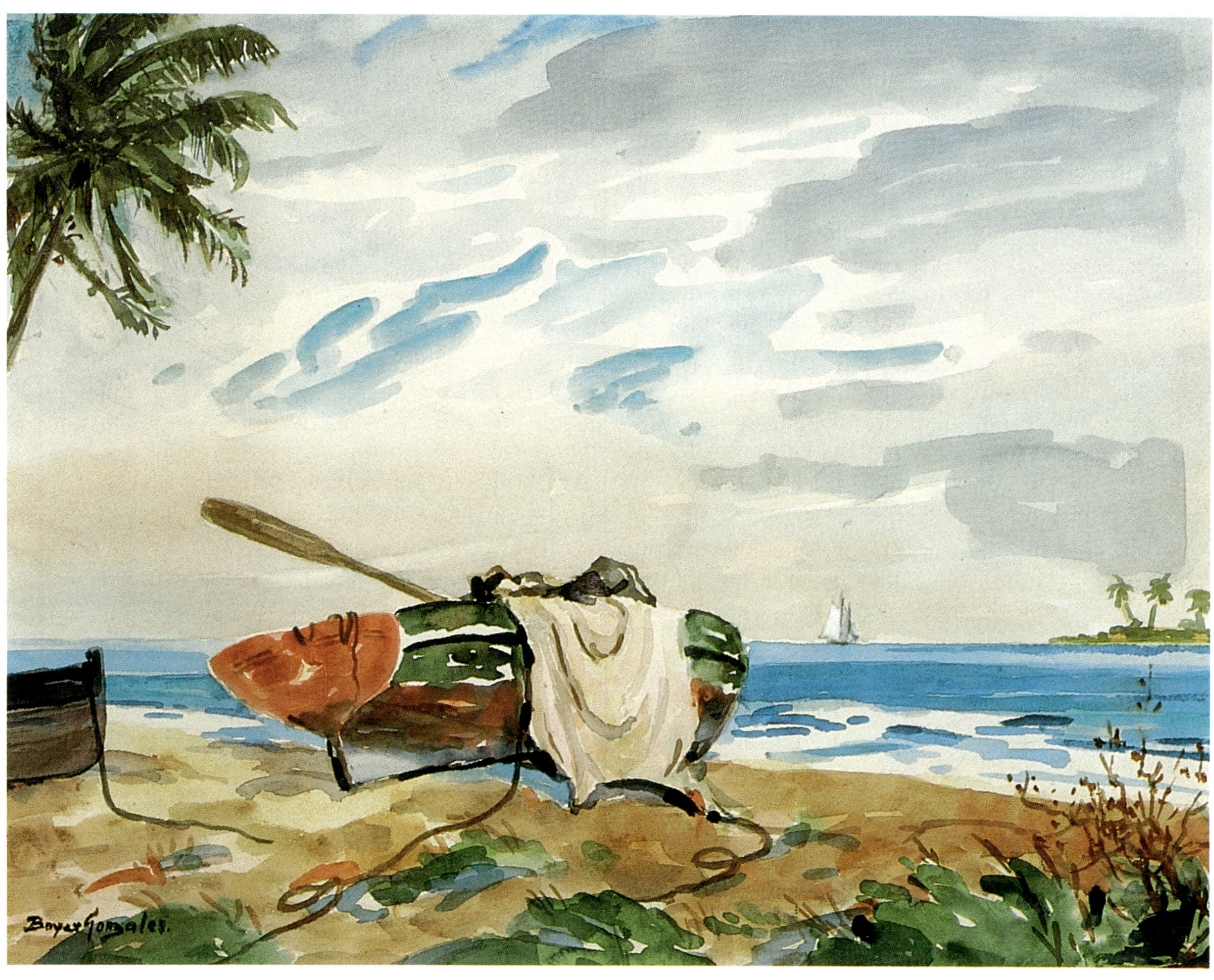

Beached Boat, Florida, 1929

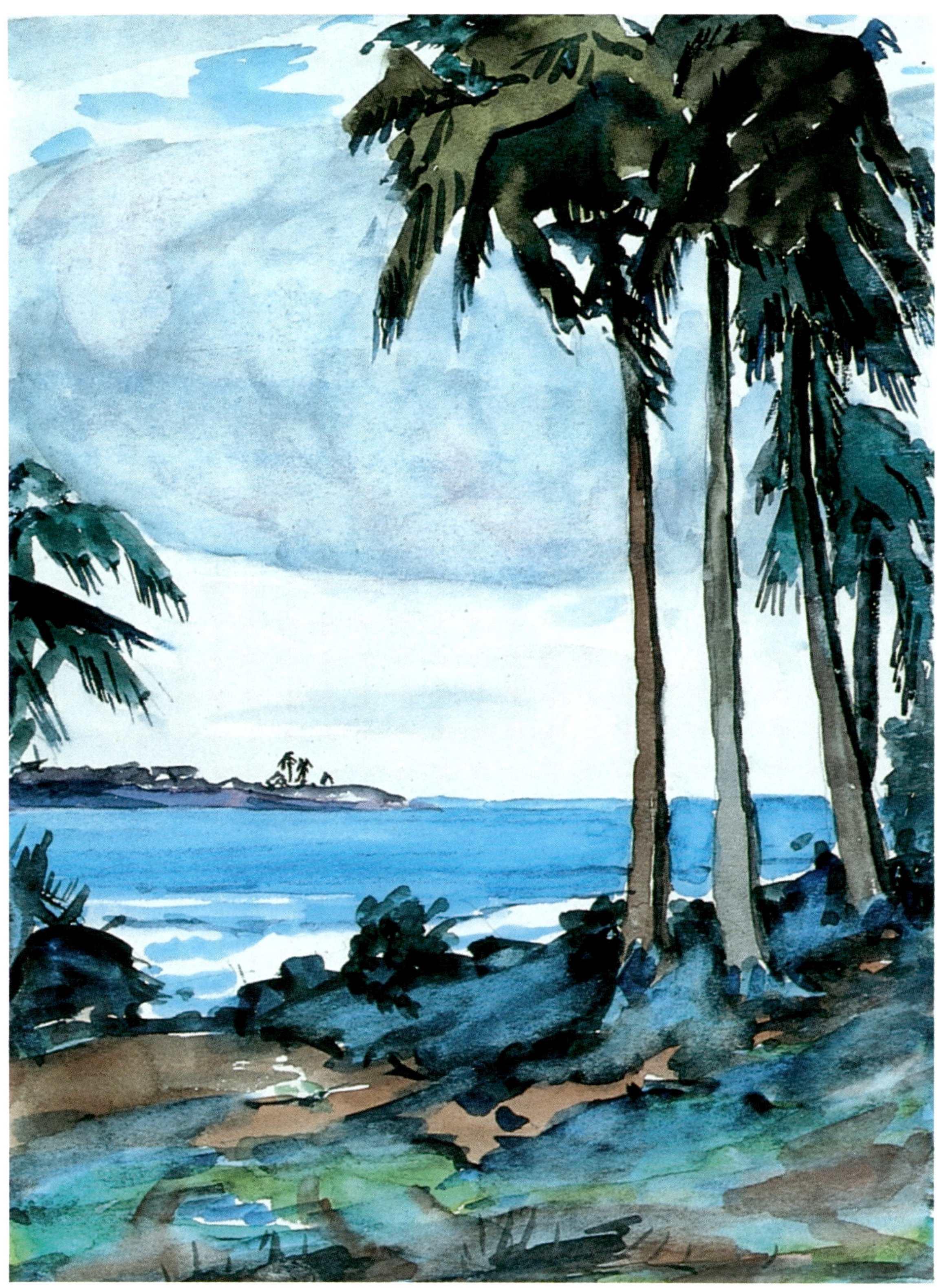

Three Palms—Florida,
ca. 1929

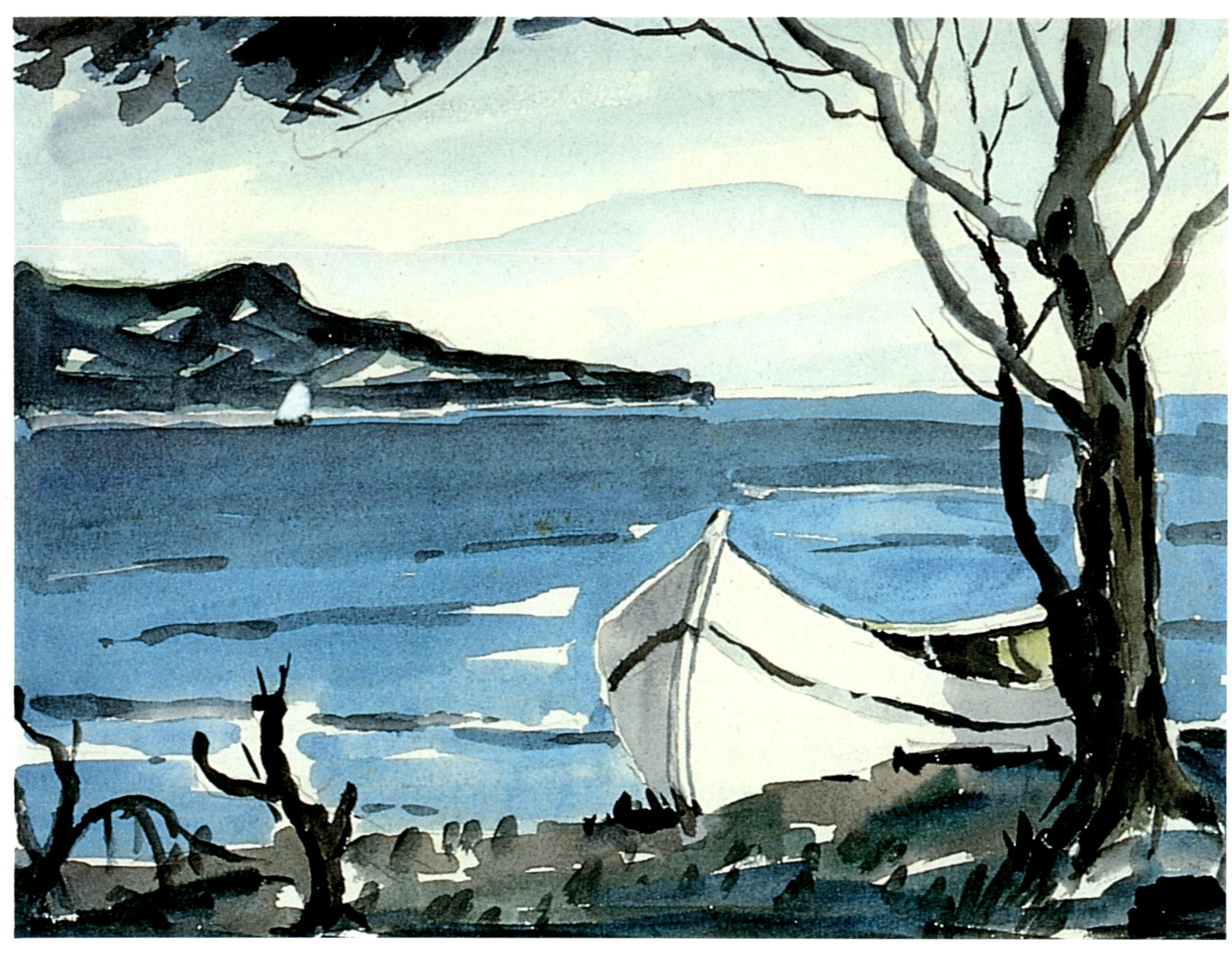

Deep Lake, Maine, ca. 1930

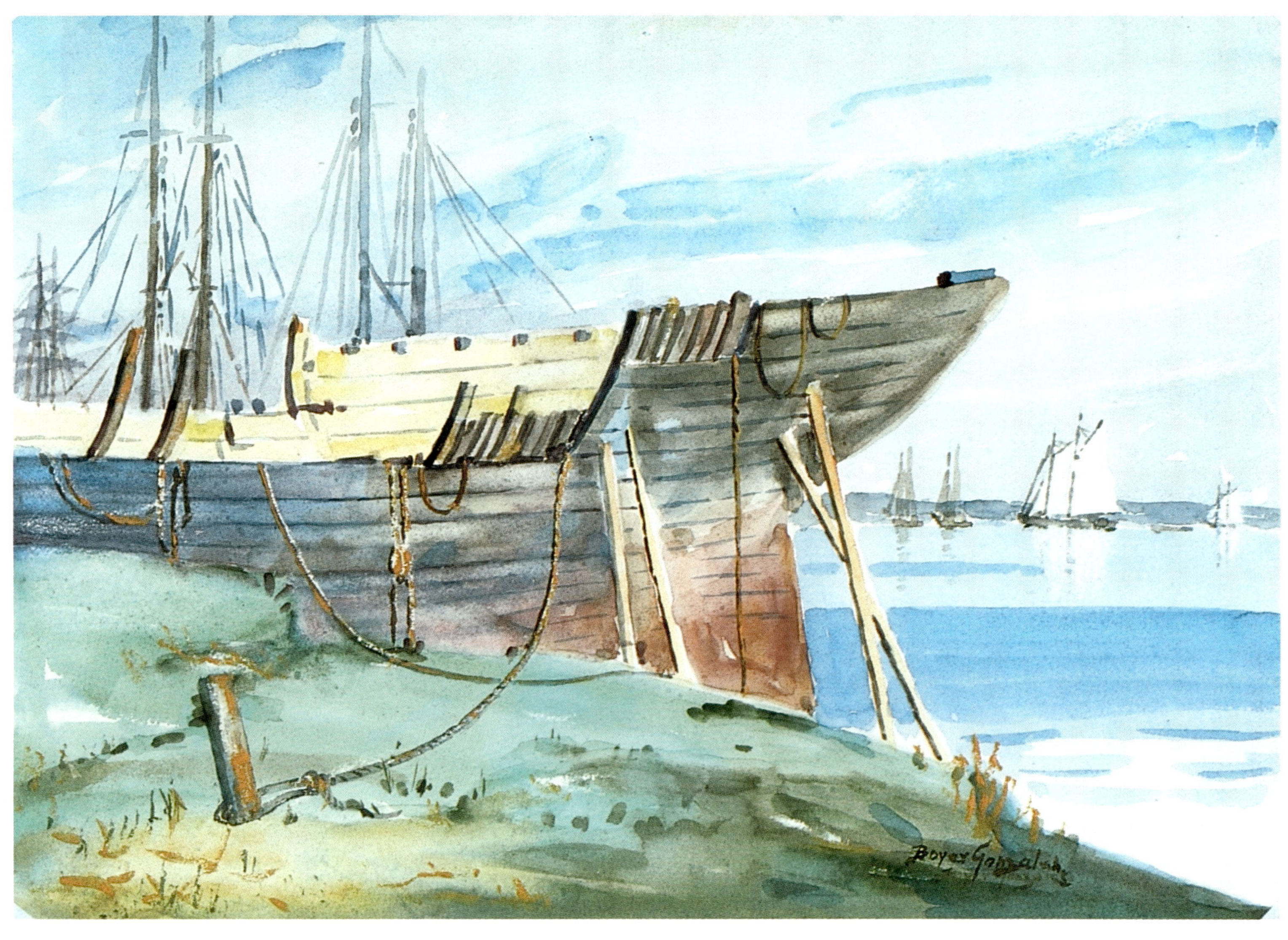

Her last port, ca. 1930

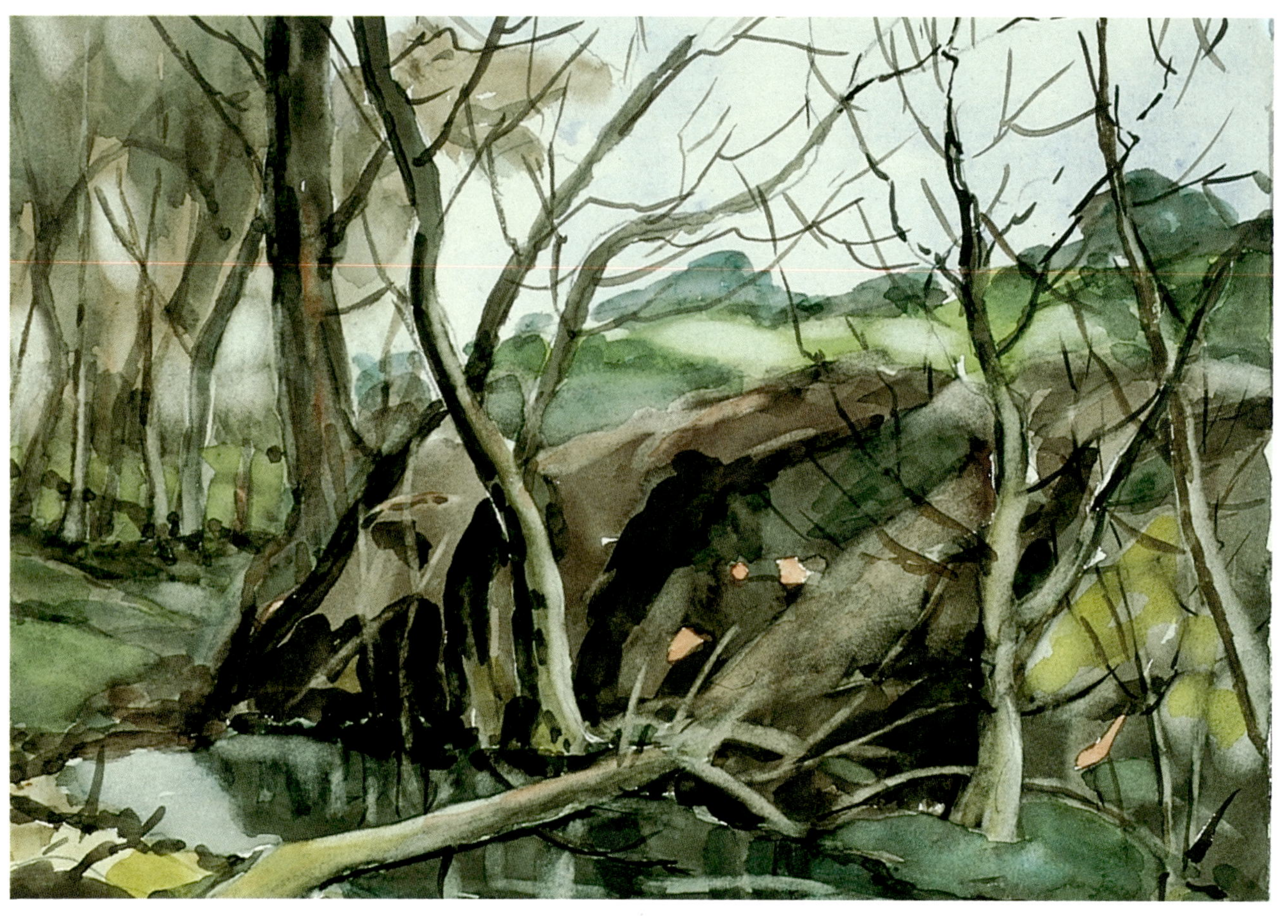

Backwater, ca. 1932

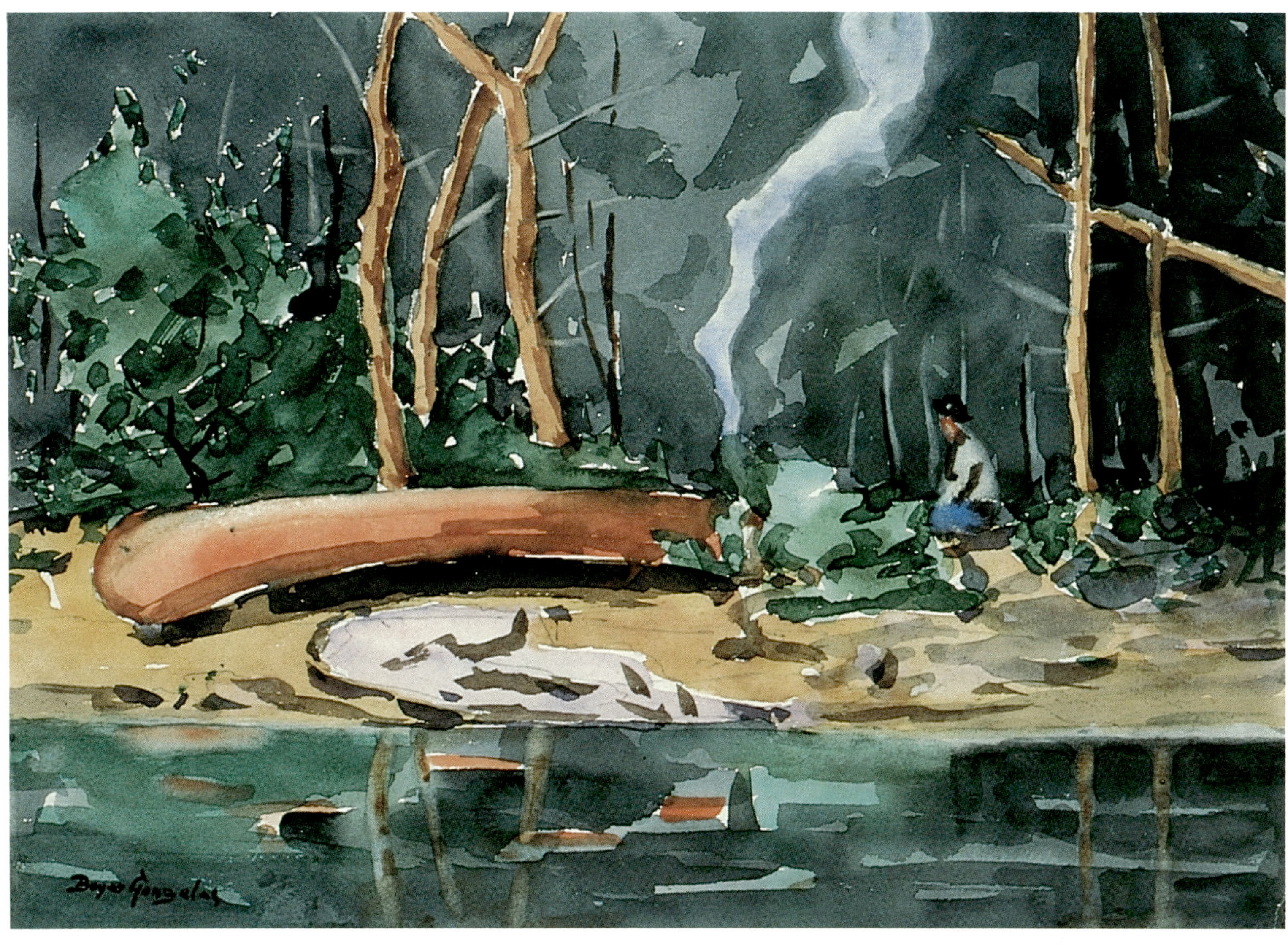

Making Camp, ca. 1932

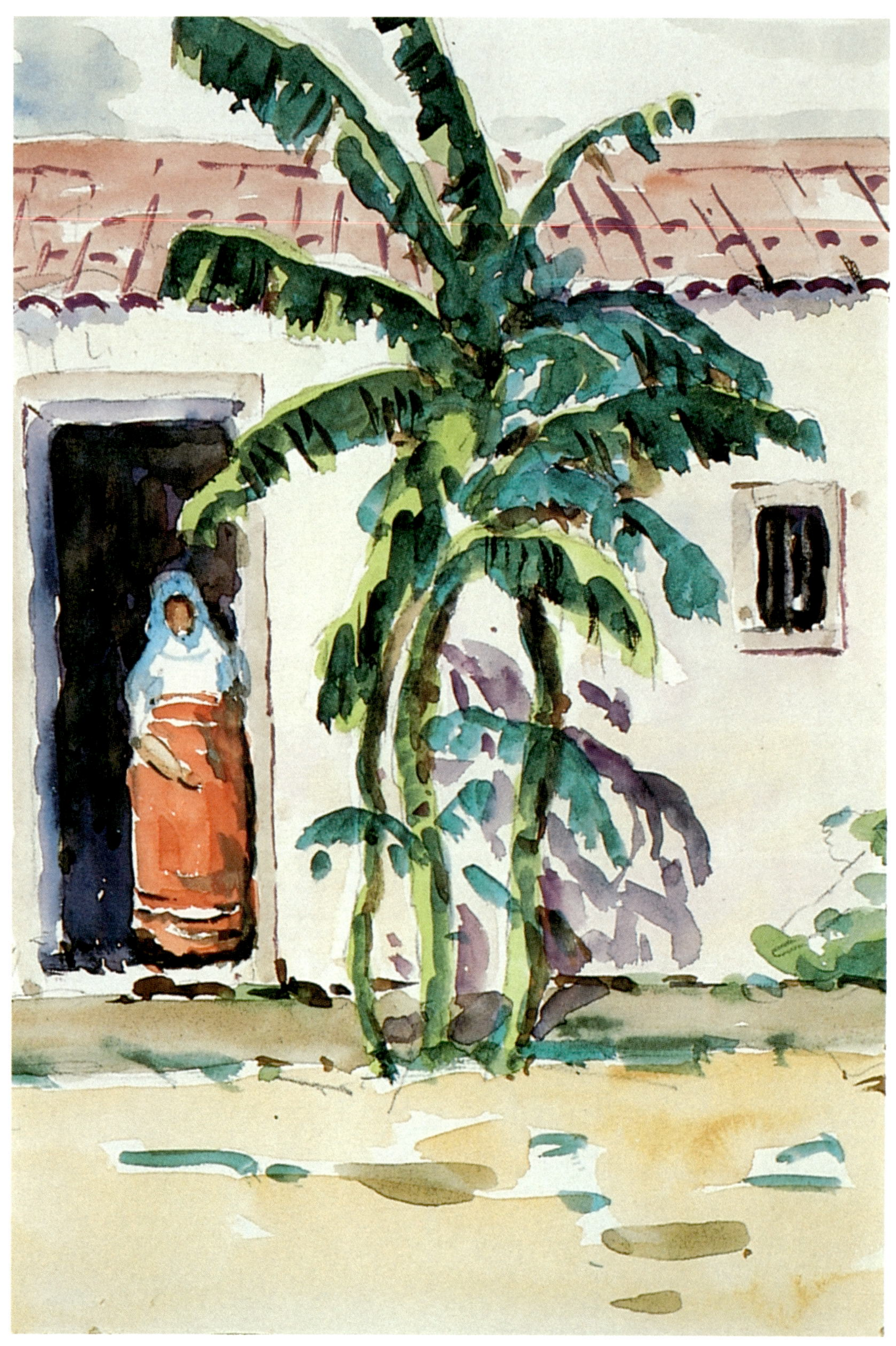

Doorway—Old Mexico, 1932

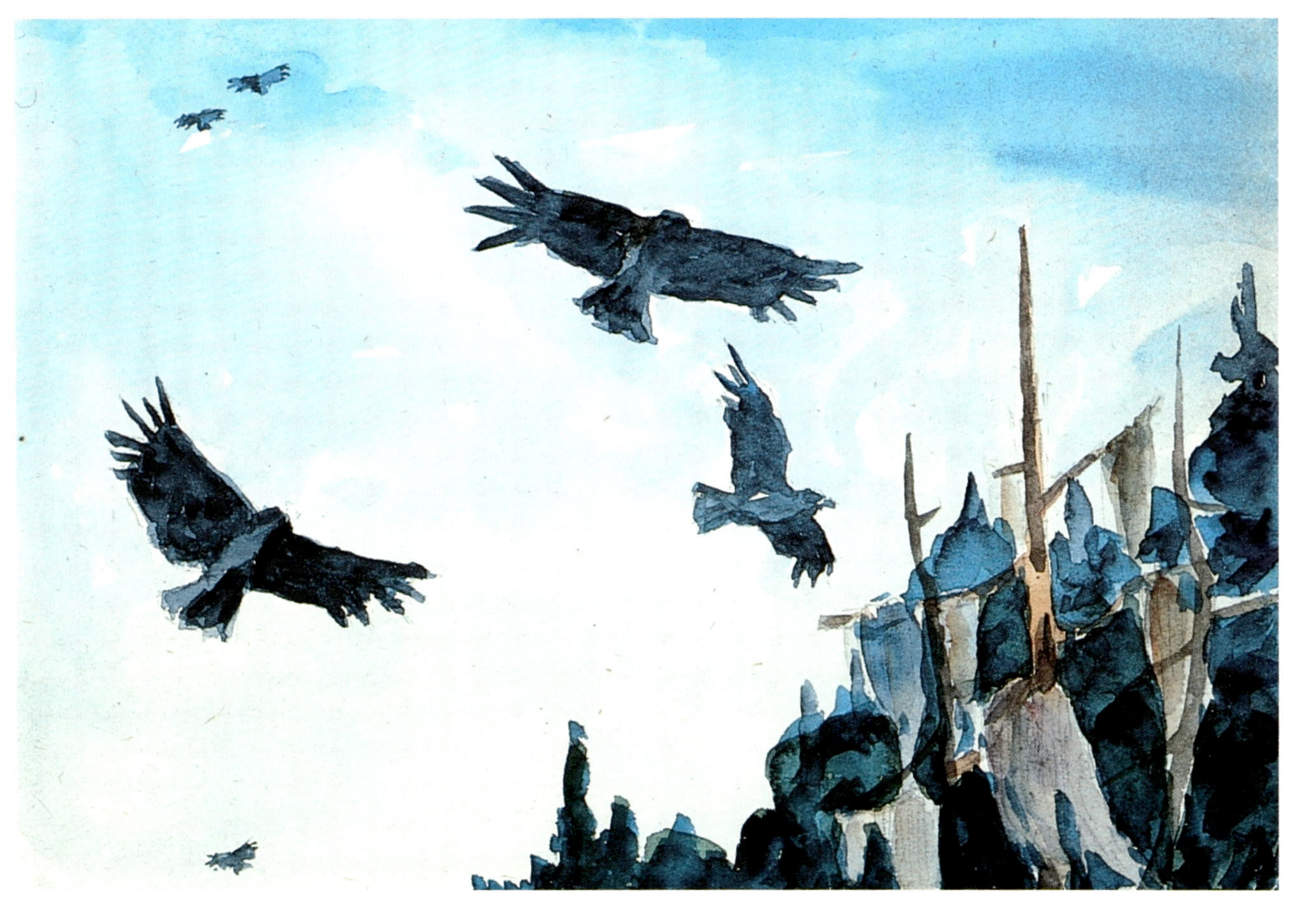

Three Crows, ca. 1933

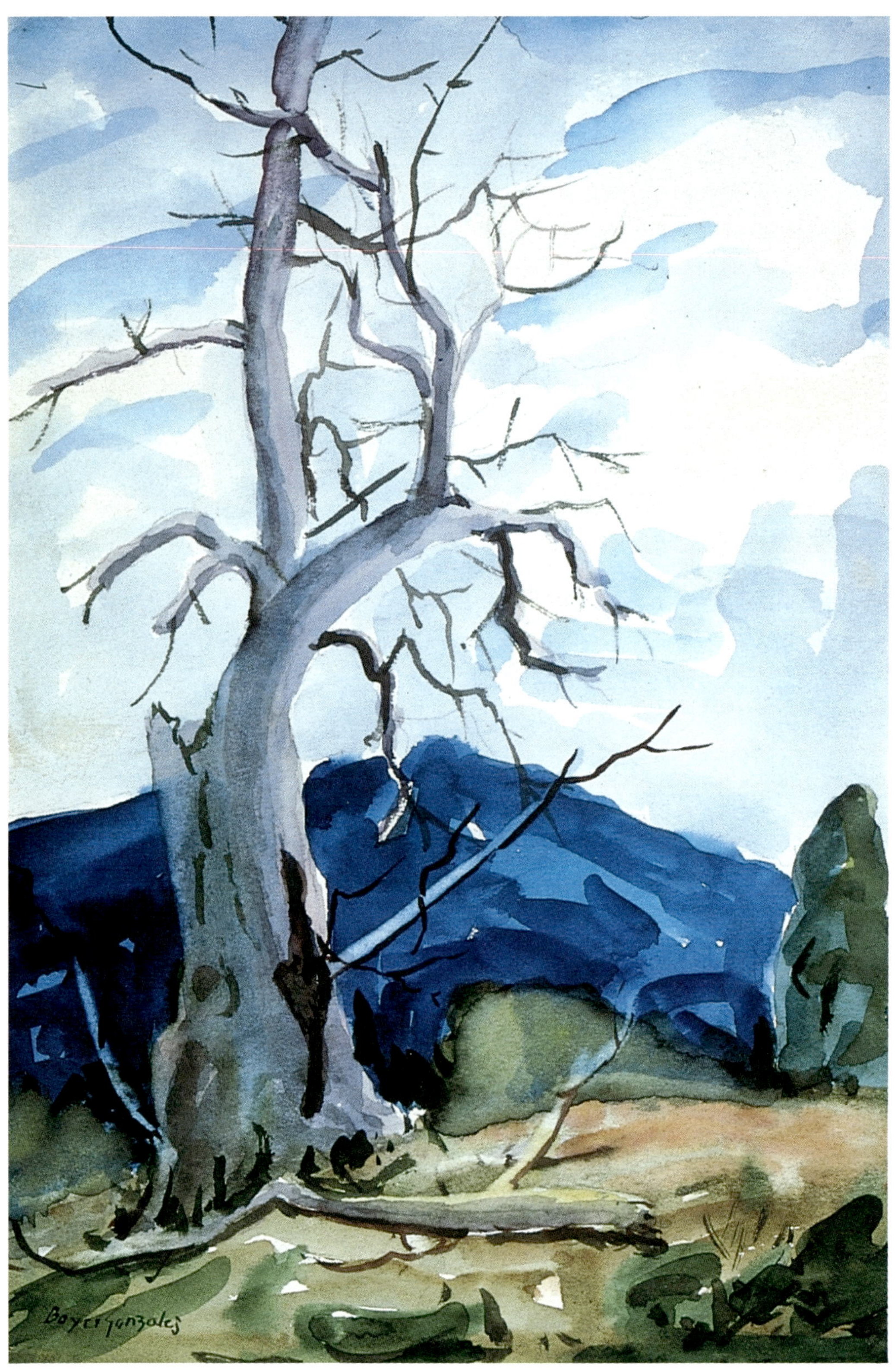

Old Chestnut Tree,
Woodstock, ca. 1933

NOTES

Preface

1. Actually the records reveal that Boyer Gonzales only went twice to Europe, in 1892 when he went alone and again in 1908 when he went with this wife on an extended tour, at which time he studied painting in Florence.
2. Boyer Gonzales, Jr.'s remarks were recorded, transcribed, and later included in the Boyer Gonzales, Jr., Subject File in the Galveston and Texas History Center of the Rosenberg Library in Galveston.
3. One of two collections of the Gonzales Family Papers catalogued in the Galveston and Texas History Center of the Rosenberg Library in Galveston, Gonzales Family Papers 89-0016, box 1, file folder 12.
4. Boyer Gonzales, Jr., Subject File.
5. Ibid.
6. Boyer Gonzales Subject File in the Galveston and Texas History Center in the Rosenberg Library.
7. Ibid.
8. Ibid.
9. Ibid.
10. Ibid.

Chapter 1. The Gonzales Family

1. *The National Cyclopaedia of American Biography* vol. XXIV, (New York: James T. White & Co., 1935), p. 90.
2. Boyer Gonzales Subject File.
3. Ibid.
4. Ibid.
5. It was this decree that also abolished the practice of slavery in Mexico, setting free all African slaves in the country. It should be noted that included in the proclamation were two groups that are often forgotten, both mixtures with African blood: the *mulatto,* a mixture of African blood with European or Caucasian blood, and the *sambo,* a mixture of African and Indian blood.
6. *Galveston Daily News,* January 17, 1890, p. 5.
7. John Henry Brown, *Indian Wars and Pioneers of Texas* (Austin: L. E. Daniel, [189?]), p. 297.
8. Ibid.
9. Ibid.
10. *The New Handbook of Texas,* vol. 5, (Austin: Texas State Historical Association, 1996), p. 855.
11. Brown, *Indian Wars,* p. 298.
12. Historic New Orleans Collection, New Orleans, Louisiana.
13. Louisiana Collection of the New Orleans Public Library, New Orleans, Louisiana.
14. Boyer Gonzales Subject File.
15. Louisiana Collection of the New Orleans Public Library.
16. Boyer Gonzales Subject File.
17. Gonzales Family Papers 89-0016, box 2, file folder 8.

18. Boyer Gonzales Subject File.

19. *Galveston Daily News*, January 5, 1895, p. 8.

20. Gonzales Family Papers 89-0016, box 2, file folder 32.

21. *Cameron County [Texas] Records of Real Estate*, vol. e., (n.p., n.d.), p. 533; Boyer Gonzales Subject File.

22. Col. Harry Kidder White, U.S.M.C., ed., *Official Records of the Union and Confederate Navies in the War of the Rebellion*, series II, vol. 3, (Washington D.C.: Government Printing Office, 1922), p. 12.

23. Gonzales Family Papers 87-0035, box 4, file folder 8. When the war ended, of course, both bonds, which were loans to the Confederate government, were declared null and void and Gonzales's certificates became worthless. In January of 1862, Gonzales's cotton business was less than eight years old, yet he had enough money to invest $4,800 in the venture, quite a sizable amount of money. That same amount of money in 1991 would be worth nearly $65,000, Matt Connor, "March of Dollars," *Forbes, FYI*, November 25, 1991, p. 40.

24. Boyer Gonzales Subject File.

25. Francis Richard Lubbock, *Six Decades in Texas* (Austin: Ben C. Jones & Co., 1900), p. 346.

26. Lubbock, *Six Decades*, p. 348.

27. Ibid.

28. Ibid.

29. Ibid.

30. *Galveston Daily News*, January 2, 1862, p. 2.

31. Boyer Gonzales Subject File.

32. Charles W. Stewart, ed., *Official Records of the Union and Confederate Navies in the War of the Rebellion*, series I, vol. 18, (Washington D.C.: Government Printing Office, 1904), p. 829.

33. British Consulate, Galveston Records, 1861–65, photocopies in the Galveston and Texas History Center of the Rosenberg Library of British Foreign Office Records in possession of the Library of Congress, Washington, D.C.

34. Boyer Gonzales Subject File.

35. Ibid.

36. Ibid.

37. Ibid.

38. *Galveston Daily News*, January 5, 1895, p. 8.

Chapter 2. Thomas Gonzales, Cotton Merchant

1. *Galveston Cotton Exchange and Board of Trade 1872–1899* (Galveston: Knapp Brothers: Stationers and Printers, n.d). p. 19.

2. Galveston County Records, Galveston County Court House, Galveston, Texas.

3. Trinity Episcopal Church [Galveston] Records, Galveston and Texas History Center, Rosenberg Library.

4. Boyer Gonzales Subject File.

5. Gonzales Family Papers 87-0035, box 4, folder file 11.

6. Boyer Gonzales Subject File.

7. Gonzales Family Papers 89-0016, box 2, file folder 27.

8. Gonzales Family Papers 87-0035, box 3, file folder 11.

9. Andrew Morrison, ed., *The Industries of Galveston* (Galveston: Metropolitan Publishing Company, 1887), p. 8.

10. Morrison, *Industries of Galveston*, p. 81.

11. One dollar in 1888 was approximately equal to $15 in 1991, meaning that the total loan plus interest would be valued at approximately $105,000 in 1991. Matt Connor, "March of Dollars," *Forbes: FYI*, November 25, 1991, p. 40.

12. *Groce v Gonzales*, 17540, County of Galveston District Court 1049 (1895).

13. *Galveston Daily News*, January 17, 1890, p. 5.

14. Trinity Episcopal Church [Galveston] Records.

15. Gonzales Family Papers 87-0035, box 4, file folder 11.

16. University of Washington Libraries, Special Collections and Preservations, Seattle Washington, FM-5.

17. Gonzales Family Papers 87-0035, box 1, file folder 5.

18. It was not unusual for a young man born to such a well-educated family to be well-read even though he had very little formal education as did the Gonzales children. In this entry, he adapts the last line from Milton's elegy "Lycidas" to suit his purposes: "Tomorrow to fresh woods and pastures new" becomes "greener fields and pastures new."

19. Joe Levy and his brother Ben, in addition to renting horses and buggies, were undertakers, selling metallic caskets and cases as well as burial robes and coffins. That establishment had offices on the north east corner of Twenty-first and Winnie. They advertised they had a "Child's white hearse and harness, with white horses, and fine hearses for adults, to hire at all times."

20. In 1991, the $35 outing in 1883 would cost $525.
21. Gonzales Family Papers 87-0035, box 2, file folder 11.
22. The sketch book contains the earliest known works by Gonzales. If there were any works completed before 1883, it is most likely that they were lost when the great fire of 1885 destroyed the Gonzales home at Nineteenth and Avenue N. There is no evidence that he ever studied art as youth; in fact, he had no formal training until he was twenty-nine years old when he spent two weeks during the summer of 1894 studying with William J. Whittemore at an artists colony in Annisquam, Massachusetts.
23. Gonzales Family Papers 89-0016, box 2, file folder 14.

Chapter 3. The Grand Tour of Europe
1. Gonzales Family Papers 87-0035, box 1, file folder 6.
2. Sir Henry Landseer (1802–73) was recognized as England's foremost animal painter and sculptor. In 1867, he completed the bronze lions for the base of the monument to Lord Nelson in Trafalgar Square in London.
3. Gonzales Family Papers 89-0016, box 1, file folder 9.

Chapter 4. Chicago's Columbian Exposition of 1893
1. Henry Justin Smith, *Chicago's Great Century* (Chicago: Consolidated Publishing, Inc., 1933), p. 108-109.
2. Carolyn Kinder Carr, *Revisiting the White City* (Washington, D.C.: National Museum of American Art and the National Portrait Gallery, 1993), p. 12–13.
3. Carr, *Revisiting the White City,* p. 100.
4. Gonzales Family Papers 98-0016, box 2, file folder 22.
5. Boyer Gonzales Papers 90-0001+, box 1, file folder 1, Galveston and Texas History Center, Rosenberg Library.
6. Philip C. Beam, *Winslow Homer at Prout's Neck* (Boston: Little Brown and Company, 1966), p. 112.
7. Gonzales Family Papers 87-0035, box 1, file folder 7.
8. Gonzales Family Papers 89-0016, box 2, file folder 23.
9. *Galveston Daily News,* January 5, 1895, p. 8.
10. Brown, *Indian Wars,* p. 297–98.

Chapter 5. Gonzales and Mexico: A Burst of Color
1. Boyer Gonzales Subject File.
2. Gonzales Family Papers 89-0016, box 2, file folder 28.

3. Gonzales Family Papers 89-0016, box 2, file folder 22.
4. Ibid.
5. Ibid.
6. *Groce vs. Gonzales,* 17540, County of Galveston District Court 1049 (1895).
7. Gonzales Family Papers 89-0016, box 1, file folder 14.
8. The Galveston County death records indicate that he was buried in the family plot in the Episcopal cemetery with his wife, daughter Edith, who died at the age of six in 1867 during a yellow fever epidemic, and his son Thomas Edward, who died at the age of thirty-four in 1892. However, the church has no records of his grave. His body was evidently placed in a receiving vault and held until the family readied another plot at a Lakeview cemetery which was completed in February, 1897. At that time, Gonzales's wife and children were removed from the Episcopal cemetery and re-interred in the new vault along with Thomas.
9. Boyer Gonzales Papers 90-0001+, box 1, file folder 2.
10. Gonzales Family Papers 88-0016, box 1, file folder 14.
11. Boyer Gonzales Papers 90-0001+, box 1, file folder 3.
12. Boyer Gonzales Papers 90-0001+, box 1, file folder 4.
13. Boyer Gonzales Papers 90-0001+, box 1, file folder 5.
14. Of Sam, Philip C. Beam has written: "Almost a member of the family was Winslow's dog Sam, a white wire-haired terrier with a black head which the artist bought as a pup in England. When Winslow had to leave Prout's Neck in the winter his primary concern was for Sam's welfare, and he boarded him at the West Point House like a gentleman. He was as long lived as any Homer, for he died in 1899 at the age of eighteen. The two were inseparable, and it was a question as to whether Winslow owned Sam or Sam owned Winslow." Beam, *Winslow Homer at Prout's Neck,* p. 54.
15. Gonzales Family Papers 89-0016, box 1, file folder 14.
16. Boyer Gonzales Papers 90-0001+, box 1, file folder 6.
17. Boyer Gonzales Papers 90-0001+, box 1, file folder 7.
18. Boyer Gonzales Papers 90-0001+, box 1, file folder 8.
19. Gonzales Family Papers 87-0035, box 1, file folder 5.
20. Gonzales Family Papers 89-0016, box 2, file folder 15.
21. Boyer Gonzales Papers 90-0001+, box 1, file folder 9.
22. Gonzales Family Papers 89-0016, box 2, file folder 4.
23. Gonzales Family Papers 87-0035, box 1, file folder 8.

24. Wedding book in possession of Lise Darst, granddaughter of the Robertsons.
25. Trinity Episcopal Church [Galveston] Records.
26. Gonzales Family Papers 89-0016, box 2, file folder 16.
27. Photocopy of marriage certificate; Boyer Gonzales Subject File.
28. Gonzales Family Papers 89-0016, box 1, file folder 5.
29. Boyer Gonzales Papers 90-0001+, box 1, file folder 10.
30. Gonzales Family Papers 89-0016, box 2, file folder 13.

Chapter 6. A Honeymoon in Europe
1. Gonzales Family Papers 89-0016, box 2, file folder 14.
2. Gonzales Family Papers 89-0016, box 1, file folder 12.
3. Gonzales Family Papers 89-0016, box 1, file folder 6.
4. Gonzales Family Papers 89-0016, box 1, file folder 12.
5. Gonzales Family Papers 89-0016, box 1, file folder 6.
6. Gonzales Family Papers 89-0016, box 1, file folder 12.
7. Gonzales Family Papers 89-0016, box 1, file folder 7.
8. Gonzales Family Papers 87-0035, box 1, file folder 5.
9. Gonzales Family Papers 87-0035, box 1, file folder 8.
10. Gonzales Family Papers 89-0016, box 1, file folder 14.
11. Homer had spent much of 1881 and 1882 in England where he sketched and painted in the thirteenth-century fishing village of Tynemouth, in Northumberland at the mouth of the Tyne River.
12. Gonzales Family Papers 87-0035, box 1, file folder 8.
13. Gonzales Family Papers 87-0035, box 1, file folder 5.
14. Gonzales Family Papers 87-0035, box 1, file folder 8.
15. Ibid.
16. Ibid.
17. Ibid.
18. Ibid.
19. Gonzales Family Papers 89-0016, box 1, file folder 8.
20. Gonzales Family Papers 87-0035, box 1, file folder 10.
21. Gonzales Family Papers 87-0035, box 1, file folder 9.
22. Ibid.
23. Gonzales Family Papers 87-0035, box 3, file folder 24.
24. Boyer Gonzales Subject File; Harrison on Gonzales at Houston exhibit, 1927.
25. Gonzales Family Papers 87-0035, box 1, file folder 9.
26. Gonzales Family Papers 87-0035, box 1, file folder 10.

27. Boyer Gonzales, Jr., Subject File.
28. Gonzales Family Papers 87-0035, box 1, file folder 9.

Afterword
1. Regarding Homer's visiting Galveston, Mattie Kelley, registrar of the Bowdoin College Museum of Art in New Brunswick, Maine, which has extensive Homer archives, wrote on March 13, 1996, to Edward Simmen that "there are no specific references to any trips to Texas in the Homer correspondence [in the archives]." She added, "The Museum owns one of Homer's day books, a journal in which he recorded costs, references to the weather and thumbnail sketches of paintings. In a series of thumbnail sketches of some of his paintings on a page dated July 5th, 1902, one is entitled *After the Tornado, Texas.* However, since Homer later titled the painting *After the Tornado, Bahamas,* this does not seem to be definitive proof that he painted the work in Texas." She continued, "I asked Phil Beam [author of *Winslow Homer at Prout's Neck*] about the trips to Texas last week and he indicated that he had been told years ago by Homer family members that Winslow Homer did travel to Galveston to visit his brother. He relayed an anecdote to me of Homer purchasing ponies for two of his nephews [Arthur Homer's two sons] while in Texas." [A copy of the letter is in the Boyer Gonzales Subject File in the Galveston and Texas History Center at the Rosenberg Library, Galveston, Texas.] In addition, in their recent exhibition catalogue from National Gallery of Art, Nickolai Cikovsky and Franklin Kelly write: "There is speculation that Homer may have at one time visited his brother on one of his later trips to Key West, Florida. The Mallory line Key West Steamer also went to Galveston" [Nickolai Cikovsky and Franklin Kelly, *Winslow Homer* (Washington, D.C.: National Gallery of Art, 1995), p. 95.] Mattie Kelley concluded her letter to Simmen: "I am sorry to be so vague. This seems to be an unanswered question." Regarding the sketch in Homer's day book dated July 5, 1902, *After the Tornado, Texas,* it should be added that if Homer had been in Galveston at that time, he would not have seen his brother. After having lost his rope business in the 1900 storm, Arthur Homer, in 1901, sold his home and with his family returned to Massachusetts.